The
Value
Connection

Founded in 1807, John Wiley & Sons is the oldest independent publishing company in the United States. With offices in North America, Europe, Australia and Asia, Wiley is globally committed to developing and marketing print and electronic products and services for our customers' professional and personal knowledge and understanding.

The Wiley Trading series features books by traders who have survived the market's ever changing temperament and have prospered—some by reinventing systems, others by getting back to basics. Whether a novice trader, professional, or somewhere in-between, these books will provide the advice and strategies needed to prosper today and well into the future.

For a list of available titles, visit our Web site at www.WileyFinance.com.

The Value Connection

A Four-Step Market Screening Method to Match Good Companies with Good Stocks

MARC H. GERSTEIN

WILEY

John Wiley & Sons, Inc.

Published by John Wiley & Sons, Inc., Hoboken, New Jersey.
Published simultaneously in Canada.

For general information on our other products and services, or technical support, please contact our Customer Care Department within the United States at 800-762-2974, outside the United States at 317-572-3993 or fax 317-572-4002.

Wiley also publishes its books in a variety of electronic formats. Some content that appears in print may not be available in electronic books.

For more information about Wiley products, visit our web site at www.wiley.com.

Library of Congress Cataloging-in-Publication Data:
Gerstein, Marc H.
    The value connection : a four-step market screening method to match good companies with good stocks / Marc H. Gerstein.
        p.   cm.
    ISBN 0-471-32364-0 (CLOTH)
    1. Stocks—United States.   2. Investments—United States.
    3. Investment analysis—United States   I. Title.
        HG4910.G476   2003
        332.63'2042—dc21   2003001700

Printed in the United States of America.

10   9   8   7   6   5   4   3   2   1

Contents

Acknowledgments

This is a book that bridges the gap between classic stock valuation theory and the modern information revolution. Accordingly, it owes much to the work and writings of many who, one way or another, address the field of value investing. At the forefront are such pioneers as Benjamin Graham and David Dodd, followed by modern investment superstars such as Warren Buffett, Peter Lynch, Martin Whitman, John Neff, Mario Gabelli, and Charles Royce.

Closer to home is the Multex team that produces the data and tools that make this value connection investment method possible. Leading the way are Isaak Karaev and Jeffrey Geisenheimer, CEO and CFO, respectively, of Multex, and Homi M. Byramji, head of the Multex Content and Applications (CAP) group and a key architect of much of this method's virtual structure. I'm also grateful for the efforts of the many dynamic professionals in the CAP organization, including, but certainly not limited to, Mukul Gulati, John Schirripa, Peter Sluka, David Coluccio, Haksu Kim, Gladimyr Sully, Michael Sferratore, Bryan Smith, and Jerry Czarzasty.

But there's much more to this method than the creation and production of the necessary data and tools. It must be delivered to you in a smooth, efficient manner, a task that is far more complex than many realize. Meeting the challenge at Multex is the Consumer group, spearheaded by Azahr Rafee. David Listman manages the Multex Investor web site with the help of Michael Hickins, who oversees the site's content. Other key members of the Multex Investor team include Chris Ball, Mary Nichols, Vlad Bar, Lana Fedorinchik, Ingrid Michelsen, Tom Dowe, and David Smith. Kudos, too, to Matthew Waldman, Joel Williamson, and Darren Newton and the rest of the Multex design group. I'm also grateful to Nancy DePiano, Samantha Topping, Steven Schwartz, Sheri Levy, and Rosalina Yap, who work hard to bring Multex Investor to the world at large, and to Walker Jacobs and his staff, whose efforts make so much of the site free to you, the investor.

As this book goes to press, the ability of the Multex team to deliver the value connection increases exponentially as we proudly join the Reuters family, headed by CEO Tom Glocer. Although best known as the world's largest international multimedia news agency, more than 90 percent of Reuters' revenue comes from its financial services business, which will enhance and be enhanced by the Multex assets.

Especially noteworthy are the efforts of Multex colleagues Alex Karavousanos, Richard (Rick) Smith, and Vladimir Jornitski. Alex was a champion of screening even before it moved online, back when it was primarily a CD product. And today, he works hard to develop new ways to bring to the investing public the benefits that can be obtained through screening. Rick and Vlad were likewise instrumental in bringing Multex information to the world, a mission they've been pursuing since before the MultexInvestor site existed in its current form. Indeed, as these words are written, they continue to regularly burn the midnight oil envisioning and implementing still newer and better ways of making the concepts presented in this book real.

Speaking of making things real, there's the actual book you now hold in your hands. That was made possible by Pamela van Giessen and the rest of the team at John Wiley & Sons. I'm especially grateful to my agents, Robert Diforio, Marilyn Allen, and Coleen O'Shea, who recognize ideas in quick outlines and hasty e-mails, and push me to do what it takes to bring them to full fruition.

On a personal level, I'm grateful for the support of Michael Elling and Christopher Feeney, who helped me refine and focus many of the ideas that sometimes floated a bit too freely in my mind, and Lauren Keyson, for the friendship and perspective she regularly provides.

Finally, it's hard to imagine anything worthwhile coming into being without the continuing support of my parents, Bernard and Connie, my sister Leah, and my niece Emma. Thanks, too, to Heidi, who continually drives me to be more Web savvy than before, and Sheldon, who doesn't let a little thing like a bear market prevent him from investing based on my screens.

MARC H. GERSTEIN

Introduction

Value investing is usually thought of as buying a stock for less than it is really worth. That's a nice goal. Often, though, the approach has been distorted to the point where an obsession with low price, or more specifically, low price-related stock valuation metrics, became an end in itself. But in truth, company quality has always been relevant and the value connection method presented here brings this issue to the forefront. The word "connection," every bit as important as the word "value," refers to the relationship between the stock price and the quality of what we get for our money. In other words, we seek to match good stocks with good companies.

BEYOND THE OBVIOUS

The idea of matching good stocks with good companies sounds so obvious as to hardly be worth discussing. But in practice, the results of such an effort can be quite surprising to those who cling to stereotypical price-obsessed ideas about value. William Miller, who heads Legg Mason's mutual fund unit and manages the Legg Mason Value Trust, is a poignant example. During the late 1990s, his fund owned such names as Amazon.com, Amgen, Dell Computer, and Nokia, all of which were a far cry from the kinds of stocks many expected to see in a value-oriented portfolio.

Janet Lowe, in *The Man Who Beats the S&P* (John Wiley & Sons, 2002), explores Miller's investment style in depth. On pages 62–63, she cites remarks he made for the March 2000 issue of *Kiplinger's* magazine where he related a conversation in which his decision to own Dell in lieu of Gateway was challenged because Dell's price/earnings (P/E) ratio was three times higher. In response, Miller focused on company quality. At that time, Dell's return on capital was five times higher than Gateway's. Viewed in that light, Dell's P/E only three times higher was a bargain. In other words, Miller paid a higher price because he perceived Dell as offering more, much more, for the money.

The idea of getting one's money's worth is what led Miller to start buying

Amazon.com, seen by many as the penultimate antivalue stock, when it was priced at $80 per share. Miller and his team study company financials extensively. They determine private market liquidation values and analyze cash flows based on a variety of 5- to 10-year scenarios. So Miller was certainly aware of Amazon.com's losses. In fact, he was more aware than some of his critics. Janet Lowe describes (on page 114 of *The Man Who Beats the S&P*) a conference in 2000 where Miller distributed a questionnaire asking fund managers to guess the cumulative losses Amazon.com had incurred since its inception. The responses ranged from $200 million to $4 billion. In fact, the correct answer at the time was $62 million. Moving beyond the numbers, Miller also considers qualitative factors such as products, competitive positioning, strategies, and the business environment including industry dynamics and regulatory frameworks. In his opinion, Amazon.com fared well when viewed this way. It was building a critical mass of customers and hence becoming an entrenched e-commerce leader. It had sufficient capital to withstand early losses and continue building its business. And the necessary capital investments would be disproportionately small (compared to bricks-and-mortar retailing) relative to the financial rewards.

Miller concluded that over the long term, the company was sufficiently good that an investment in Amazon.com, even at what we now describe as bubble-era share prices, would ultimately give investors their money's worth. Internet stocks collapsed, though, and Amazon.com shares dropped well below Miller's average (approximately $30 per share) purchase price. But value investors tend to be more patient than many others. As time continues to pass, the company may yet translate its market-leading position into the sort of profits that will ultimately give Miller's fund a good return on the investment, even based on the prices he paid. On the other hand, it is possible that Miller's Amazon.com decision may turn out wrong, even over a long time horizon. That is a normal aspect of the investment process. It happens to everybody regardless of style. What's important, here, is that we recognize the extent to which Miller factors company quality (what shareholders get for their money) into his assessment of value.

The approach that caused Miller to buy Amazon.com does not always lead to high valuation metrics. As of September 30, 2002, the Morningstar.com web site pegged the average price/earnings ratio—based on projected earnings per share (EPS)—for his fund's holdings at a mere 10.4, a 40 percent discount to the S&P 500. But he certainly gets his money's worth. Morningstar.com also computed the overall long-term projected EPS growth rate for the companies in the portfolio as being 23.1 percent (a 40 percent premium to the S&P 500).

This indicates that rather than taking a doctrinaire approach to traditional valuation metrics, Miller really is looking individually at each situation and making judgments as to whether the stock prices, whether high or low by conventional measures, are warranted by his assessment of company prospects. Sometimes, the companies Miller liked were also favored by the investment community as a whole. Other times, they were in Wall Street's doghouse. But on the whole, the matches Miller made between what his fund paid and what it got for its money were on target. Even the new economy crash, which dented Miller's most recent track record, was not sufficient, as of November 1, 2002, to offset the fact that over the prior 10 years, the Legg Mason Value Trust produced an excellent load-adjusted annual return of 15.16 percent. That was 5.29 percentage points per year better than the S&P 500.

GETTING OUR MONEY'S WORTH

There is no single "correct" way to get one's money's worth in the stock market. William Miller takes a case-by-case approach and, if necessary, is willing to accept what most consider a very high price tag if warranted by his assessment of company quality. The key is that high or low, there must be a money's-worth match. This is hardly a novel concept. We think when we shop for cars, apparel, houses, television sets, and so forth. Some of us buy upscale. Some shop downscale. Others prefer midlevel shopping experiences. Ultimately, shopping for stocks is the same. We pick our shopping experience, check the price, examine the merchandise, and decide if we're getting our money's worth.

Charles Royce, who recently sold Royce & Company with its stable of small-company mutual funds to Legg Mason, also uses company quality, rather than stock valuation metrics, as his starting point. On page 200 of *Value Investing with the Masters* (New York Institute of Finance, 2002) by Kirk Kazanjian, Royce told the author, "I don't wake up in the morning saying 'The whole world should sell at nine times earnings and if it doesn't, I won't buy it.' I need to understand the qualitative dimensions of a company before I'm ready to talk about valuation. If I can get a deep confidence in the qualitative part of the company, I will address the valuation questions after that." Much of his qualitative inquiry centers on developing conviction regarding the future sustainability of strong corporate returns on capital.

So on the surface, one might expect funds managed by Miller and the Royce organization to own stocks that are similar in all respects except for market capitalization. But as it turns out, the portfolios are quite different. At September 30, 2002, Royce's flagship Pennsylvania Mutual Fund had an overall beta of 0.61. (A beta of 1.00 would mean that from a statistical standpoint, the portfolio's volatility is equal to that of the S&P 500 index. A beta of 0.61 means the fund's volatility is only 61 percent of the index's volatility.) The beta of the Legg Mason Value Trust was 1.10, meaning that the fund was 10 percent more volatile than the blue-chip S&P 500 index. This is especially interesting since one might have expected the Royce investments to be more volatile given that those companies are much smaller and often less known. The upshot: Even investors with similar inclinations who "shop" in similar, in this case high-quality, "stores" can have different tastes and wind up with different kinds of merchandise.

John Neff, who managed the Vanguard Windsor Fund from 1964 through 1995, also stresses the importance of company quality. In his book *John Neff on Investing* (John Wiley & Sons, 1999), he describes typical Windsor investments as "good companies with solid market positions and evidence of room to grow" (page 76). From a quantitative standpoint, he favors earnings growth that comes not so much from wider margins (where improvement cannot persist indefinitely), but from sales growth. And he prefers sales growth that comes not only from gains in units sold, but also from having and exercising the power to raise prices. Neff also believes return on equity "furnishes the best single yardstick of what management has accomplished with money that belongs to shareholders." This approach to company analysis seems very compatible with what Miller and Royce do. When it comes to assessing the stocks, however, the picture changes. On page 83 of his book, Neff states that "[t]he investing process has to start somewhere. In my case, all ladders start in the dusty rag and bone shop of the market, where the supply of cheap stock replenishes itself daily." Because low valuation metrics represent Neff's starting point, the typical Vanguard Windsor portfolio looked very different from that of the Legg Mason Value Trust. Yet Neff, acting on the basis of different priorities, also accumulated an impressive long-term track record. During his 31-year tenure at Windsor, the fund posted an average annual return of 13.6 percent, which was 2.9 percentage points better than the return posted by the S&P 500 over that same period.

Martin Whitman, manager of the Third Avenue Value Fund, also is a stickler for company quality. In *Value Investing with the Masters*, his ideas regarding company quality are described in terms of a strong financial position, good stockholder-oriented management, and an understandable business. But when it comes to the price he's willing to pay, Whitman told Kazanjian that "[w]e try not to pay more than 50 cents on the dollar for each dollar we think the security would be worth if the business were to go private or be taken over" (page 266).

These star managers differ in emphasis. But the substance of what they do is the same. They seek to get their money's worth. They don't necessarily shop in the same stores. One might assume that Miller and Royce might spend a lot of time shopping in upscale neighborhoods while Neff and Whitman might frequent the discount outlets. But where they shop, or even whether one sticks to the same neighborhood or goes back and forth, is less important than the fact that they consciously strive to get their money's worth. This, not a mindless quest for low P/E, is the essence of value investing.

THEY DON'T ALL DO IT

An extreme antivalue view was propounded during the late 1990s by David and Tom Gardner, proprietors of the MotleyFool.com web site. In their book, *The Motley Fool's Rule Breakers, Rule Makers: The Foolish Guide to Picking Stocks* (Simon & Schuster, 1999), the Gardners articulate two categories of desirable investments. One consists of companies that are rule breakers, visionary firms that ignore the customary ways of doing business in their respective industries and invent new approaches on their own. The other group, the rule makers (in theory, rule breakers that grow up), dominate their industries. They set the norms, and others fall into line.

From a company analysis standpoint, rule maker status is based on analysis of financial statements and related qualitative factors consistent with the approaches of the value notables mentioned earlier. Assessing rule breaker status depends more on qualitative factors such as being a leader in an important emerging industry, having strong consumer appeal, and having sustainable competitive advantage due to company strengths (i.e., patents, vision, etc.) and/or inept competition. As with the rule maker tests, these rule breaker attributes would probably strike most investors as being desirable.

The interesting aspect of the Gardners' approach relates to stock valuation. The rule maker investing strategy is silent on the question. Presumably, if the company measures up to rule maker tests, buy the shares at whatever price they fetch in the marketplace. The rule breaker strategy is bolder. Here, before buying a stock, "you *must* find documentary proof that [the stock] *is grossly overvalued, according to the financial media*" (page 127, emphasis in original).

Times have changed. The late-1990s stock market bubble collapsed, and the Gardners switched gears. Today, they acknowledge that value does count. In *The Motley Fool's What to Do with Your Money Now: Ten Steps to Staying Up in a Down Market* (Simon & Schuster, 2002), they state that "[e]schewing valuation by knocking it off your list saying, 'This is a great company like AOL or GE!'—pursuing growth at any cost—is not a dependable way to beat the stock market averages over time" (page 49).

Even so, views less extreme than those originally advocated on Motley Fool remain widespread. We see it every day as investors flock to shares of companies that issue positive earnings-related announcements. Many buy solely in response to the good news. Little or no consideration is given to whether the price being paid for the shares is excessive relative to what one gets (the quality of the company). Conversely, shares are sold in response to unfavorable announcements even though the prices may be disproportionately low relative to corporate quality.

THE AGENDA

The value connection method presented here is about getting our money's worth from the stocks we buy, holding them while they continue to deliver, and selling when they cease to do so. The emphasis is on the method, ways of assessing companies, ways of assessing stock prices, and ways of determining, in individual situations, whether the price is aligned with what we get. This approach applies whether we shop in the upscale district, middle-market stores, or discount outlets.

But before diving into the heart of the matter, it's important that we make sure we start on the same page. Value means different things to different people. Chapter 1 starts us off by reviewing basic notions of stock valuation and discussing their respective pros and cons. Chapter 2 outlines a game plan for day-to-day implementation of the value connection based on the four-step method I originally presented in *Screening the Market: A Four-Step Method to Find, Analyze, Buy, and Sell Stocks* (John Wiley & Sons, 2002). The rest of the book will examine, in detail, ways to find, analyze, buy, and sell value connection stocks.

Warming Up

## CHAPTER 1

On the Same Page

The value connection method is about getting our money's worth when we buy stocks. We seek a reasonable relationship between what we pay for a share and what we get as a result of our stock ownership. As we'll see, this is tied to the profits earned by the corporation. Hence the relationship between price and earnings will be crucial.

Many regard this relationship, expressed through the price/earnings (P/E) ratio, as inadequate or simplistic. I agree that in the highly imperfect workaday worlds of business and investing, there are often good reasons to consider things other than P/E. But we should stay aware of the importance of the price-and-earnings relationship, and whenever we switch to another metric, it behooves us to understand why P/E comes up short, and why the alternative approach is better for the situation at hand.

Let's start with a review of the most fundamental principles of value, which are based on the stream of corporate earnings.

IVORY TOWER ORIGINS

Interestingly, the purest valuation theory does not explicitly involve P/E. That's because earnings do not flow directly into the hands of the shareholders. Legally, the corporation that earns the profit is completely separate from the shareholder/owners. The law treats a corporation as a completely separate person.

There are three ways corporate wealth can be conferred upon owners (the shareholders). One is liquidation, where the company ceases to conduct business, sells its assets, repays its outstanding obligations, and distributes whatever is left to shareholders. In the usual situation where the corporation stays in existence and continues to conduct business, there are two ways shareholders can tap into the firm's wealth. The direct method is payment of a dividend (which comes from the profit earned by the company). The other, the indirect way, is for the shareholder to sell his/her stake. Presumably, though, the price received will be based on the buyer's assessment of dividend payment prospects or liquidation proceeds. And even in liquidation, prices received will reflect buyers' assessments of income the assets can yield to them. So one way or another, we're back to dividend, the part of the corporate profit that actually passes into shareholders' hands.

The Dividend Discount Model

We evaluate the dividend stream through an approach commonly referred to as "discounted cash flow." Our goal is to calculate the "present value" of the cash we expect to receive from our share ownership.

To understand the concept of present value, consider the intuitively obvious fact that receipt of $1,000 today is not the same as receiving $1,000 a year from now. This would be so even if we could be completely certain the obligation would be honored a year hence. If one-year interest rates are 5 percent, we could invest $1,000 today and have $1,050 one year hence. If we start with $952.38 today and invest it at 5 percent, we'll have $1,000 at the end of a year. Hence $952.38 is the present value of $1,000 assuming a one-year time frame and a 5 percent "discount" rate. If we assume a two-year waiting period, the present value of $1,000 would drop to $907.03. That's the amount we'd have to start with if we want to have $1,000 after investing for two years at a 5 percent compound annual interest rate.

Mathematical models have been developed to calculate fair prices for fixed income securities based on the present value of each interest payment and the present value of the debt principal that gets repaid at some point in the future. Stocks are similar in that we can look at the present values of expected dividend payments. But stocks have no maturity date. The closest we can come to principal repayment is the present value of proceeds we expect to receive when we sell the shares later on. But in contrast to the situation with debt (fixed income securities such as bonds), stock resale proceeds are not usually fixed by contract. Instead, the price is based on the present values of dividends and eventual stock sale proceeds the future buyer will expect to receive. Another complication lies in the fact that dividend payments, unlike bond interest, are expected to grow over time.

The classic approach to addressing such issues is known as the Gordon Dividend Discount Model (DDM). It values stocks based on a simple formula:

$$P = D/(R - G)$$

where P = stock price
D = dividend
R = required rate of annual return
G = projected dividend growth rate

The calculation itself can easily be done using inexpensive handheld calculators. That, in and of itself, is a red flag. To borrow an oft-used investment cliché, if it were really that easy, we'd all be rich. But we're not. So it can't really be as easy as it looks. Indeed, it's not, as we'll see.

Beyond the Dividend Discount Model

The DDM assumes the growth rate (G) is less than the required rate of return (R). Otherwise, the stock would have a negative value, a patently absurd result. Theoreticians are not troubled. They say high growth rates are necessarily temporary and that any growth rate used in this supposedly perpetual model ought to be more permanently sustainable, and hence low enough to avoid producing a negative denominator for the fraction.

Even if we could make reliable assumptions about what such a permanently sustainable growth rate should be, real-world investors would never be content to use it. There's simply too much opportunity to prosper by reacting to the wider variety of growth patterns, whether permanently sustainable or not, that we see every day. Also, many high-quality companies pay little or no dividends.

Hence it is essential that we modify our approach to dividend-based valuation to accommodate these day-to-day realities. Such adaptations are well described in *Security Analysis on Wall Street: A Comprehensive Guide to Today's Valuation Methods* by Jeffrey C. Hooke (John Wiley & Sons, 1998) and *Investment Valuation: Tools and Techniques for Determining the Value of Any Asset* by Aswath Damodaran (John Wiley & Sons, 1996; 2d ed. 2002). A popular theme is the multipart approach. Here's how a three-period variation would work.

- Assume in period one, the corporation reinvests all of its profits (i.e., paying no dividends) to facilitate rapid growth and a better stream of dividends (than what would be the case if dividends were paid immediately) that will start in the future. For the time being, there is nothing we can directly use for purposes of computing a value. All we can do is make assumptions about how fast earnings will grow. That will give us a projected EPS level for the start of the second period. (If the company is losing money now, we project revenue growth and make assumptions that the company will break into the black at or before the start of period two. At that time, estimate EPS by multiplying an assumed net margin by the projected sales number and then dividing by the number of shares.) For now, let's assume period one lasts five years.

- The corporation pays its first dividend in the sixth year, which is the start of period two. The payout ratio (the dividend as a percent of earnings) is not yet at what will ultimately be a long-term sustainable level. So we are not going to plug this dividend into a DDM-like formula. But we do recognize that the shareholder gets the dividend so we factor it into stock valuation. We do that by using the present value of this payment. Throughout period two, the payout ratio will gradually rise to a "permanent" level. Also, the rate of earnings growth will decelerate from the unusually rapid period-one pace to the long-term, permanent, "mature rate." The investor makes assumptions about how this progress will occur year by year. For each year in this transition period, calculate the dividend that is expected to be paid (multiply projected profits by an assumed payout ratio), and add its present value to the here-and-now estimate of stock valuation.
- We assume period three, which starts, say, in year 11, is the mature phase characterized by a permanently stable rate of dividend growth that is less than the required rate of return. Now, we can use the strict DDM formula. The present value of this amount is added to the here-and-now estimate of stock valuation.

That's it. We have an objectively derived value for a company that is growing rapidly at present, and may even be losing money. We stretched the DDM mathematics as far as we'll ever need. (If we're looking at an initial public offering for a company that's barely out of, or even in, the development phase, no problem; extend periods one or two to 10 years or 20 years or however many are needed to make the math work.)

Are you satisfied? I hope not.

Most investors know full well how hard it is to project sales and/or earnings just one quarter into the future. Does anybody really want to commit funds based on assumptions stretching 11 years and beyond? And is there any rational way any investor can decide on the probable lengths of periods one and two, not to mention crucial patterns of transition? We need one set of assumptions regarding the pace at which the payout ratio makes a transition from zero at the end of period one to a permanent level at the start of period three. We also need to decide how quickly and smoothly earnings growth decelerates from the rapid period-one pace to the mature period-three rate. It's fun to make up spreadsheets and fiddle with things like this. But if you do it, make sure you confine such efforts to entertainment. In *Value Investing: From Graham to Buffett and Beyond* by Bruce C. N. Greenwald, Judd Kahn, Paul D. Sonkin, and Michael van Biema (John Wiley & Sons, 2001), the authors reject such approaches because of "the glaring inconsistency between the precision of the algebra and the gross uncertainties infecting the variables that drive the model" (pages 32–33). Amen!

Back to P/E

As impractical as the math can be, it's vital in one respect. It reminds us of the inextricable link between share prices and earnings.

The three-period model just described, although cumbersome, is the approach that is closest to the day-to-day reality of the equity markets. The plain, simple fact is that many corporations see themselves as growth companies and retain a lot of (and in many cases, all) profit. And shareholders as a whole approve this to such an extent that they act as if EPS does pass into their hands and they choose to give it back to the corporation for reinvestment—hence the importance of the basic price-and-earnings relationship, the P/E ratio.

Let's go back to the basic DDM formula and reshuffle it to compute a theoretically correct P/E ratio. Here, again, is our starting point.

$$P = D/(R - G)$$

Since we have seen that earnings, more particularly earnings per share (EPS) supplanted dividend as the object of investment community focus, let's rewrite the equation:

$$P = (\text{EPS} \times \text{Payout Ratio})/(R - G)$$

(EPS × Payout Ratio) is, of course, identical to dividend. If EPS is \$1.00 and the payout ratio is 25 percent, we can express the dividend quickly as \$0.25, or the long way: \$1.00 × 0.25.

Let's now reminisce to our youthful school days, back when the algebra teachers simplified things (so they told us) by dividing each side of an equation by the same item. We'll divide each side of the preceding equation by EPS. Doing so, we get:

$$P/\text{EPS} = \text{Payout Ratio}/(R - G)$$

To accommodate adult habits, we make a purely cosmetic change. We'll refer to EPS as E.

$$P/E = \text{Payout Ratio}/(R - G)$$

This is a theoretically pure formula for calculating what a stock's P/E ought to be.

We're not actually going to use this formula, since it carries all the same baggage we encountered with the basic DDM model. We need to use a multiperiod variation to accommodate companies that don't pay dividends and for situations where the growth rate is higher than the required rate of return or where the growth rate changes over time. And we face all the practical difficulties involved in predicting these items.

But the formula is worth examining because it shows us some things that are crucial for our day-to-day stock valuation efforts. First, we see that P/E ratios should move in the opposite direction from interest rates, an important component of R. If R goes up, the lower part of the fraction, the denominator, moves higher. And if the denominator is higher, then the overall value, the P/E, falls. The reverse occurs when interest rates fall (the denominator decreases and the P/E moves higher).

This is nice, but it just confirms what investment practitioners have long understood. We also see confirmation of some traditional ideas about the way growth should impact a P/E. When G goes up, the denominator of the fraction gets smaller, and a smaller denominator translates to a higher P/E. When G goes down, the denominator goes up and P/E gets smaller. Again, we're confirming what we already knew.

Now, consider the price/earnings-to-growth (PEG) ratio. It's widely assumed that to be correct, a P/E ratio ought to be equal to the growth rate. Put another way, it is often said that the ideal PEG ratio is 1.00. Look at the formula. We see right away that the traditional assumption is not mathematically correct. The formula contains another variable, R, the required rate of return (influenced by interest rates).

Hence we cannot say that there is a single correct relationship between P/E and G. If interest rates go up, the P/E will fall; so, too, will the PEG ratio. If rates go down, P/E rises; so, too, does the PEG ratio. One might say rising interest rates will suppress economic activity and depress profit growth such that the P/E will fall in tandem with growth. (Conversely, falling interest rates would stimulate the economy and profit growth.) But would the change in P/E really match the change in growth resulting from the change in interest rates? In fact, how do we know how much change we can expect in growth based on a particular shift in interest rates? Moreover, what do you think the chances are you could find two economists who'd give the same response? Perhaps an answer can be derived. But even if that's doable, we've still introduced a layer of complexity that takes us far away from the simplistic notion that PEG ratios should always be equal to 1.00.

A Free Ride

Notice that so far, we haven't paid much attention to R. This, too, is subject to our ability to make reliable assumptions. One classic approach to determining R, the capital asset pricing model (CAPM), uses the following formula:

$$R = RF + (RP \times B)$$

where R = required return
          RF = risk-free rate of return
          RP = risk premium
          B = beta assigned to the individual stock being
              examined

Analysis of return starts with the risk-free interest rate, usually a rate applicable to U.S. Treasury securities. We can debate which maturity to use. This can be a critical issue at a time when the yield curve is steep (i.e., when long-term rates are materially higher or lower than short-term rates). But practitioners can generally get away with using the rate on Treasuries that matches a theoretical three- to five-year holding period.

Nobody can be expected to forgo an opportunity to own risk-free securities in favor of stocks, which have risk, if the returns are the same. So stocks have to offer higher prospective returns. The extent to which projected overall stock market returns exceed the risk-free rate of return (RF) is known as the risk premium (RP). How high RP should be is subjective, but that's manageable. Historically, risk premiums have been in the 4 percent to 5 percent range. Many use that range. But investors are free to set higher or lesser levels if they so desire.

Beta is a statistical measure of share price volatility in relation to the "market" (a stock with a beta of 1.20 is deemed 20 percent more volatile than the overall market, a beta of 0.95 suggests 5 percent less volatility, etc.). That's the most challenging assumption. Traditionally, we relied on historical data comparing share price movements to market movements. But such relationships are not necessarily stable over time. Hence beta users would do well to heed the mutual fund advertising party line, "Past performance does not assure future results."

If we can't rely on the past, what can we do? How can anybody make a credible forecast that IBM will be 10 percent more volatile or 5 percent less volatile than the S&P 500 over a particular future time horizon? (Remember, we're not necessarily forecasting the volatility of IBM's earnings, which would be hard enough. We're interested in the relative volatility of its stock price, which involves market sentiment toward it as well as all other stocks.) In fact, we could quarrel with the entire concept of acade-

mic risk measurement that assumes upward volatility is as bad as downward volatility. Most investors are thrilled to see exorbitant upside volatility and are averse only to the downward movements.

There is no easy answer to the beta question. (We can even debate
how to define the "market." The S&P 500 serves as a widely accepted
proxy, but investors can substitute another index if they so desire.) Some
investors simply set all betas equal to 1.00. This assumes all stocks will exhibit the same degree of volatility as the overall market. But that's not necessarily the best approach. Common sense suggests that all else being
equal, more volatile stocks should have lower P/Es. A higher beta (which
drives R higher and thereby reduces P/E) accomplishes this. Many quanti-
tatively inclined investors find it useful to use imperfect betas based on
historical data rather than nothing at all.

Hence there is uncertainty throughout the CAPM, so R is a "soft" number, like the others. But the questions here are not as troubling as they are
elsewhere in the DDM-based approaches. Risk-free rates are widely
known. And it's not unreasonable to assume a general equity risk premium
in line with the historically observed 45 percent range. Beta is challenging
but not materially more so than any other assumptions investors must
make. Chapter 8 examines a value connection technique that uses CAPM
in such a way as to minimize the impact of the most challenging forecasting issues.

Can't Live without Them

As we've seen, the ivory-tower approaches are chock-full of problems.
Clearly, it's hard to live with them. But the many who followed approaches
such as that presented in *The Motley Fool's Rule Breakers*, *Rule Makers*,
which completely ignored the relationship between stock prices and earnings, found how harsh life can be without some kind of valuation anchor.

Ironically, as troublesome as the ivory-tower math can be, pragmatic
real-world adaptations of these concepts can work very well in practice.
An example is the belief that PEG ratios should equal 1.00. As we've seen,
mathematically, that notion is, to put it bluntly, wrong. Ad hoc calculations I've done suggest that PEG ratios in the 1.50 to 2.00 range are often
quite acceptable. Therefore, seeking a PEG ratio equal to or less than 1.00
adds more discipline than necessary to the process. But as we saw with
the collapse of the 1990s market bubble, there are worse things an investor can do than be too attentive to value. So in practice, those who focus on stocks that have PEG ratios equal to or below 1.00, and are
appropriately attentive to company quality issues (often a big if), can and
do achieve success.

The benefit of the ivory-tower approaches isn't so much in the math but in the mere fact that they keep our attention focused on the need to have share prices relate rationally to some measure of wealth creation. Since so many investors ignore this, those who pay attention to it can prosper even if the nature of the relationships they use is largely subjective.

COMPANY-CENTRIC VALUATION

The ivory-tower approaches can be considered "investor-centric" since they focus on wealth that flows into shareholders' hands: dividends (in fact) or EPS (in theory). There is another set of approaches—"company-centric" approaches that focus on the corporate entity itself. Deep down, company-centric and investor-centric approaches are one and the same since it is assumed that at the end of the day, wealth created by the corporation will eventually move into the investor's hands. But the distinction is useful for analytic convenience; company-centric approaches focus our attention on the way the corporation conducts business and the value of its assets, rather than on mathematical relationships between a shareholder's outlay and the returns he/she gets.

Many find company-centric valuation approaches appealing because they raise questions we are accustomed to addressing when doing stock analysis. This is evident from the work of Greenwald et al., who offer in *Value Investing* a strong company-centric presentation that, following the tradition of Benjamin Graham and David Dodd, "is based on a thorough grasp of the economic situation in which the company finds itself [and] puts more emphasis on information about the firm that is solid and certain" (page 35). Their method is based on three elements: the value of the assets, earnings power value, and the value of growth.

Value of the Assets

The first line of inquiry is the balance sheet, which tells us what the company is worth. The problem is that many of the stated valuations owe more to accounting conventions than to what the assets could actually fetch in the real-life transactions. So, according to Greenwald et al., we start by making whatever adjustments are needed to align the official numbers to real-world values. Working from the top of the balance sheet to the bottom, we progress from valuation questions that are easy (cash is worth exactly what the balance sheet says it's worth) to those that are difficult, such as goodwill or physical plant. As we move through the process, we replace book numbers with more realistic alternatives such as liquidation cost or, for a going concern, replacement cost.

Earnings Power Value

The earnings power value (EPV) of a firm is computed using the following formula.

$$EPV = AE/R$$

where AE = adjusted earnings
R = required return

At first glance, this seems similar to the ivory-tower approaches we examined earlier. The difference lies in four adjustments we make to earnings:

1. Eliminate nonrecurring items.
2. Align depreciation expense with what the company really has to spend to maintain the physical asset base.
3. Account for the fact that the earnings being examined may reflect a time when the business cycle was at an unsustainably high or low point. (So we increase or decrease the reported figure in order to get a result that is more representative of the company's normal level of performance.)
4. Allow for the value of a "franchise," if any, as discussed next.

Under normal circumstances, we expect EPV to be equal to (and thereby confirm) the asset-based valuation. If EPV is less, it means management needs to do more to generate the level of profit that should be obtained given the nature of the company's resources. If EPV exceeds asset value, we determine whether the difference is supported by a special "franchise" that will prevent competitors from chipping away until the company's EPV is equal to asset value.

Value of Growth

Thus far, we have not discussed growth. Greenwald et al. isolate this issue for two reasons. First, growth involves assumptions less reliable than those discussed earlier (which are based on factors that can be observed in the present). Second, the only kind of growth worth incorporating into stock valuation is where the increase in earnings exceeds the additional capital necessary to support the new business. If we get this far, we evaluate the strategic underpinnings of the company's franchise and build in a margin of safety to accommodate uncertainties in this area. The margin of uncertainty is based on the extent to which the present value of projected cash flows (which incorporate growth assumptions) exceeds the EPV (which assumes zero growth). At that point, variables incorporating expected growth are added to the EPV computation.

Doability

There can be little doubt that the valuation efforts based on these three elements are considerably more doable than those based on the ivory-tower models. Asset replacement values can be estimated by looking at real-world marketplace transactions. Required return can be calculated based on available data (using the CAPM). The existence and quality of a franchise can be analyzed based on such factors as government license, unique cost structures that cannot be replicated by competitors, customers that are captive by virtue of habit, the burden of finding alternative suppliers, or costs of switching to another provider.

These are issues about which we can make reasonable assumptions. Difference of opinion is possible. But a debate over whether customer habit gives XYZ Company a sustainable competitive advantage seems far more rational than debate over the accuracy of an assumption that XYZ will grow 25 percent for five years, moderate smoothly over the next five years to a 6 percent growth rate, and stay there forever.

But we're not completely out of the woods. Although the company-centric judgments are a lot more sensible than the ivory-tower ones, they are still challenging. Many investors are not able to reliably make judgments about asset replacement costs or the factors that go into a franchise unless they have direct professional experience in the industry in question. And even within a particular milieu, there's plenty of room for difference of opinion.

IN THE EYE OF THE BEHOLDER

Ultimately, no matter how hard we try to be objective, the truth is that stock valuation is far more subjective than is widely acknowledged. We might even go so far as to say the value of a stock is largely in the eye of the beholder. While many may find this hard to accept given this topic's mathematical heritage, the notion is actually quite standard in other disciplines. Consider, for example, the definition of value presented by Lakshman Krishnamurthi, in Chapter 12 (page 281) of *Kellogg on Marketing*, (Northwestern University Kellogg Marketing Faculty Treatise, Dawn Iacobucci, Ed.; John Wiley & Sons, 2001).

Value is the "art" part of pricing. It is idiosyncratic. One person may have a high value for a Mazda Miata, another may have no value for it. Value is relative. There are no absolutes. . . . The value that a customer derives from a product or service is a function of the quality delivered by the product or service which in turn is obtained from the economic, functional, and psychological benefits provided by the product or service.

Actually, in the real world, the value of a Mazda Miata is established in the same manner as a share of corporate stock; both are based on supply and demand. As the number of people who are attracted by a Miata's quality attributes increases, the greater is the probability that demand will relate to supply in such a way as to establish a relatively high price. Similarly, as the number of investors who are attracted to a company's quality attributes increases, the greater the probability that demand will relate to supply in such a way as to establish relatively high valuation metrics for the shares.

It's tempting to see this as a license to chase shares of a hot company no matter how richly valued they may be based on the notion that if supply and demand combine in a stock price that equates to a P/E of 200, then that's a correct value. Part of the art of valuation is recognizing when demand is motivated by factors that are irrational and probably unsustainable. If a Yugo sold for the same price as a comparably equipped Miata, Yugo shoppers would eventually come to realize they wouldn't be getting their money's worth and they'd shift their attention to the Miata, at least until in the collective opinion of the car-buying public the price of the Yugo was fair compared to that of the Miata.

But markets are rarely, if ever, in perfect equilibrium. Usually, prices vacillate back and forth between being too high or too low. So car shoppers will have opportunities to overpay. And undoubtedly, some careless buyers won't do their homework and will, indeed, wind up paying a high price for a low-end car. The stock market works the same way. Many buyers do not diligently evaluate what they get (the quality of the company) in return for what they pay. And over the long term, their fortunes fare similarly to those who pay top dollar for low-end merchandise. They get burned. Many who chased new economy stocks in the late 1990s can attest to that.

Good decision making involves capable assessment of a product's attributes. Yugos and Miatas can be assessed on the basis of such attributes as size, interior comfort, motor power, ease of handling, appearance, and so on. There is no absolutely objective way to say a particular combination of attributes should equate to a specific price. The most we can hope for in a properly functioning market is that buyers and sellers will fairly consider what each car's collection of attributes means to them and achieve a supply-demand match that reflects the sum total of all these decisions. When assessing companies, consideration is given to such attributes as growth trends and prospects, return on capital, financial risk, margin, turnover, and so on. As in the car market, different investors will decide how desirable different attribute combinations are to them. But this kind of subjectivity is a far cry from the new economy bubble, when many gave no credible consideration to bona fide corporate attributes.

Throughout this book, we'll hone in on important attributes of company quality and the relationship between the company and the price at which the stock trades. Our method grows from the investor-centric and company-centric concepts described in this chapter, but does not attempt to reduce either to a rigid formula. Instead, we'll strive to work with both the art and the science of value.

## CHAPTER 2

The Four-Step Screening Method

We implement the value connection with a four-step screening method. We use both investor-centric principles (measures of economic benefit accruing as a result of share ownership) and company-centric concepts (wealth that accumulates within the corporate entity) to help us identify potentially "good stocks." Company-centric principles are also used to help us find potentially "good companies." We also weigh and balance to determine whether the price we're being asked to pay is reasonable in light of what we are getting.

The four steps are based on the approach I presented in *Screening the Market*. This system is unique in its steadfast commitment to the principle of doability. As is the case with any other investment method, you will be asked to consider many questions. The difference here is that I fully expect you to be perfectly capable of answering each and every question posed.

The four steps are based on the life cycle of an investment. These are things every investor does, whether or not he/she openly articulates or acknowledges what is being done. Here are the steps:

- **Step 1: Find.** There are many available investment books that teach how to decide whether a particular stock is attractive. This method does that as well. But an important aspect of its uniqueness is that it does not take for granted that investors are being reasonable in deciding what stocks to examine. It presents a systematic approach for deciding which stocks are worthy of being looked at in the first place.

- **Step 2: Analyze.** Here, we look individually at the stocks uncovered in Step 1 (Find), and for each, make a determination as to whether it is attractive. Convincing investors to engage in Step 2 (Analyze) is easy since this is what most see as the meat of the process. The more interesting issue is how one goes about performing the analysis. This method advocates an approach that deemphasizes worthwhile but unanswerable questions such as the competence of a company's management, the quality of its work force, the uniqueness of its technologies, and so on, and emphasizes use of a doable protocol based on readily available financial and descriptive data reports.
- **Step 3: Buy.** It is widely assumed that if a stock passes muster under our analytic standards, we should buy it, and that we should avoid stocks that don't measure up. Rarely, though, are things that simple. Almost every stock we see will have some qualities we like and others we find disturbing. This method takes the position that all buy-or-avoid decisions are based on a balancing of pros and cons in a manner consistent with our investment objectives, and introduces a set of procedures to help us accomplish that task.
- **Step 4: Sell.** This is a widely misunderstood process that is often based less on rational analysis and more on folklore, such as ride your winners, dump your losers. This method eschews folklore and takes the position that the sell-versus-hold decision is very similar to buy-versus-avoid. In each case, investors determine whether the company is worthwhile in light of the current stock price. Step 4 does this by applying an Alert-Update-Reconsider discipline that is similar to Find-Analyze-Buy.

We'll turn now to a more detailed explanation of each step. Then, the rest of the book will explore, in greater detail, how each of the market-screening method's four steps can be applied to the value connection investment style.

Here, now, is an overview of how the four-step method can be used to match good companies with good stocks.

STEP 1: FIND . . . POTENTIALLY ATTRACTIVE VALUE CONNECTIONS

It's nice to be good at evaluating stocks. But how do we decide which ones to look at? As of this writing, Multex's U.S. database already has more than 9,000 companies, and its new global database will eventually more than double that number. No matter who we are, what we seek, what style(s) we choose to pursue, we all have a very important thing in common. We need a method that brings some companies to our attention and excludes others.

Sometimes, this method is very casual, or downright unconscious. If someone says, "I look at such-and-such stocks because these are the ones I've heard of, but I can't recall offhand how I happened to have learned of their existence," we can still say this person has a method of finding stocks. Most serious investors would consider this an extremely poor method. But it's still a method. Another person may say, "I look at such-and-such stocks because they have P/E ratios below their respective industry averages and the companies have above-average growth rates." This, too, is a method, a much better one at that.

The latter approach to finding stocks is superior because it is purposeful. The investor has identified a set of personal investment goals, has given serious thought to how those goals can translate into specific investment characteristics, and has found a way to put this program into action in the real world, probably through stock screening, that is, use of a computer program that sifts through a database and identifies stocks meeting a set of tests we articulate.

A generation ago, only large institutional investors had access to such programs and databases. Things are much different today. One area in which the information revolution is all it's cracked up to be, and perhaps more, is the way it makes stock screening accessible to a very broad universe of investors. Some perfectly workable applications and databases can be accessed for free or for nominal fees. Those willing to pay a few hundred dollars can get access to good-quality screeners. And for those who feel unwilling or unable to create their own screens from scratch, there are many excellent regularly (often daily) updated preset screens available, again for free or at a reasonable cost.

This book assumes you will use stock screens (ones you create for yourself and/or preset screens) to find potentially attractive value connections. A comprehensive discussion of stock screening is contained in *Screening the Market*. But even if you have not read that book, the material presented here is sufficient to enable you to find the right opportunities. Chapter 3 describes how to use the kinds of screening applications you're likely to encounter. Chapters 4 and 5 show you how to create the sort of screens that will identify good companies and good stocks, or recognize if a preset screen is sound. Chapters 6 and 7 will help you combine these approaches and enhance your efforts by introducing secondary and alternative themes drawn from other investment styles.

STEP 2: ANALYZE . . . SPECIFIC IDEAS TO SEE IF THE VALUE CONNECTION IS SOUND

One shortcoming of screening is the fact that not every program includes every possible test. Sooner or later, we're bound to find ourselves stymied by the fact that the screening application we use or preset screens to which we have access do not include certain data tests we wish we could apply. Believe it or not, this is not a major obstacle. We can apply the screening method successfully even if we are not able to perfectly implement our preferences in Step 1 (Find). The solution is to accept whatever imperfections exist in the screening process and use Step 2 (Analyze), the company-by-company review, to consider factors that never made it into the screen.

Also, no screen can ever be treated as a hard-and-fast buy list. Computers, by their very nature, apply criteria in a rigid way. For example, a screen seeking P/Es below 10.0 may include ABC Company, with a P/E of, say, 8.5. But the ratio may be calculated with reference to EPS for a period that includes one quarter in which the company reported unusually high and clearly unsustainable results (perhaps because of a large gain resulting from sale of an asset). Absent the one odd quarter, the company's P/E usually runs in the neighborhood of 20.0. In listing ABC Company, the screen complies with the letter of the law; its P/E is, indeed, below 10.0. But computers are not able to assess the spirit of the law and are therefore unable to understand that ABC Company is not really the sort of thing we're looking for.

Even where screens wind up complying with the spirit, as well as the letter, of the law, we still can't treat the result set as a list of automatic buys. Stocks meeting our value expectations may be unsuitable for any one of a number of other reasons such as poor company balance sheets, a likelihood of significant future business deterioration, and so on. The book includes some additional screening tests to address such situations. But we can't filter out every potential negative. If we try, we'll wind up with so many tests, no companies will be able to pass all of them. So we'll rely on Step 2 (Analyze) to weed out some of the undesirables that inevitably make it through Step 1 (Find).

The heart of Step 2 (Analyze) is examination of a series of data presentations readily available on the Internet. To the uninitiated, the quantity of information may appear overpowering. But if we understand at the outset what we're looking for, the task becomes easily manageable. We'll organize our inquiry based on the metaphor presented in the Introduction, a shopping trip where we seek to get our money's worth on what we buy.

1. **Check the price.** We'll start out by examining a set of relevant stock valuation metrics. Some, such as P/E, are obvious. Others are less mainstream, and sometimes we won't be able to simply look at what's

posted on the Internet and will have to calculate the ratios ourselves. But that will be easy, since all the information we'll need in order to create all the ratios is very widely accessible. The computations, detailed in Appendix A to Chapter 8, easily lend themselves to use in a spreadsheet template. Some of us might even be able to automate some of the work using auxiliary features of screening programs.

2. **Assess the merchandise.** This is the procedure introduced in *Screening the Market*, the review of company-oriented data reports. Chapter 8 includes a review of this procedure for those who are not already familiar with it. The information we seek, such as fundamental results and trends, price charts, news summaries, and business descriptions, is readily available on the Internet. Accordingly, this is a highly doable task. That doesn't mean we're going to act like investment automatons. Even the most objective information usually lends itself to a wide range of interpretations. Hence we are not relieved of responsibility for exercising judgment. But at least the opinions we draw, whichever way they lean, are based on a solid foundation of fact.

3. **Determine if we are getting our money's worth.** We'll wrap up with an expectation analysis that shows us how much future earnings growth is needed to justify today's stock price, something that can easily be accomplished through a spreadsheet template that will be described in Appendix B to Chapter 8. We'll use what we learned in our merchandise assessment to help us determine whether we believe the company can meet or exceed this growth target.

Note the assumption that we start by assessing price (i.e., determining if we have a good stock), and then assess whether we have a good company. This is done strictly for convenience. Just as many shoppers examine merchandise before they look at the price tag, we, too, can flip the process and assess company quality before we consider share valuation metrics. As with any shopping experience, the sequence is a matter of taste. The important thing is that we make two separate assessments, one focusing on the stock and the other focusing on the company. Regardless of which is done first, we'll ultimately reach the same point, a decision as to whether we're getting our money's worth.

STEP 3: BUY . . . THE BEST VALUE CONNECTED OPPORTUNITIES

In Step 3 (Buy), we apply a systematic decision process to the task of balancing pros and cons that are almost inevitable in any stock we see. This is a vital step. Many investment systems are flawed in that they leave the reader assuming he or she will purchase those stocks that pass whatever tests the investor chooses to apply. The problem with this approach is that it fails to show how to deal with the situations investors are much more likely to find in the real world, stocks that look good in some respects but bad in others.

Identifying appropriate buys involves more than simply tallying pros and cons. Whether a particular fact has positive, neutral, or negative investment implications can vary depending on one's investment style. There are two sides to every stock market transaction—a buyer and a seller. Some market participants are, indeed, guilty of faulty analysis. But often, differences between buyers and sellers reflect different ways of assessing shared facts based on differing goals.

Screening the Market presents a framework based on three Analysis Keys, each of which is a yes/no question covering an important aspect of the investment analysis. The first Analysis Key asks if the insights you gained through Step 2 (Analyze) indicate that the situation fits your original investment theme, the spirit of the law as well as the letter. The second Analysis Key asks whether additional factors beyond the original theme impact the investment situation in a positive way. Analysis Key 3 turns the tables and asks whether the situation is free of additional factors that have negative impact on the investment story.

After answering the three questions, we will have three yes/no answers for each stock we analyzed. *Screening the Market* places each possible combination on one of eight Decision Paths. The highest path, representing the best possible scenario, is a stock that satisfies our original goal, offers additional positives beyond those we had hoped to get, and carries no negative baggage. These stocks are clear-cut buys. The worst scenario, the one we'll avoid at all costs, is the stock that does not really offer what we originally hoped to get, offers no alternative benefits to compensate, and has other kinds of negative baggage. The real balancing results from the fact that few stocks will wind up on the highest or lowest paths. Most will be somewhere in the middle.

Chapters 9 and 10 explain more comprehensively how to apply the Analysis Keys and Decision Paths to the value connection method.

STEP 4: SELL . . . STOCKS FOR WHICH THE VALUE CONNECTION HAS WEAKENED

For many, hold-versus-sell decisions are very challenging. The main reason is because investors are often obsessed with the rearview mirror, a focus on what they paid for the stock and whether they have a gain or loss. This leads to often-contradictory "rules" such as ride your winners versus taking profits, or dump your losers versus averaging down.

Instead, investors should look to the future. Is the stock a worthwhile investment based on today's price and a current assessment of company quality? The price paid in the past is water under the bridge. There's nothing that can be done about it. And it is certainly irrelevant to the key issue—what the stock is likely to do in the future. (Obviously, the prices we paid are relevant if the shares are held in taxable accounts. But too many inappropriate hold-versus-sell decisions can easily leave us worse off than we'd be if we simply made the right investment decisions and let tax consequences fall where they may.)

We'll focus on relevant factors by, in effect, tuning in to the other side of a potential sale. Imagine there's another investor out there who shares our goals, our risk tolerances, our style, and so forth, but does not at present own shares of XYZ Company, a stock we are thinking about selling. Now, imagine that XYZ has come to the attention of the other person for the first time. He or she will analyze the stock and apply the Analysis Keys and Decision Paths in a way quite similar to the way we'd do it (because our goals are the same). Finally, imagine what conclusion this other person might reach. The more bullish that imaginary investor ought to be, the more reluctant we should be to sell. If the other investor would find the stock unappealing, that's our cue that we should sell.

Since we're being asked to try to see the stock through the eyes of another potential buyer, it should come as little surprise that Step 4 (Sell), explained more fully in Chapters 11 and 12, is adapted from the three steps that were used to purchase the stock. It's based on three phases: Alert, Update, and Reconsider.

Sell Phase 1 (Alert) is analogous to Step 1 (Find). It is designed to call our attention to situations requiring a hold-versus-sell decision. Alerts can be triggered by screens designed to uncover sell opportunities, events such as earnings announcements or sharp and sudden movements in the stock price, or the passage of time (we may adopt a policy of automatically reviewing any position we haven't updated in, say, three months). Sell Phase 2 (Update) is analogous to Step 2 (Analyze). We follow the same data-oriented analytic approach we used the first time. But now, the specifics of what we now see reflect updates due to the passage of time. Sell Phase 3 (Reconsider) is analogous to Step 3 (Buy); we use three Update Keys similar to the original Analysis Keys. Then, we'll use a series of Reconsideration Paths based on the combinations of yes/no answers to the Update Keys. As with the original Decision Paths, the Reconsideration Paths range from best (obvious holds) to worst (stocks that should be most quickly sold).

Find . . . Potentially Attractive Value Connections

## CHAPTER 3

Tools of
the Trade

S tep 1 (Find) involves use of stock screens to help us identify potentially attractive investment opportunities. There are three ways to
approach this task. The best is to gain access to one or more applications and build our own screens. In the alternative, we can choose from
among the preset screens that normally accompany these programs.
There's also an in-between approach; we can use preset screens as a starting point and then edit them to suit our personal preferences.

BAD NEWS, GOOD NEWS

I'm going to get some bad news out of the way quickly. No matter what
screener is used, you will find yourself unable to apply some of the ideas
presented in this book. As we'll see later on, the things we can do with a
particular program depend on its inventory of variables (data items
against which companies are tested) and on the presence or absence of
auxiliary features such as report customization and the ability to ex-
port/import user-defined lists or portfolios. All screeners today are better
than they were 20 years ago, but even now no individual application is
perfect. And besides, even if you find a perfect screener that can do
everything, you would still have to limit your choices lest you trap yourself into a quest for perfection that drives the number of passing companies down to zero.

The good news is that everyone can, and should, use all of the ideas
presented here even if they cannot be incorporated into screening tests.
To some extent, auxiliary program features provide useful work-around

opportunities (which will be introduced later in this chapter and explained in greater detail in the appendix to the chapter). More importantly, screening is presented here not as the be-all and end-all of the process, but as the first step in a four-step method. It's perfectly acceptable to implement Step 1 (Find) by using screens that only approximate your ideas about what makes for a good investment because we'll have ample opportunity to more precisely refine your lists of candidates in Step 2 (Analyze) and Step 3 (Buy).

HOW STOCK SCREENS WORK

For those who are new to stock screening, a summary of the topic will be presented in this book. A more comprehensive presentation can be found in *Screening the Market*. As was the case there, sample tests presented here will not follow strictly the linguistic conventions of any particular application. Instead, they will be presented in a plain-English adaptation of the terminology used in the Multex screeners.

Commonly referenced time periods will be expressed using the following abbreviations:

TTM   Trailing 12 months
MRQ   Most recent quarter

Screeners search databases and identify situations having certain qualities we specify. For example, we might ask the program to identify shares of all companies having a three-year EPS growth rate equal to or greater than 20 percent. The typical screener would require us to express this as a statement that could be evaluated by the computer as being true or false. In creating such expressions, the programs typically utilize the following standard mathematical notations.

=   Equal to
<>   Not equal to
>   Greater than
>=   Greater than or equal to
<   Less than
<=   Less than or equal to
/   Divided by
*   Multiplied by

Based on that, our 20 percent growth rate test might look like this:

3 Year EPS Growth Rate >= 20%

Often, a single test such as this will leave us with more passing stocks than we have time to examine. To reduce the list to a manageable size, screens usually contain more than one test. Let's assume our complete screen is:

3 Year EPS Growth >= 20%
3 Year Sales Growth >= 20%
P/E <= 15
Dividend Yield >= 2%

Here is what the computer will do in response to this series of tests.

- It will start with a master list containing all stocks in the database. Assume, in this example, we begin with 10,000 stocks.
- It will evaluate each stock to determine if the company's three-year EPS growth rate is equal to or greater than 20 percent. If so, the stock stays in the list. If not, the stock is discarded. Let's assume this step reduces the list to 900 stocks.
- The program will evaluate each of the remaining 900 stocks to determine if the company's three-year rate of sales growth is equal to or greater than 20 percent. If so, the stock stays in the list. If not, the stock is discarded. Let's assume this step reduces the list to 450 stocks.
- Now the program looks at each of the remaining 450 stocks to see if the P/E is equal to or below 15. If so, the stock stays in the list. If not, the stock is discarded. Let's assume this step reduces the list to 200 stocks.
- Finally, the program examines each of the remaining 200 stocks to see if the dividend yield is at least 2 percent. If so, the stock stays in the list. If not, the stock is discarded. Let's assume this step reduces the list to 35 stocks.

Now, we have exactly what we wanted. We were interested in growth companies whose shares traded at or below 15 times earnings and yielded at least 2 percent. The screener examined 10,000 stocks and found 35 that met our requirements.

You probably noticed that not every stock got a chance to be reviewed under every test. In fact, 9,100 stocks never made it past the first cut. But this does not impact the composition of the final list. If we reshuffle the tests, the best that nonconforming stocks can do is to stay alive a bit longer. But by the time we're finished, they'll all be gone. To make the final list, each stock must pass each test.

But there's lots of leeway to determine how strict or lenient each test will be. The more lenient we are, the larger our final list will be. Let's see how this works by modifying our sample screen.

3 Year EPS Growth > = 20% OR 3 Year Sales Growth > = 20%
P/E <= 15
Dividend Yield >= 2%

The theme is the same; growth stocks with modest P/E ratios and decent yields. But we've taken a somewhat more relaxed attitude toward the growth test. Now, instead of requiring that sales growth and EPS growth each be equal to or greater than 20 percent, we allow the stock to pass muster if just one of those rates meets the 20 percent threshold. This is not an exception to the rule that each stock must pass each test. That's still the case. But now we substituted one lenient test in place of two strict growth tests.

SCREENING STRATEGIES

For those new to screening, even simple applications can look intimidating due to what might appear to be an overwhelming number of different things that can be done. Don't worry. Picking and choosing becomes much easier if we approach screening with a clear strategy based on two important sets of decisions: the kinds of tests we use, and the way we combine tests into themes.

Different Kinds of Tests

Some tests are better than others. In choosing among the available screeners, consider the kinds of tests each lets you create and strike your own personal balance between sophistication and cost.

Basic Testing   The tests contained in the sample screens just illustrated are direct tests, where one thing (three-year EPS growth) is compared to another (20 percent). This is a simple, straightforward approach, and it is available in any screener. But ease and potency do not necessarily go hand in hand. For example, consider why you would choose to set a growth hurdle at 20 percent. Why not 25 percent or 30 percent? Come to think of it, why not 15 percent? Considering the rate at which the economy as a whole grows, rates of inflation, and other factors, a company that can grow 15 percent a year nowadays is doing quite well.

Comparative Testing   This approach spares us the need to wrestle with such questions. There are two kinds of comparative tests. A cross-sectional approach would look like this:

3 Year EPS Growth Rate > = Industry Average 3 Year EPS Growth Rate

This is a much more potent inquiry than the simple test. A company growing 20 percent a year would be deemed inadequate and rejected if the industry as a whole is growing at a 30 percent rate. Conversely, a company growing 15 percent a year would pass the test if, say, the industry average growth rate is 12 percent. That's the kind of company we'll be looking for—companies that look good, not because they have the good fortune of being in the right place at the right time (i.e., being in a hot industry and benefiting from the rising-tide-lifts-all-boats phenomenon) but because they have company-specific strengths.

Some screeners handle cross-sectional comparison via the relative strength approach. Consider a test like this.

3 Year EPS Growth Relative Strength > = 70

This would mean that the company's three-year EPS growth rate is better than those of at least 70 percent of the others in the group. When using relative strength, make a point of checking the definitions provided by the screener (in help sections or a glossary). For one thing, you need to know which group the company is being compared to. It can be the industry, the sector, the S&P 500, or the entire data universe. Also, there are different ways of expressing relative strength. Some applications express the exact same concept this way:

3 Year EPS Growth Rank < = 30

Translated into English, this version of the test would require that no more than 30 percent of the companies in the group have better three-year EPS growth rates than the company in question.

Here's the other kind of comparison, the time-series approach.

TTM EPS Growth Rate > = 3 Year EPS Growth Rate

This test is also potent, but in a manner that differs from the cross-sectional inquiry. Here, we compare a company's shorter-term, more recent performance to its own longer-term record. The example seeks companies that are improving over time. A company whose EPS grew 20 percent in the past year would look impressive if this pace represents acceleration from, say, a 10 percent three-year rate. It would look less impressive if it were in the process of decelerating from, perhaps, a 30 percent three-year growth rate.

Behavioral Testing   Here, we don't care about the data points per se, but are instead interested in the way data points stand as evidence of the subjective reactions of others in the investment community who have examined a company and its stock. We infer what they think based on how they behave. This is an important line of inquiry. Screening is often seen as limited by a focus on numeric information only. Clearly, investing is not a pure science. It contains large elements of art, as reflected in subjective judgments, especially about future prospects. Intelligent use of behavioral tests can bring subjectivity far deeper into the screening process than many realize.

Consider the following test.

P/E > (Industry Average P/E) * 1.5

At first glance, such a test, seeking shares whose P/E ratios are at least 50 percent higher than their respective industry averages, seems contrary to the needs of a value investor. But we're living today in the information age. Sixty years ago, it may have been plausible to assume that a stock could be richly valued because many investors didn't know better. That's not the case today. In fact, such a P/E could be interpreted as evidence that investors who are looking at the totality of the situation see reason to believe this company is substantially better than its peers. It's possible this conclusion may be counterbalanced by other evidence to the contrary. Additional screening tests, as well as our activities in Step 2 (Analyze), will provide ample opportunity to see if that's the case. But skillful use of behavioral testing can uncover interesting value connection opportunities that might otherwise be missed.

Screening Themes

Suppose, in creating a screen, our primary goal is to invest in shares that have modest valuation metrics. We might start with a screen that looks like this.

TTM P/E < (Industry Average TTM P/E) * .75
TTM P/E/3 Year EPS Growth Rate < 1

Primary Theme   The first test requires that each stock's P/E be no greater than 75 percent of the industry average P/E. The second test requires that PEG (price/earnings-to-growth) ratios be less than 1.00. Both of these tests relate to our goal, low valuation metrics. These constitute the screen's primary theme.

I actually created this screen as I wrote the manuscript. As of that time, 1,079 stocks (out of a total of 9,215) passed muster. Such a list is too big to be useful. We could add more valuation tests (relating share price to sales, book values, cash flow, etc.). We could also make the existing tests more stringent. Perhaps we should reduce the PEG threshold to .50. But it's not necessarily constructive to go overboard with any one theme.

Secondary and Alternative Themes Any time we seek low valuation metrics, we are in danger of finding stocks that deserve to be cheap because of poor company quality or prospects. We can address this with secondary and/or alternative themes. A secondary theme is one that is generally consistent with (albeit not identical to) the primary theme. An alternative theme is one that is opposed (or at least unrelated) to the primary theme.

Let's add the following tests to the sample screen.

3 Year EPS Growth > Industry Average 3 Year EPS Growth
Long-Term Debt Ratio < Industry Average LT Debt Ratio
Share Price Change Last 4 Weeks > Industry Average 4 Week Share
    Price Change

All three are alternative tests since they are unrelated to the primary value theme. They combine to reduce the list to 69 stocks, a still large but now somewhat manageable size. Admittedly, in working the list down from 1,079 to 69 we strayed from pure value. But we did not hurt ourselves. We made our list better.

Consider that in percentage terms, the first two value tests eliminated 88 percent of the total database. That's a pretty good day's work for our efforts involving P/E. And we knew it would be imprudent to stop there, since the list probably included many poor quality companies. The long-term growth and balance sheet tests eliminated many fundamental dogs. And the share price test (strong recent performance compared to industry peers) indicates that those who have been looking at the situation in the past month like what they see (i.e., it serves as behavioral evidence to the effect that the immediate company's fundamental position is at least acceptable).

This alone ought not induce us to buy any of the 69 remaining stocks. But the list as presently constituted, very low P/E ratios based on industry and growth comparison, coupled with additional tests that combine to produce at least some inference of acceptable quality, gives us a good head start for Step 2 (Analyze). We're certainly better off than we would have been had we just made the primary theme more stringent and continued to leave ourselves fully exposed to the possibility that many bad companies will crowd their way into our lists.

Layered Screening   This is a variation on the idea of secondary and alternative themes. In conventional screening, secondary and alternative tests are combined with primary tests in a single screen. The layered approach involves use of multiple screens and is especially well suited for the value connection.

For example, we may locate three favored value-oriented good-stock screens we like, and, perhaps, a half-dozen screens aimed at different aspects of the good-company theme. These screens may in total produce, say, 250 stocks. We'd collect all these names into a "user portfolio," and load it into one of the applications that can accept imported lists. Then, instead of screening on the entire database, we'd set the program to screen only on our custom-created value connection portfolio. We'll make the final cut using a new layer-two screen aimed at an entirely different theme, such as the following example, which is based on sentiment.

Consensus Estimate of Current Quarter EPS > Consensus 4 Weeks Ago

Consensus Analyst Rating Is More Bullish Than Where It Stood 4 Weeks Ago

Short Interest < Prior Month Short Interest

Share Price Change Last 4 Weeks > Industry Average 4 Week Share Price Change

It could be argued that an important aspect of the value connection's appeal is that it frees us from the burden of chasing the stocks that are popular now, which is the sort we'd uncover if we applied these four tests to a full database. But when we apply them to a limited subset consisting of stocks that already appeared in at least one of a group of value connection screens, the sentiment tests take on an entirely new flavor. This layer-two screen doesn't merely produce a list of well-favored stocks; it produces a list of well-favored value connection stocks. Put another way, it produces a list of value connection stocks that are likely to appeal not merely to value investors, but also to investors who pursue other styles. Considering the Wall Street community's long-standing preoccupation with short-term earnings trends, chances are any stock that satisfies this layer-two sentiment screen has at least some appeal to those who utilize that approach. And since all stock prices are ultimately based on supply and demand, it seems logical that all else being equal, we should favor stocks appealing to as many different kinds of investors as possible (the ones most likely to attract greater demand).

WORKING WITH SPECIFIC SCREENING APPLICATIONS

A variety of programs are available, mainly over the Internet. Years ago, access to these programs, and the databases with which they work, were prohibitively expensive to all but the largest institutional investors. But nowadays, screeners are accessible to all who want to use them. It's still the case that the best applications are the costliest. But modern programs are so advanced, even the lower-end applications that are free or inexpensive (less than $300 per year) can be used to implement the value connection. And given the plunge in hardware prices, personal computers priced for first-time home users have more than enough power to handle any of these programs. (The hardest work is done on remote servers.)

Learning to Use the Interface

Every screening application has its own unique interface. But the process is so heavily dominated by common features, it's easy to figure out how to work with any application if you understand the key themes.

Each screening test has four components: (1) a category, (2) a variable, (3) a relationship, and (4) a base or threshold. Let's see how these apply to the following sample test.

3 Year EPS Growth Rate >= 20%

1. **Category:** Most screening applications group their offerings into a convenient number of categories. These do not impact the tests themselves or the lists. They are presented for the sole purpose of helping users quickly find what they are looking for. In our sample, we would start by looking for a category that has a label such as "Growth Rates."

2. **Variables:** Variables are the basic building blocks of the screens. They represent the data items computers can use to evaluate stocks. In the sample test, "3 Year EPS Growth Rate" is the variable. The variables that are offered by a particular screener figure prominently in an assessment of whether the program is a good one. Many screeners offer variables for three-year growth rates. But suppose we want to screen for companies whose 15-year growth rates are equal to or greater than 20 percent. Most screeners do not offer 15-year growth rate variables, so chances are we will not be able to screen this way. (The only

screener I know of that allows for such a test is a top-dollar institutional offering, and even there, we would have to mathematically "construct" the growth rate formula on our own using present and past EPS figures.)

3. **Relationship:** This is the means by which we identify the nature of the comparison we want the computer to make in order to determine whether the stock should be kept in the list or discarded. In the sample test, >= (greater than or equal to) is the relationship. Most relationships are mathematical, consistent with the list presented earlier. Some screeners also allow us to specify relationship based on the sorting concept. In other words, we might construct a test requiring that the three-year EPS growth rate be "as high as possible" or that the P/E be "as low as possible." Screeners that allow this typically limit the number of stocks that can appear on a list. We might, as an example, wind up using conventional tests (based on mathematical relationships) to set sales and EPS growth rate thresholds, and then using a sort-oriented test to produce a final list consisting of the 25 growth stocks having the lowest P/Es in a lowest to highest P/E sort.

4. **Base:** This is what the variable is compared to. In the case of our sample test, the base is 20 percent. The simplest kind of base is a number. That's how we constructed our sample tests. Some programs will allow you to use more sophisticated bases. For example, we might want to have a test that compares one variable to another variable.

3 Year EPS Growth Rate >= 3 Year Sales Growth Rate

Here we want companies whose earnings per share have been growing more rapidly than sales. The variable is "3 Year EPS Growth Rate" and the base is "3 Year Sales Growth Rate." Top-of-the-line applications will allow you to go a step further and adjust the bases using multiplication factors. Consider the following example.

3 Year EPS Growth Rate >= (3 Year Sales Growth Rate) * 1.25

Here, the base is the three-year rate of sales growth multiplied by 1.25. Put another way, we'd say the base is set at a level 25 percent above the three-year sales growth rate. So translating that test to plain English, we would say we seek companies whose three-year rates of earnings growth are at least 25 percent greater than their three-year rates of sales growth.

Note, though, that care is needed in situations where a variable used as part of the base might be negative, as in this example. If the three-year sales growth rate is –10 percent, the base would be –12.5 percent ($1.25 \times -10 = -12.5$). Hence a company with a –12 percent EPS growth rate would make the screen even though –12 is worse than –10. We can guard against this by adding another test that requires the company's three-year EPS growth rate to be at least zero. Or, if we want to accept companies with growth rates that are less negative than the industry average, we could add another test requiring that the company's EPS growth rate be at least .75 times that of the industry average. Often this test will be redundant. But a company with a –12 percent EPS growth rate would now be excluded (–12 is not greater than or equal to –7.5).

This framework should help you navigate your way through any screening interface you encounter. Terminology varies from one program to the next. But the elements (category, variable, relationship, and base) should be present in all. Once you have created your tests, look for a prompt that allows you to communicate to the program that you want it to apply the tests to the database. (Some programs will run the screen again and again every time you specify a test while others will wait for you to click on a button that says "Run," "Submit," or something like that.)

Beyond these basics, there are other features that are available in some screeners and not others. Here are the most important ones.

- **Saving Screens:** No matter how avid a screening enthusiast you are, you are likely to spend only a little bit of time creating screens. Once you have a collection of screens you like, you will, for the most part, return to them again and again to see which stocks appear based on the most up-to-date data. Hence it is a major convenience if your favorite application allows you to save your screens for immediate retrieval at later times. Most applications let you do this. However, even as of this writing, there are some programs that don't include this feature. So look for it, and if it's absent, you'll have to balance its omission against other features that might appeal to you.
- **Reports/Layouts:** The main task of a screener is to identify companies that meet all of your tests. So at the very least you'd like to get a list of stocks that make the grade. Actually, though, all of today's screeners go beyond this bare-bones minimum. They identify the stocks and also give you basic information about each. Individual applications vary in terms of how much control you get regarding which items of information are displayed and how you can sort. Some applications even allow you to store your favorite report layouts for future use. Usually, you can choose to sort on any of the data items. For example, you may create a good value-oriented screen that produces a list of 50 companies. If you don't have time to analyze all of them, you may sort based on, say, projected EPS growth and work your way down from the top of the list company by company for as many as you have time to examine.

- **User Portfolios/Import/Export:** Most of the time, screens are designed to query the entire database. But there will be occasions when you want to apply your tests to smaller subsets, often referred to by the programs as user portfolios or custom lists. Therefore, some applications allow you to store your screen results as portfolios and export them in text and/or spreadsheet format, and import any such files created from other sources. This is indispensable for layered screening. And it can prove very handy if you wish to work with different programs having different core competencies. For example, you might use Program A to create a screen that makes heavy use of relative-strength type variables, export the results as a user portfolio, and import it into Program B, which does a better job of allowing you to screen based on company fundamentals. In the latter application, you'd run your fundamental screen on a subset of the database defined as those companies that passed the relative strength screen created with the other application. Export can also be useful to those who like to sort the results by something other than the default presentation (usually company name or stock ticker). Suppose, for example, I want to sort from lowest P/E-to-sales growth ratio to highest. I can't think of any present-day screener that provides this ratio as a data item. But in some applications, you can put sales growth and P/E into your report layouts and download to a spreadsheet. Then, you can calculate the ratio via Excel formula and sort on the column containing the ratio you just calculated.
- **Proprietary Analytics:** Several applications include sets of proprietary ratings or grades based on a variety of investment themes. In some ways, these are similar to screens in that they attempt to make inferences about investment merit based on a variety of data-oriented tests. But there is one very important difference. With screens, each test is equally important. With ratings or grades, the relative importance of the tests often varies and in many cases is determined based on statistical testing to determine which sets of data characteristics have been associated with various levels of investment performance during a sample period. Generally, providers of these analytics offer enough explanation to enable you to get a general sense of the factors upon which the ratings or grades are based. But to preserve the value of their intellectual property, they typically withhold the details. As of today, the providers have not been revealing the results of performance testing. Therefore, our willingness to use these analytics requires a leap of faith. But because this is a four-step method, we would not buy or sell based on proprietary analytics alone regardless of how much information is disclosed. If the explanations given are sufficient to make us comfortable that they are based on factors we deem wor-

thy of consideration, ratings can be helpful to our Step 1 (Find) efforts, especially when judiciously used as secondary or alternative tests. For example, a four-test good-company screen can be enhanced by a single alternative test based on a value rating.

Choosing an Application

My primary frame of reference when I discuss stock screening is the Multex premium screener, the one I regularly use. There are two very low-cost products able to produce comparable screens. One is the SmartMoney Select.com subscription screener ($49.95 per year). Another is Stock Investor Pro, a CD-screener, updatable weekly via Internet data download, produced by the American Association of Individual Investors (AAII). Including the annual AAII membership, it costs $247 per year. My preference for these applications is based primarily on their powerful capabilities in implementing the full range of screening strategies discussed earlier.

The free screener on MultexInvestor.com is limited in terms of comparative screening. But it offers import/export capabilities. Therefore, you can use the layered approach to run simple screens against large user portfolios consisting of stocks included in preset screens constructed with the Multex premium screener (made available for free on the MultexInvestor.com web site) and/or other applications.

The MSN Money screener (free at http://moneycentral.msn.com) and Morningstar.com's Premium Stock Selector ($109 per year or $11.95 per month) contain some comparative screening capabilities, but not enough to make such comparisons a cornerstone of a screening strategy. Nevertheless, both have other virtues that make them worthy of consideration. Both feature interesting arrays of proprietary ratings (to be discussed in Chapters 4 and 5) that can be used as screening variables. This feature is especially noteworthy in the case of Morningstar since much of what it offers is consistent with the value connection philosophy.

ProSearch by INVESTools ($249 per year) offers a very basic level of functionality in the way it accommodates value connection concepts. The word "basic" may come off as a backhand sort of compliment. But practitioners of alternative or layered screening may find it worthwhile to accept "basic" value connection variables if you can combine them with outstanding opportunities to utilize sophisticated alternative themes based on technical price/volume trends. Don't worry about losing your grip on core good-stock, good-company ideals. An important benefit of the four-step method is that we don't have to rely on screening, the heart of Step 1 (Find), to carry the whole load. It's okay to take a "lite" approach to value connection screening, find stocks that are outstanding in other respects, and tighten up on value connection principles in Step 2 (Analyze).

If you are completely new to screening and want to dip your toe into it as gradually as possible, check the free screener available on Quicken.com. Its menu of variables, as well as its ability to handle comparative screening, while not great, is above par compared to other entry-level simple screeners.

BEYOND THE LIMITS

Some screening tasks are very easy to implement. For example, any program will allow us to create a test seeking stocks whose price/earnings (P/E) ratios are equal to or below 20. And many will allow us to seek P/E ratios that are below a comparative benchmark such as the industry, sector, market, or database average.

But suppose we want to use a concept like net working capital (NWC), which we can define as current assets minus total liabilities. I'd love to be able to create the following screening test.

Price-to-Net Working Capital per Share <= Industry Average Price-to-Net Working Capital per Share

Unfortunately, I cannot do this today with any of the applications mentioned. None have net working capital as a built-in screening variable. Obviously, we can defer consideration of this ratio to Step 2 (Analyze), where all the data we need to make this calculation on our own is widely available. But we need not give up on using such concepts in Step 1 (Find). With a little ingenuity, and sometimes a bit of extra effort, we can squeeze more out of several of these screeners.

Next, I'll introduce two techniques that can be used with the Multex premium screener, with Stock Investor Pro, and with SmartMoney Select.com. But keep your eyes open. Screeners are continually being improved, so in the future additional applications may offer the features necessary to implement these suggestions.

Let's assume we want to use the ratio of share price to net working capital per share (P/NWC) as part of our Step 1 (Find) activities. One way or another, we'll have to create our nonstandard P/NWC variable. Once we do that, we can utilize two work-around techniques.

1. **Sorting:** Create a screen that does not include the P/NWC ratio. Then, sort the resulting list based on P/NWC, and when you move on to Step 2 (Analyze), give higher priority to stocks whose ratios rank low on the list.

2. **Homework:** This involves doing some legwork that enables us to create plausible numeric tests. For example, as of this writing, about 3,100 companies out of nearly 9,200 in the Multex database had positive net working capital (current assets in excess of total liabilities). Among these situations, the average P/NWC ratio was 19. If we limit consideration to S&P 500 companies, the ratio drops to 14. We might use that information to create a pair of tests like this:

> Price/Net Working Capital > 0
> P/NWC <= 10

This is not a perfect substitute for being able to test for P/NWC ratios that are below each company's respective industry average ratio. And we still cannot offer a precise rationale for setting the numeric threshold at 10, 8, or 13. But we can, at least, say 10 is not arbitrary. Knowing the average P/NWC ratios for the database and S&P 500 suffice to let us defend 10 as well below the database midpoint. That's good enough, since screening need not be all science. It can include elements of art.

Step-by-step examples of both techniques are provided in the appendix to the chapter.

We won't necessarily need to make such extra effort for a widely available variable like P/E, where most applications give us considerable flexibility in the kinds of tests we can build based on this ratio. But these techniques do expand our ability to incorporate less mainstream concepts into Step 1 (Find). And it bears repeating that even if you use a screener that cannot accommodate the sorting and homework techniques, all the concepts, mainstream and otherwise, discussed are usable in Step 2 (Analyze).

APPENDIX TO CHAPTER 3

Special Techniques for Screening Based on Nonmainstream Valuation Metrics

Assume we are interested in finding stocks that seem attractive based on the relationship between share price and net working capital (current assets minus total liabilities) per share: the price/net working capital (P/NWC) ratio. This ratio is not included as a variable in today's screening applications. But using one or both of the following methods, we can still utilize P/NWC in Step 1 (Find).

SORTING

The idea here is to screen based on other tests and use P/NWC to help us prioritize among stocks on the resulting list.

Create the P/NWC Variable

To date, I have not encountered any screener that includes this ratio among its variables. But some applications do include data items we can use to calculate the ratio, as well as a user-defined variable feature that allows us to store these calculations for easy one-step future retrieval. The Multex premium screener and Stock Investor Pro can both accommodate these tasks (the latter program refers to these as "custom fields"). The most direct way to create our user-defined P/NWC variable is to specify and save a definition formula that looks like this:

Price/((Current Assets – Total Liabilities)/# Shares)

Note, though, that we may at times want to look directly at net working capital without dealing with the share price. In that case, we would create and store a variable labeled "Net Working Capital" based on the following definition:

Current Assets – Total Liabilities

Since one user-defined variable can be used as part of the formula for another user-defined variable, we can create a "Net Working Capital per Share" variable using the following formula:

Net Working Capital/# Shares

Finally, we can create the main user-defined variable called P/NWC, which would use one of the following definitions.

Price/Net Working Capital per Share

Price/(Net Working Capital/# Shares)

Run a Screen That Does Not Include P/NWC

Here's an example.

1. P/E <= Industry Average P/E
2. PEG <= 1.5
3. TTM Return on Investment > Industry Average TTM ROI
4. 5 Year ROI > Industry Average 5 Year ROI
5. 1 Year EPS Growth > Industry Average 1 Year EPS Growth
6. 5 Year EPS Growth > Industry Average 5 Year EPS Growth

Tests 1 and 2 express our primary good-stock theme. Tests 3 and 4 express a secondary good-company theme. Tests 5 and 6 express an alternative theme (growth). At the time of this writing, the screen produced 193 names.

Open the Results Report

Different screeners will include different information in this report, and some let you customize. The default report layout in the Multex premium application shows, for each company in the list, the data items used in the screen. In other words, we get what looks like a spreadsheet. Each row lists one of the companies, and there are columns for P/E, Industry Average P/E, PEG, and so on. Stock Investor Pro and SmartMoneySelect.com offer a preselected group of data items in the default report layout. Both programs allow you to switch to other preset layouts or create your own custom report.

Add P/NWC to the Results Report

Access a feature in the screening applications that lets you add data items of your choice to the report. Add P/NWC.

Sort on P/NWC

Specify an ascending sort (from lowest number to highest). For many companies, total liabilities exceed current assets. That produces a negative number for net working capital. These aren't the kinds of situations we're interested in, so we eyeball the list to find the place where the P/NWC ratio becomes positive. In the sample screen created for this example, the 60 lowest P/NWC entries were negative. So my focus for Step 2 (Analyze) starts with the 61st company, the one with the lowest positive number in the P/NWC column.

AN ALTERNATIVE SORTING METHOD

Suppose we use a screener that provides the necessary data items, but does not permit us to combine them as user-defined variables. This is the case with SmartMoneySelect.com. The Excel download feature provides a good solution. Here's how we would implement it.

Run a Screen That Does Not Include P/NWC

The SmartMoneySelect.com variables are defined a bit differently, but we could set up a screen that is generally similar to the one described in the preceding section.

1. P/E in Bottom 50% within Industry
2. PEG <= 1.5
3. TTM Return on Capital in Top 50% within Industry
4. 1 Year EPS Growth in Top 50% within Industry
5. 5 Year EPS Growth in Top 50% within Industry

Create a Report

Clicking on the "Make Report" icon will open a second window containing a spreadsheet-type layout with a company on each row, and a series of columns containing a standard set of data items selected by SmartMoney.

Add Data Items to the Report

Clicking on an "Edit Columns" link will take you to a screen showing all data items that can be included in the report. The items used in the default layout are already checked. We can leave these checked or uncheck them, as we choose. Regardless, we add checks to boxes next to Liabilities, Current Assets (in the Balance Sheet category), and Shares Outstanding (in the Ownership category). We'll also need the share price, but that's already checked as part of the default layout.

Create an Excel Spreadsheet

SmartMoneySelect.com's report page contains an "Export" link allowing you to choose between Excel and text formats. Choose Excel.

Complete the Job in Excel

Open the spreadsheet version of the layout. Establish a new column for P/NWC and create the ratio using an Excel formula built like this:

P/NWC = Cells in the price column/(((Cells in the current assets column – Cells in the liabilities column)/Cells in the shares outstanding column)

Use Excel's sort capabilities to do a lowest-to-highest sort on the column containing P/NWC. Eyeball the list until you find the smallest positive number.

HOMEWORK

This approach assumes we will create a numerical screening test for P/NWC. But rather than choosing a threshold arbitrarily or by trial and error, we will conduct a preliminary investigation to give us a realistic idea of how high or low P/NWC ratios run. This establishes a context that will help us make a more thoughtful choice when we select a numeric base.

Establish the Data Set

The Multex premium screener and Stock Investor Pro allow us to work with the entire database. But let's suppose we know we're interested in small stocks. We would then create a screen that looks like this.

1. Market Capitalization <= $1 billion
2. Market Capitalization >= $50 million

In SmartMoneySelect.com, you'll have no choice but to use a head-start screen like this since that program will not allow a report to contain more than 300 companies.

Create and Download the Results Report

Use the procedure just described to open the default results report and add P/NWC. In the Multex premium screener or Stock Investor Pro, the result set could be the entire screening database if you so choose. Otherwise, it will be the list generated by our head-start screen. Whatever the case, download into Excel.

Calculate Summary Statistics in Excel

Open the spreadsheet. Use Excel functionality to calculate the average P/NWC.

In the Multex screeners, the spreadsheet download might be deemed redundant, since averages for all data columns can be computed by the screeners. Average is a calculation that can be greatly distorted by extremely high or low numbers within the group. Median (the midpoint of a high-to-low sort) is a measure that guards against this. The Multex screeners cannot calculate medians, but Excel can. Also, if we download first to Excel, it's easy to make sure our calculation of the average excludes negative numbers, if that's what we want to do. When the screener computes an average, it automatically uses all data items in the column.

## CHAPTER 4

Screening for
Good Stocks

W e're now ready to examine the data items we can use to screen for good stocks, those with reasonable valuation metrics. We'll start by applying the ivory-tower investor-centric principles discussed in Chapter 1. We won't actually use the mathematical models, but we will work with the relevant data and explore ways to relate share prices to earnings and other measures of company financial performance. Then, we'll turn our attention to company-centric approaches that relate share prices to various asset-oriented measures.

USING, DECONSTRUCTING, AND SUPPLEMENTING P/E

Although the purest ivory-tower models value stocks on the basis of dividends, in the real world the ratio of price to earnings per share (P/E) has become paramount. There are other ratios that often supplement or are used in place of P/E, such as price to sales, price to cash flow or free cash flow, and price to earnings before interest, taxes, depreciation, and amortization (EBITDA) or earnings before interest and taxes (EBIT). But even when these ratios are used, P/E is never far from the scene. Either we use P/E along with whatever alternatives we select, or we should explain, at least to ourselves, why P/E is not being used. Hence we'll start by looking at P/E, which casts a very long shadow.

Screening for P/E

Many who consider P/E think in terms of relationships such as this:

P/E < 20

But this screening test is not nearly as basic as it might seem. Why should we assume 20 is a reasonable benchmark? In some market environments, 20 would be considered too high. In others, it would be a bargain. And it might systematically eliminate high-growth industries that usually command above-average P/E ratios. All in all, I suggest that numerical P/E tests be avoided whenever possible.

Comparative testing will align our screens much more directly with the principle of seeking our money's worth. There are two kinds of comparisons we'll use: the growth comparison and the peer comparison.

Growth Comparison   Investors have long understood that shares of companies that grow more quickly command higher P/E ratios. In Chapter 1, we saw that this goes far beyond investment culture. The relationship between P/E and growth is well established in the classic mathematical valuation models.

So if a P/E looks modest compared to a credible growth forecast for the company, we can assume we're looking at a reasonably valued stock. If we can't find any or enough stocks that look attractive under this standard, we could assume that this is because the market as a whole is overvalued. Conversely, if we find an abundance of attractively valued stocks, we can probably make bullish assumptions for the market as a whole. Remember, though, that in order to work, the growth forecasts must be credible. This often-neglected requirement will figure very prominently in Chapter 8, when we discuss Step 2 (Analyze).

Even before we address the growth forecast, we have to refine our understanding of what makes for a desirable P/E-to-growth (PEG) ratio. Many in the investment community take for granted the notion that the matter is simple, that the PEG ratio should be no higher than 1.00. Put another way, it is widely assumed that the P/E should be equal to or less than the growth rate.

As we saw in Chapter 1, the 1.00 PEG ideal is just that, an ideal. It does not spring from any legitimate mathematical rationale. Indeed, the fact that P/Es are influenced by another item that does not vary in lockstep with growth (interest rates) means we cannot define any strict relationship between P/E and growth. The best I've been able to do is crunch numbers on an ad hoc basis and observe that PEG ratios in the 1.50 to 2.00 range often turn out to be reasonable.

But PEG can still help us as long as we keep our eyes open to its limitations. We do this by recognizing that it's a guide, not a commandment carved in stone. Accordingly, we'll try to favor companies whose PEG ratios are lower than those of others that are under consideration. And in our highly imperfect world, we learn from experience that there are far worse errors investors can make than to insist that PEG ratios be at least within hailing distance of the popular 1.00 threshold. If enough market participants believe in the 1.00 PEG threshold, then principles of supply and demand, the ultimate determinant of all share prices, make it relevant regardless of whether mathematicians approve.

But we will not be rigid. We will keep our minds open to accepting PEGs above 1.00 if other factors support such a conclusion. Conversely, if the stock doesn't look quite right based on factors that are important to us, we will not allow a PEG at or below 1.00 to overrule these other considerations.

Generally speaking, screening tests based on the growth comparison will look like this:

PEG Ratio <= 1.25

Prepackaged screening variables for PEG are a mixed blessing. They are convenient, especially if we are inclined to create comparative PEG-based tests such as:

PEG Ratio <= Industry Average PEG Ratio

One downside of such tests is that credibility is hard to assess. While we can easily look at the growth rate used to calculate an individual company's PEG ratio, it's hard to do likewise for aggregate ratios, such as industry, sector, or market averages.

Also, prepackaged PEG variables distract us from the fact that there's more than one way to create such a ratio. We can calculate P/E by dividing price by trailing 12 months (TTM) EPS or consensus EPS estimates for a future period. And the growth rate used in the ratio could be a projection of near-term EPS growth, a projection of long-term EPS growth, or a historical growth rate computed for past time periods (e.g., TTM, the prior three years, the prior five years).

Speaking for myself, I like to use forward-looking PEG ratios because the success or failure of a stock investment will depend on what happens in the future. I like to use P/Es calculated based on the consensus estimate of EPS for the next fiscal year (this allows me to bypass temporary oddities that may be impacting near-term results). And the growth number I prefer is based on a long-term projection. Ultimately, though, whether you agree with these choices is far less important than the fact that you at least make thoughtful decisions about how you'd like to calculate the PEG ratio.

Accordingly, I suggest that you make your choices and then build a PEG test that takes the form of one of these examples:

P/E/Growth <= 1.25

P/E <= Growth * 1.25

Peer Comparison   This activity relies on the wisdom of the marketplace to tell us how much we should expect to pay for a dollar of economic value (e.g., earnings). This, arguably, is the purest form of valuation, not just for stocks, but for all kinds of goods and services. This is consistent with the legal definition of fair market value as what a willing buyer would pay and a willing seller would seek assuming both are free to transact or not transact as they see fit. This is how commodities are valued. This is how houses are valued. This is how restaurant meals and movie tickets are valued.

In Chapter 1, we discussed the Kellogg view that value is in the eye of the beholder. Relative stock valuation looks at the world to determine what other beholders have been willing to pay for similar shares and reasons that the observed what-you-pay and what-you-get relationships make for good precedent.

Such a notion may offend mathematicians. But my own experience suggests that it should be very pleasing to investors. On Multex Investor.com, I maintain one screen based primarily on the P/E-to-growth comparison. From early 2000 through the end of 2002, it beat the S&P 500 by about 70 percentage points. But as impressive as that was, another screen, one based primarily on peer comparison, beat the S&P 500 by approximately 120 percentage points!

When creating screening tests based on this approach, we compare company P/E ratios to those of an appropriate peer group. Here are some examples.

P/E <= Industry Average P/E

P/E <= Sector Average P/E

P/E <= S&P 500 P/E

Relative P/E <= 50

P/E in Bottom 35% within Industry

There is, of course, a major omission from this system. Suppose the peer group on the whole is overvalued. In that case, we could still wind up overpaying for this particular stock. This hasn't proven a problem for the peer-comparison screen referred to earlier during 2000–2002, a period when the market harshly punished investors who held overvalued stocks. (Besides beating the S&P 500, the performance of this screen was impressive even in an absolute sense; it rose 85 percent.) Even so, one can never completely dismiss this issue.

Then again, this question isn't unique to stocks. It applies to all kinds of valuation. Consider houses. Suppose in a particular region home prices rise to the point where the average monthly carrying cost is $3,000. I find one house that I can get at a price that would give me a monthly carrying cost of $2,500. It appears that I found an undervalued house! But before buying, I need to consider whether the market as a whole is overheated. Suppose I study the local economy and learn that the kinds of people most likely to desire this particular property can afford to pay only $1,700 per month for housing. In the real world, real estate values might not adjust immediately to this underlying economic reality. Banks tend to relax lending standards during booms (much to the chagrin of banking regulators), and buyers, tending to believe that a new era is dawning, may redefine traditional notions of how much they have to pay for housing. So for a while they live on savings. But that sort of thing can't last indefinitely. Sooner or later, home prices must align with affordability. Either the region must experience an economic boom to enable homeowners to spend more on housing, or the real estate market must come down.

Although real estate is not our field of inquiry, this discussion reveals exactly how we must view stock valuation. First, let's consider what we've done with our housing example. We've split our analysis into two parts. One involved identification of a house that was attractively priced relative to peers, or as they say in real estate, comparables. But before plunging in, we looked separately at the dynamics underlying the market as a whole. Ultimately, we concluded that the house in question (the one with the $2,500 monthly carrying cost) is cheap compared with the rest of the market. But we still refrain from chasing that so-called bargain because the market as a whole might fall. A $2,500 monthly carrying cost would not turn out to be appealing if, after we purchase, the market average falls from $3,000 to $1,700.

Anybody who has exposure to academic finance recognizes this line of inquiry. Stock valuation is really a two-part exercise, since all share price movements reflect a combination of general-market and stock-specific factors. Peer comparison helps us identify stocks that are attractive based on stock-specific factors. Then, we need a way to recognize that sometimes even the best relative values should still be avoided. (Those who, in 2000, bought Internet stocks that seemed most favorably valued relative to the Internet group as a whole still incurred huge losses.) Fortunately, our use of a four-step method spares us the burden of addressing this in Step 1 (Find). The expectation analysis we'll discuss in Chapter 8 as part of Step 2 (Analyze) and Chapter 10 as part of Step 3 (Buy) will provide ample warning if we're about to buy the supposedly best of a badly overvalued group.

The E in P/E

In Chapter 1, we saw that the relationship between share prices and EPS, the P/E relationship, is central to stock valuation. It's not as pure a measure of wealth as dividend, but in the workaday world, it's the item on which most investors focus. Interestingly, though, many are uncomfortable with P/E. Often companies report more than one version of EPS, creating uncertainties as to which one should be used in the P/E computation. And no matter what version of EPS we use, we're likely to come face-to-face with the fact that there's a difference between what the company earns (or loses) and how much cash comes into (or flows out of) the corporation. Many regard it as a badge of honor to reject earnings (and the accounting assumptions used to compute them) in order to focus on the actual cash numbers, saying something like "I'm only going to value shares based on what's real, and cash inflows/outflows are real."

Before exploring the issues surrounding EPS, we can easily dispose of one P/E alternative, the earnings yield, which is EPS divided by stock price. Mathematically, this is the converse of P/E. If EPS is $0.75 and the share price is $18, it's equally correct to say the P/E is 24 ($18 divided by $0.75) or that the earnings yield is 4.2 percent ($0.75 divided by $18).

Our tendency to favor P/E is more a matter of habit than of methodological conviction. But some resist convention and claim we should use earnings yield. It's true a 4.2 percent earnings yield can be more conveniently compared to returns on fixed income investments. But the comparison is less useful than meets the eye. Interest payments are generally constant. EPS are expected to grow over time. To truly compare an earnings yield to a fixed income yield, we'd have to factor in growth assumptions by adjusting the former according to a model such as the DDM (and all the tenuous assumptions that accompany it).

There's nothing wrong with doing that. But we would lose out on the convenience we thought we could get by comparing an earnings yield to an interest yield. Hence there's no significant incentive to depart from the popular preference for P/E over earnings yield. We will therefore proceed based on investment community convention that uses P/E.

Varieties of E Do not expect to be able to calculate a single correct P/E for a stock. That's because we have to make choices as to which EPS number we will use.

- **Should we calculate P/E ratios based on forward-looking or historic EPS?** Assume XYZ Company's stock trades at 30 and its EPS was $1.20 over the trailing 12 months (TTM); analysts are expecting it to earn $1.30 during the current fiscal year and to soar to $2.35 next year. At various times, I've used all three EPS figures in my P/E calculations. So if a particular screening application omits some choices, one need not be shy about using whatever is available. But assuming we use an application that lets us pick and choose, my preference is to use the estimate of the next year's EPS (in this example, the $2.35 figure) since that item will heavily influence the future direction of the stock. Based on TTM EPS and the estimate of current-year EPS, XYZ Company's P/Es work out to 25.0 and 23.1, respectively, which, at first glance, don't seem especially appealing. But the P/E based on the estimate of next year's EPS is only 12.8. If our efforts in Step 2 (Analyze) convince us that the estimate is credible, the 12.8 P/E would seem very attractive. And the stock could present an especially nice opportunity if most of the investment community is focusing on P/E calculations of 25.0 or 23.1.

  If we screened based on P/Es calculated using TTM or current-year EPS, we might never be prompted to look at XYZ Company in the first place. Hence using the most forward-looking P/E variable that's included in our screener can tune us in to ideas others might miss. The disadvantage to screening this way is that not all applications allow us to make forward-PEG comparisons to industry, sector, or market averages. Hopefully, in the future more screeners will allow us to do this. But for the time being, if we want comparisons of this sort, we may be limited to use of the TTM P/E ratio.

- **Should we calculate P/E ratios based on generally accepted accounting principles (GAAP) earnings or on another measure that weeds out nonrecurring items?** From a Step 1 (Find) standpoint, today's screening applications usually cause us to screen TTM P/E ratios based on GAAP EPS. But this is not necessarily a bad thing. Write-offs (i.e., costs of plant closings, employee severance costs, losses on asset sales, recognition on the books of asset value deterioration, etc.) often reflect past problems or management errors. It is fair to consider this as part of an evaluation of the company's overall success or failure. Unusual gains, on the other hand, inflate EPS and make P/Es seem more attractive than they really are. Based on the current state of screening programs, we cannot address this in Step 1

(Find). But we can and certainly should note such data oddities in Step 2 (Analyze).

Meanwhile, when we screen based on estimates, the applications use normalized earnings (also known as operating earnings, recurring earnings, or core earnings). That's because this is the basis upon which analysts make their estimates. Normalization of earnings is a very controversial topic as this is being written. Critics claim such numbers obscure oddities that investors ought to be worrying about. They have a good point when it comes to looking at historic results. But when it comes to estimates, this issue becomes more challenging. Analysts generally cannot predict if or when companies will experience odd or unusual events. As of this writing, there is talk of analysts trying to do just that. If they do change the way they make estimates, that will be reflected in the screening databases.

Cash versus Accrual   Once we choose which EPS we will use for our P/E assessment (assuming more than one choice is made available to us), we have a bigger issue to face: whether we should be trying to use any definition of P/E at all. The main objection many have to using this ratio is the fact that noncash accounting accruals are often used as part of the EPS calculation. Although this sounds troublesome to those who want to value stock based on what is real (cash generation), if we think about the accruals, we'll see that they are more sensible than many realize.

Suppose I decide, this year, to go into the business of manufacturing shirts. Assume my direct costs (raw materials and salaries of employees who do the manufacturing) amount to $20 per shirt and that each can be sold for $30. Assume I sell 500,000 shirts. That means my revenue is $15 million and my direct costs are $10 million. But I cannot say my profit is $5 million. I accounted only for direct costs, or cost of goods sold. There are additional expenses. Assume I as CEO pay myself an annual salary of $300,000 to run the business. I also employ executives to handle finance and marketing at annual salaries of $150,000 each. Our salaries, which total $600,000, are overhead and have to be subtracted from the $5 million in direct (gross) profit bringing our operating total down to $4.4 million.

We've addressed one accounting issue (distinguishing between direct costs and overhead). But the situation is still very straightforward—$15 million of bona fide cash came in the door, and $10.6 million of bona fide cash went out. So there's absolutely no ambiguity about the status of the remaining $4.4 million. It's real live cash that can be reinvested in the business or distributed as dividends to shareholders.

However, we can't really get through our first year with only $10.6 million worth of expenditures. Assume that to get started we had to spend $50 million to build a factory. Therefore, we really spent $60.6 million, not

$10.6 million. So on a cash basis, we lost $45.6 million. But if we can find some way to at least temporarily fund the gap, we'll do a lot better next year. Even if we slow a bit, and get only $12 million worth of revenue, we'll make money. We won't have to spend for the factory, so our year two costs will be only $10.6 million, leaving us $1.4 million in the black. If we stay above water like this in year three and beyond, and hopefully improve, we'll be fine.

This is an accurate depiction of cash flows. But it does not necessarily paint a proper picture of the company's ability to generate economic wealth. Year one looks horrible and years two and beyond look good, not because that's really the way business is (it is actually worse in year two) but because we have not properly matched expenses against the revenues generated as a result of the outlays.

Expenses in year one were drastically overstated. We did spend $50 million on the factory, but the plant is likely to be productive for 20 years (after which time we'll assume it will be obsolete and worthless). It seems unfair to ask a single year to bear the entire burden of an expenditure that will help produce 20 years' worth of revenue. That's exactly how the accounting profession feels. Accountants address the issue through the concept of depreciation. We'll assume the factory produces revenue and gradually approaches obsolescence (i.e., depreciates) at an even pace through the estimated 20-year "useful life." So when we compute year one profits, we won't include the entire $50 million plant cost. We'll divide $50 million by 20 (number of years of useful life) and recognize a depreciation charge of $2.5 million ($50 million divided by 20). We'll recognize the same $2.5 million charge in each subsequent year.

So in truth, the year one profit is $1.9 million ($15 million revenue minus $10.6 million in direct and overhead costs minus $2.5 million in depreciation). In year two, we lose $1.1 million ($12 million in revenue minus $10.6 million in direct and overhead costs minus $2.5 million in depreciation).

To calculate depreciation, we used some admittedly subjective estimates and judgments. (Maybe we should assume a useful life of 15 years, or 25. Perhaps the value will be more than zero at the end of the useful life, in which case, instead of depreciating the entire cost, we'd depreciate only the difference between cost and estimated salvage value. And the "straight line" approach that produces the same charge year in and year out isn't the only method we can choose; we could decide to depreciate more in some years than others.) Despite this, depreciation gives us a more accurate picture of the economic performance of the company. Focusing only on cash flow led us to believe year two was better than year one and that the year two revenue decline was not such a big deal. Using so-called artificial depreciation allowances showed us something we really did need to see— that the revenue decline in year two is not acceptable and signals trouble.

This is an example of how the techniques and assumptions upon which conventional EPS is based are not arbitrary. They are designed to try to accurately match revenues and expenses. If we fail to think about this, we'll wind up overrating the company's performance in some years and underrating it in others. EPS is not perfect. We can and do wonder about the assumptions made to calculate it. But at least it does represent an effort, a serious effort at that, to give a valid economic picture of how well or poorly a company is doing.

That doesn't mean EPS is the only thing we should look at. There are times when we may want to look at components of company performance, in which case other measures may be preferable. For example, creditors don't necessarily care about the full view of a company's performance. They are mainly interested in whether the corporation can generate enough cash to satisfy the borrowings (regardless of how accountants match revenues and expenses). Somebody who considers acquiring the corporation might have a different view: The $50 million factory-creation expense is in the past. The only relevant issue is whether the company generates enough cash every year to keep it in good working shape. Hence measures other than EPS are useful. Even so, we should not casually dismiss EPS as shallow or old-fashioned, as so many nowadays try to do. EPS and P/E ratios definitely are important.

The foregoing establishes a proper context for looking at alternatives to P/E, which we'll now examine. Note that different sources can, and often do, define these terms differently. Hence it is crucial that you check glossaries or help screens that accompany any web sites or applications you use, so you know exactly what the numbers represent.

Screening Based on P/E Alternatives

We'll now consider the following P/E alternatives:

- Earnings before interest, taxes, depreciation, and amortization.
- Earnings before interest and taxes.
- Cash flow.
- Free cash flow.
- Sales.

In all cases, creating screening tests based on P/E alternatives is very straightforward. We can create basic numeric tests. And several applications permit us to create comparative tests such as these:

P/Sales <= Industry Average P/Sales

P/EBIT per Share <= Sector Average P/EBIT per Share

P/Free Cash Flow per Share <= S&P 500 P/Free Cash Flow per Share

As of today, when using the P/E alternatives in Step 1 (Find), we'll always be calculating the ratios based on TTM results rather than estimates of future tallies. But that may change in the future if analyst estimates of sales, cash flows, and so on find their way into screening databases.

Now that we have disposed of the easy issue, how to build screening tests, let's consider the more challenging questions, the benefits and drawbacks in using P/E alternatives.

Earnings before Interest, Taxes, Depreciation, and Amortization (EBITDA)

This is a measure that many companies hope investors will look at. And in some cases, this has, indeed, been the metric of choice among many in the investment community when they wish to analyze performance of companies whose EPS numbers are in the red. In theory, it gives a reasonably pure picture of the performance of the business, since it omits three items that supposedly distract us from this inquiry:

1. **Interest Expense:** Arguably, this is not relevant to assessing the cash generation capabilities of a business. This expense can be considerable or zero with the result depending entirely on strategic choices to use or not use debt capital.
2. **Depreciation:** This is the noncash accounting accrual for gradual obsolescence of physical assets.
3. **Amortization:** This is a depreciation-like charge that is used to gradually reduce the stated value of intangible assets.

EBITDA is a measure that should be used with caution. We'll consider the pros and cons of eliminating interest expense from consideration. But as noted earlier, depreciation and amortization, despite their limitations, give us a good sense of how revenues and expenses match up, thereby painting a fair picture of economic performance in a world where we simply cannot pretend that assets are obtained for free.

Back in the 1980s, when I was covering cable TV stocks, I recall a difference of opinion I had with an executive at one of the major companies. He acted offended by my reluctance to value the stock based on "operating earnings" (the company defined this term in a way that is very similar to EBITDA). I kept arguing that I could not value a stock based on a measure that ignores interest expense. "The shareholders don't own that money," I pointed out. "That belongs to the creditors." According to the executive, I simply didn't understand. Looking back now, I think the problem was that I *did* understand.

Nowadays, many criticize tendencies on the part of corporations to report something called pro forma earnings. Once upon a time, this was a perfectly reputable measure.

"Pro forma" is a Latin phrase that translates to "as a matter of form." Companies traditionally report pro forma numbers to show what past results would have looked like if circumstances were different from what was really the case. Usually, companies planning to make acquisitions do this to show what prior years' results would have looked like had the merger occurred several years earlier. Nowadays, though, the concept has been distorted and the label "pro forma" is often attached to a set of financial statements that resembles the sort of vintage-1980s cable TV reports I disliked. So if you're uncomfortable using modern pro forma results, chances are you won't want to use EBITDA.

Earnings before Interest and Taxes (EBIT)

This is a more reasonable measure of the ongoing economic performance of a business (including asset-related costs) without the distraction of strategic decisions relating to how the business is capitalized (debt or equity). But if we are evaluating a company as a going concern, this measure suffers from its failure to account for interest, which must be paid.

EBIT is most useful in assessing companies as acquisition candidates. Presumably, a buyer would pay off the debt, thereby eliminating ongoing interest expense. But even this assumption should be taken with a grain of salt. Where will the buyer get the money to pay off the debt? Will he/she have to borrow money from someplace else? It's tempting for shareholders who want to take the money and run to avoid thinking about where the buyer gets the money. But if we're looking at a stock trying to figure out what it might be worth to an acquirer, we cannot ignore the latter's cost of capital. A company with $100 million in annual EBIT cannot be acquired by somebody whose cost of capital would be $150 million. (Those of us who thought otherwise back in the 1980s learned just as harsh a lesson as new-economy investors did in 2000–2002.)

Cash Flow

This is usually defined as net income plus depreciation and amortization. It has the virtue of including capital costs (interest). But it falsely assumes asset costs are zero.

Free Cash Flow

This metric is a better measure of cash inflows and outflows. It can be defined as net income plus depreciation and amortization minus capital expenditures minus dividends paid.

Multex takes a more pure approach. It starts with cash from operations, an item from the Statement of Cash Flows that represents net income adjusted for a wide variety of cash-related issues that don't regularly show up on the income statement. Obviously, depreciation and amortization are added back since those are noncash accruals. We also adjust for changes in working capital, such as increases in accounts payable (which enhance a company's cash position) and decreases in accounts receivable (which reduce the cash position). As noted, though, cash from operations is just a starting point. We also subtract capital expenditures and dividend payments.

This is a good measure of cash inflows and outflows and is the metric of choice if that is what we wish to examine. The problem is that it can be volatile in ways that do not reflect the underlying health of the business. That's because large multiyear expenditures are not matched against revenues in each year (as was the case in the shirt manufacturing example).

Sales

Sales, more specifically price/sales ratios, were widely used during the late 1990s new economy bubble. Many of that era's most favored companies were deep in the red (hence P/E ratios could not be computed), and many didn't even show positive results in terms of cash flow, free cash flow, EBIT, or EBITDA. But except for the greenest of start-ups, every company has some level of sales. Hence we can always compute price/sales ratios.

After that bubble burst, price/sales went out of favor. But we ought not throw the baby out with the bathwater. The fact that the ratio was misused by some should not blind us to the fact that it can be quite helpful.

Not all companies with negative EPS are like new economy bubble firms. There are many that fall into the red temporarily. Sometimes this happens because of overall business conditions. Other times it happens because of company-specific problems. There are also situations where unusual charges cause the GAAP EPS numbers used in screening databases to fall below zero. And even where EPS stays above zero, there are times when the foregoing issues can cause the number to be very small. Consider a company with a stock price of $15 whose EPS is usually in the $0.50 to $0.60 range. Assume, though, that for some reason during the past year, EPS temporarily slid to $0.02. Mathematically, there is a correct

P/E—in this case, 750. But this ratio is not even remotely representative of the usual levels. The market recognizes this. That's why the stock may be trading at $15, instead of, say, less than a dollar. Investors recognize that $0.02 is an aberration that does not reflect the company's typical level of earning power.

Either way, we're often dealing with real companies that over prolonged time periods produce real shareholder wealth and deserve to have their shares rationally valued. Asset-based valuations (which will be discussed later in this chapter) are one answer. But price/sales can be pressed into service as a useful alternative when P/E is temporarily unavailable. We can't be certain that every trailing 12 month (TTM) sales number is really representative of the company's regular economic prowess. Business conditions influence sales as well as earnings. But changes in sales aren't nearly as pronounced as changes in the bottom line. Even if the price/sales ratio is imperfect, there are many occasions when it can be preferable to a completely dysfunctional P/E number.

DIVIDENDS

Dividends, the portion of corporate earnings that passes directly into the hands of shareholders, is, of course, the most classic basis for measuring the value of a stock. As noted in Chapter 1, it appears as if the world has moved beyond this important basis. But it would be a mistake to completely dismiss it. And indeed, as this is written, there are indications that dividends may be returning, if not to center stage, at least out of the dusty backstage closets. Any future move from Washington to alleviate the tax disadvantage (where the same money is taxed first as income to the corporation, and a second time as income to the shareholders who receive the dividends) would help.

Admittedly, the resumption of dividend talk in 2002 occurred in the context of a bear market. At such times, the benefits of yield protection become very tempting. Conventional wisdom would hold that a $1.25-per-share dividend reduces downside risk to a stock priced, say, at $25. The 5 percent yield is already very high by today's standards and would presumably attract enough investors to prevent much, if any, decline in the share price.

This is not a foolproof theory. If profits are under enough pressure, the dividend could be reduced, or at least the market may fear a reduced payout. Even in the latter case, the stock would decline, notwithstanding that the yield could climb to eye-catching levels. But despite these situations, the presence of a meaningful dividend yield usually helps support stock prices.

In a mid-2002 study, I compared quarterly share total return (capital gains/losses plus dividend yield, if any) for two groups of stocks. I defined a nonincome group consisting of all companies in the sample period having market capitalizations of $50 million or higher that pay no dividends at all or whose stocks had yields that were negligible (below 0.5 percent). I also defined an income group consisting of stocks whose yields were high, but not so high as to indicate market worries about a dividend cut. Table 4.1 shows the performance of each group during what was a very difficult period for the stock market.

We see that as stock prices plunged, the income group outperformed the nonincome group by a wide margin, and also featured substantially less risk.

But the study went further and showed that there's more to dividends than a bear market price cushion. Table 4.2 shows how the two groups performed during a generally bullish period for stocks.

The superiority of the income group was not so pronounced during the bullish period measured by Table 4.2. But it may come as a surprise to many to see that there was any income advantage at all, since the 1990s was a period when dividends had receded back to the deepest recesses of investment community consciousness.

When screening for dividend, it is tempting to simply aim for high yield

TABLE 4.1 Bear Market Analysis of Income Stock Relative Performance

	5/31/2000–5/31/2002	
	Median Quarterly Return	**Risk (Standard Deviation of Return)**
Income group	+3.44%	7.09%
Nonincome group	−0.82%	13.46%

TABLE 4.2 Bull Market Analysis of Income Stock Relative Performance

	5/31/1993–5/31/1998	
	Median Quarterly Return	**Risk (Standard Deviation of Return)**
Income group	+3.33%	6.45%
Nonincome group	+1.67%	10.20%

(dividend per share as a percent of the share price). We can do that through a basic numeric test requiring the yield to be above a level we specify based on our assessment of what's reasonable given the current interest rate environment. But even with dividend staging an image recovery, we're still likely to encounter slim pickings if we insist on yields that are above or even comparable to what's likely to be available in the fixed income market.

Therefore, when screening based on dividend, it's a good idea to supplement a numeric yield test with one that relates to dividend growth. For purposes of comparing dividend streams to yields on fixed income investments, many add the yield and the growth rate.

Suppose fixed income yields are 5 percent and we seek a 4 percent premium to that level. Adding the yield to the growth rate gives us an overall target of 9 percent. We might implement our strategy by using the following pair of screening tests.

1. Dividend Yield >= 2%
2. Dividend Growth Rate >= 7%

This approach is imperfect. The screen would reject a company with a 4 percent yield and a 6 percent growth rate, even though the yield plus growth rate exceed our 9 percent target. In screening applications that allow us to create complex tests (such as the Multex programs) we can get around this with the following combination:

1. Dividend Yield >= 2%
2. Dividend Growth Rate >= 9% – Dividend Yield

The dividend growth rates we've been using are based on historic data. Analyst estimates of future dividend growth are not currently disseminated. That may change in the future. But dividend trends, established by board directive, tend to be considerably more stable than earnings trends. Hence historic dividend growth rates can usually serve as a reasonable proxy for anticipated future growth.

Note, too, that if we're using numeric tests, we'll have to do some trial and error to find yield-growth combinations that produce a satisfactory present-future trade-off (higher yields are usually associated with lower growth rates and vice versa), and a satisfactory number of companies that pass these tests. At this stage, it's important that the list be big enough to withstand further winnowing as discussed later on.

Before leaving basic yield tests, we should also consider how we might use comparative techniques. A test such as the following one spares us the need to change our screen continually as market conditions evolve.

1. Dividend Yield > Industry Average Dividend Yield
2. Dividend Growth Rate > Industry Average Dividend Growth Rate

Similar tests can be constructed using screeners that make comparisons in terms of relative strength.

Such tests can be interesting because they will collect companies in a variety of industries with a variety of yield-growth trade-offs. By way of contrast, strict numeric tests are more likely to produce lists concentrated in areas like utilities, real estate, and banks, which are traditionally characterized by higher-yielding stocks.

In the case of dividend screening, we should also guard against the possibility that poor company performance may cause the directors to reduce, or even eliminate, the dividend. Consider the following test.

(Dividend Yield/Industry Average Dividend Yield) <= (5 Year Dividend Yield/Industry Average 5 Year Dividend Yield) * 1.25

The test starts with the relationship between the present yield and the present industry average yield (the present relative yield). Then, the test examines the five-year average relative yield. The casual observer might hope to see situations where the relative yield has moved up sharply. But this test has the opposite intent; it weeds out sharp increases in relative yield based on the notion that such a transition might signal investment community pessimism regarding the company's continuing ability to grow or maintain its dividend. A yield that's too high may signal bad times ahead.

Other checks and balances address trends in free cash flows, which directly impact a company's ability to maintain or enhance its dividend payments. We can create tests based on payout ratio that check to see if this measure is reasonable relative to peer comparison and/or historic trend. While, as noted earlier, free cash flow may be too volatile year in and year out to serve as a perfect substitute for EPS, income seekers would do well to check the longer-term progress. If free cash flow is trending lower, the stability of the dividend could be threatened. Look, too, at capital spending. Strong rates of historic capital spending growth are a plus since such companies may be able to afford to relax the pace of such outlays in the future.

LIQUID ASSETS

Would you pay $10 a share for a company that has $15 a share worth of cash? That sounds like a value investor's dream—getting a lot for your money (paying $10 to get $15). Would you believe that even today you can actually do this? Believe it. As this is being written, 51 companies appeared on the following single-test screen.

Share Price < Cash per Share Latest Quarter

Of course this brings to mind an old cliché that warns us about things that sound too good to be true (the idea being that they usually aren't true). Obviously, we should keep such notions in mind whenever we encounter situations like this. But for what it's worth, the data is accurate. Such stocks really do exist.

Needless to say, there's usually a catch. Often, these are troubled companies. The market deems their prospects to be so poor that it chooses to assign little or no value to ongoing business operations. And liquidation isn't always an automatic route to realizing a windfall. There would be shutdown costs and possibly large amounts of debt that would have to be repaid before proceeds (if any are left, which is often not the case) can be distributed to shareholders. This is why cash is not the only liquid asset we should examine. Alternatives are discussed later on.

We should not blind ourselves to the possibility that interesting ideas can be found just by looking at cash. Nothing on this particular 51-stock list appealed to me, but under the "never say never" principle, I'll keep my mind open to the possibility that such a screen might produce something worthwhile on a future occasion. You never know.

But the usefulness of examining cash (and other measures of liquid assets) is not limited to the prospect of an instant windfall. Suppose we pay $20 a share to own a stake in a business that has $15 a share in liquid assets. We would not have a slam dunk windfall as we would if cash per share exceeded the stock price, but we'd have a pretty good head start. If the rest of the assets (the plant, etc.) can fetch more than $5 per share, we'll come out ahead. We'll have to do some work to determine if that's doable. But we would be well ahead of where we'd be if there were only $3 per share in liquid assets, in which case the other assets would have to net $17 a share just to get us to breakeven.

Here's an alternative angle outside the context of liquidation. Suppose shares of a company earning $0.75 a share are priced at $20. At first glance, it seems that the P/E is 26.7 ($20 divided by $0.75). But if the company had $15 per share worth of liquid assets, we could subtract that from the price. In other words, we'd say $15 of our $20 purchase price is allocated to liquid assets, and that only the remaining $5 is attributable to the ongoing business. Let's assume the liquid assets are all cash and that they contribute $0.30 worth of interest income to EPS. We would therefore adjust the share price to $5 ($20 minus $15 in cash) and EPS to $0.45 ($0.75 minus $0.30 in interest income). We could then assume the P/E for the business is only 11.1 ($5 divided by $0.45).

Here are the kinds of liquid assets we can work with. Remember, in most cases, it won't be as simple as creating a standard screening test. Review the appendix to Chapter 3, which describes how to create credible numeric screening tests based on these concepts, and how to use them as a basis for sorting lists that result from other screens. (Also, if you are going to compare these items to share prices, make sure you divide the asset values by the number of shares outstanding, so you will have per-share values.) Obviously, all these concepts can easily be used as part of Step 2 (Analyze).

- **Cash:** This, of course, is the most liquid asset of all. When looking at balance sheets, we use items clearly labeled as cash. We also add "short-term investments." Typically, screening databases already do this and refer to such variables as cash and equivalents. The strength of this measure is its purity; there is no question as to its value. The weaknesses are based on uncertainty as to how much of that cash is likely to be burned by further operating losses, or used for shutdown costs and debt repayment.
- **Working Capital:** This is current assets minus current liabilities. An asset is classified as "current" if the company expects to use or dispose of it within a year. Cash, accounts receivable, and inventory are the most common kinds of current assets. Liabilities are considered "current" if the company expects to satisfy them within a year. The most common examples are accounts payable, short-term debt, and long-term debt scheduled to be paid off in the coming year.
- **Net Cash:** This is not an official balance sheet category. It is something created by investors and creditors for their own use when analyzing financial statements. Accordingly, there is no hard-and-fast definition. Stock Investor Pro defines the net cash screening variable it created as cash minus current liabilities. If we are inclined to consider potential liquid asset a windfall, this is preferable to cash because it accounts for the most immediate obligations that must be satisfied before any cash can be distributed to shareholders. Note, though, that the Stock Investor Pro definition does not account for long-term liabilities (such as long-term debt). So if we want a more pure liquidation analysis, we may want to modify the definition to be cash minus total liabilities (short-term and long-term). Another approach would be to define net cash as cash minus total debt. Our choice of definition should depend on the kinds of stocks we are trying to find. If we really are seeking liquidation, or acquisition, candidates, cash minus total liabilities or total debt would be preferable since they paint more accurate pictures of the amount of cash that would really be available for

common shareholders (excluding any cash that might be consumed by shutdown costs and preliquidation operating losses). On the other hand, if we're seeking low valuation metrics for ongoing businesses, the Stock Investor Pro definition may be better. In such a case, we would not expect long-term liabilities to be paid off.

- **Net Working Capital:** This, too, is a measure created by investors and creditors. It is usually defined as current assets minus total liabilities. It's a more relaxed version of the cash minus total liabilities approach to net cash. It is useful for liquidation or acquisition analysis because it supplements cash with other assets that ought, in the normal course of business, to be convertible to cash within a short period. Presumably, in liquidation, these assets can be sold at or near their balance sheet values. For similar reasons, it is also useful for calculating a revised operations-only P/E.

Of course a full picture of stock value must extend beyond liquid assets. Some investors do actively seek liquidation or acquisition candidates. But most expect companies to persist indefinitely as going concerns. In those cases, we have to be concerned about all assets, even those that aren't likely to be cashed out in the foreseeable future (plants, equipment, patents, licenses, etc.).

GENERAL ASSETS

The classic benchmark for general assets is book value, which is the value of everything the company owns (all assets) minus the value of everything the company owes (liabilities). In theory, if the company liquidates, it would sell all assets, repay all obligations, and have an amount equal to book value available for distribution to shareholders. In such a case, we'd be able to use price-to-book value per share as the perfect valuation metric.

Unfortunately, the real world is not nearly so simple. In calculating the book value of an asset, we start cleanly enough. We use the cost incurred to obtain the asset. But we run into trouble almost immediately thereafter. Many assets (the ones outside the current category) are meant to be on board and productive for a long time. Even in a period of modest inflation, we cannot assume that an asset is worth the same amount today as what we spent to acquire it five years ago. This, in and of itself, is not the end of the world. We could always adjust the historic cost by increasing the number according to a reputable price index.

The real problems relate to the fact that assets don't stay the same. In one sense, as time passes, they inch step by step toward obsolescence, when they will have no value, or a modest salvage value. In the real world, we instinctively understand and accept the notion that asset values often do diminish this way—hence the use of depreciation charges. But we also recognize that the path of real-world depreciation is often not as smooth as assumed in accounting formulas. And not every asset really depreciates in a true economic sense. Land, for example, may gain value based on different potential uses made possible by the way the surrounding locale evolves. Also, assets tend to be modified over time. Buildings get renovated; machines get new components. Money spent to modernize or enhance assets is added to historic cost. And, of course, the improvement gets depreciated over time.

Technology also has an impact. Widget manufacturing methods may change to the point where a newly constructed widget plant might have little resemblance to the one we built 10 years ago and gradually modernized. Assume our plant's historic cost, including the value of modernization efforts, is $300 million, and that it's halfway through an expected 20-year "useful life," so that we already have depreciated half the gross value. Assume, therefore, it is now valued on our balance sheet at $150 million. But competitors building new widget plants today are spending $400 million.

At first glance, it looks like we have a potential windfall: a widget plant that, despite its 10-year age, is still functioning nicely and is carried on our books for less than half the value of a new plant. We recognize that we have to make some allowance for the passage of time, but the gap between $400 million and $150 million seems very large. Before rejoicing in our hidden value opportunity, we'd better compare the plants. It might be the case that the new plant uses new technology to achieve levels of cost efficiency we can't approach. So, in fact, our plant may have no appeal at all to a prospective widget-making buyer. Instead, it might be sold for, say, $25 million, to someone who wants to knock down the factory and use the land for another purpose. If such a transaction occurs, we'd have to take a write-off of $125 million when we unload a factory supposedly worth $150 million and replace our asset base with only $25 million in cash. (The write-off is the device used by our accountant when we give up $150 million to get $25 million, thereby causing $125 million worth of asset value to evaporate.)

Of course such a transaction need not always have such a sad ending. Perhaps we are able to make our widget factory so efficient that somebody wants to buy it for $265 million. In such a case, our accountants would book a special $115 million gain, as we trade what we assumed was $150 worth of assets for $265 million worth of another asset (cash).

The possibilities are fascinating, and many value investors love to seek out instances of the latter situation, cases where real-world asset values exceed book values. One thing is clear for our purposes. It's not easy to use book value in the real world. But it's not impossible.

Strictly speaking, every company is completely unique. No matter how much computer processing we bring to finding and analyzing stocks, at the end of the day we're just making assumptions about things nobody can know: future performance. So it would be somewhat odd to obsess on precision. Once we become willing to approximate, we can accept the idea that companies in the same industry are similar in ways that can be useful to us.

So when I screen for value, I'm open to the idea of occasionally using the price-to-book value relationship because I can nullify the impact of accounting distortions through comparative screening techniques like this.

Most Recent Quarter Price-to-Book Value < Industry Average MRQ Price-to-Book Value

In SmartMoneySelect.com, the following more aggressive comparative book value test can be created.

MRQ Price-to-Book Value in Bottom 25% within Industry

Besides the standard industry comparison, Stock Investor Pro allows us to inquire into changes in valuation that occur over time.

MRQ Relative Strength Price-to-Book < Relative Strength Price-to-Book 1 Year Ago
MRQ Relative Strength Price-to-Book < 3 Year Average Relative Strength Price-to-Book

None of these tests would cause us to purchase the stocks. But they would be sufficient to prompt us to look more closely, which is exactly what we want to accomplish in Step 1 (Find). And it can go into the hopper as one consideration, among many others, in Step 2 (Analyze).

Tangible book value, an increasingly popular variation, is calculated as book value minus intangible assets. This metric has become more popular lately, as many believe they can help protect themselves from the impact of questionable accounting practices by refusing to value stocks based on intangibles.

Although this reasoning has emotional appeal during a time when financial scandals make too many headlines, it is not necessarily the most productive approach to investing. The plain, simple fact is that many companies today generate substantial profits from assets that don't fit generations-ago accounting conventions that were developed under the assumption that all companies were manufacturers. Licenses, patents, trademarks, copyrights, brand stature, and so on have considerable value but don't sit comfortably on corporate books that are filled with manufacturing-oriented definitions and categories. Even goodwill (which arises if one company acquires another at a price that exceeds the latter's book value) represents legitimate asset value. Given the distortions inherent in book value calculations, it's only logical to expect that an acquisition price based on the buyer's assessment of future earning power would often exceed an artificially depressed book valuation.

Accordingly, I seldom use screening tests based on tangible book value. The basic book value distortions are exaggerated even more when we stir in an unrealistic aversion to intangibles. And since company-specific issues (the presence or absence of acquisitions) can have a big impact on the presence or absence of goodwill, a major intangible category, I have less confidence in an assumption that distortions will be comparable from one company to another in the same industry. Hence comparative screening isn't much of a solution.

PROPRIETARY ANALYTICS

Among the screeners discussed in Chapter 3, the following offer value-oriented proprietary analytics.

- **MSN Money:** The key analytic here is known as the StockScouter rating. It is based on four factors: Fundamental, Ownership, Valuation, and Technical. The overall rating as well as each of the factors are available as variables in the MSN Money screener at http://moneycentral.msn.com. The Valuation grade, which runs from A (best) through F (worst), starts with considerations that should come as no surprise. It is based on P/E, price/sales, and the PEG (P/E-to-growth) ratio. But there's a twist that requires some thought. Research conducted in connection with the development of StockScouter showed that larger-capitalization stocks had more leeway than smaller issues to have high ratios and still get a good grade. I suspect the research was conducted at a time when investment community culture had a strong large-cap bias. But it's unclear if or how the merits of the StockScouter value factor would be impacted if that large-cap bias diminishes in the future.
- **Morningstar Premium Stock Selector:** This application offers a star rating for stocks (five stars is the best rating, one star the worst) based primarily on value considerations. The Morningstar web site provides a fairly detailed explanation of its approach. To summarize, Morningstar analysts estimate a fair value for each of the stocks they cover using a discounted cash flow approach driven by expected growth, expected

margins, and expectations about the nature of the asset base that will be needed to generate future profits. Then, Morningstar adds two interesting twists. First, it assumes a cost of capital that is then subtracted from projected income. The result is what it refers to as economic profit. Second, it assumes that companies with large economic profits will attract competition and that the economic profit margin will therefore decay over time. All these factors are combined into a model that computes a fair value for the stock. Stocks priced at the widest discount to fair value get five stars, stocks at a lesser discount get four stars, and so on until Morningstar gets to stocks priced at the largest premiums to fair value, which get one star. The amount of discount or premium associated with a particular star rating varies based on risk and Morningstar's assessment of the company's inherent competitive advantages (the size of its "economic moat").

The drawbacks of Morningstar's star ratings are that they require analysts to make judgments on several very challenging issues (for example, the factors upon which economic moat is assessed, such as high customer switching costs and unique corporate culture, involve very subjective judgments that are piled on top of the usual difficulties in forecasting future growth rates, costs, etc.) and that only a limited number of stocks are rated (Morningstar can rate only as many stocks as its analysts cover). The strengths are the detailed explanations (which enable users to make rational decisions as to whether the approach is consistent with their investment philosophies), the ease with which the ratings can be built into screens, and the sophistication of the approach.

- **ProSearch:** This application offers value ranks based on the PEG (P/E-to-growth) ratio, the relative P/E ratio, the relative price/book value ratio, and least squares deviation. The last is a statistical measure of the distance between a stock's current price and a mathematically calculated trend line. For the long-term value rank, three price trends are used—one for a 5-year period, another for a 10-year period, and the other for the maximum period of time based on the amount of price information contained in the database. A short-term value rank is also offered. This is designed for younger companies with shorter share price histories. It differs from the long-term value rank in terms of the trend lines used for least squares deviation calculation. The short-term value rank uses share prices measured over a three-year period and a five-year period. Use of the least squares deviations implies that stocks trading at a significant distance from their general trend lines are poised to snap back toward more normal readings. This isn't necessarily going to always happen. But at the very least the incorporation of such behavioral factors into value ratings suggests we should not ignore very high or low value ratings. We might discover something that justifies an assumption that a sustainable shift in the price trend is occurring. Such possibilities can be fleshed out with secondary and/or alternative screening tests, or in Step 2 (Analyze).

Notice that all three of these rating systems use a variety of factors. Hence it may be redundant to add additional good-stock tests. In other words, we can treat a single screening test based on one of these measures as constituting one-stop shopping for all the value-oriented tests for the screen. If good-stock screening is to be our primary theme, it's unlikely we will be content to leave the finer points of testing to a system whose details are not fully revealed to us. I believe value ratings are best used as a secondary theme in a screen whose primary tests are aimed at the good-company approach. In this context, we can tolerate not knowing or being able to edit the inner workings of the model.

## CHAPTER 5

Screening for Good Companies

This chapter will discuss the data items we can use to screen for good companies. In contrast to our experience with the good-stock concepts discussed in Chapter 4, the good-company considerations involve much less controversy. That's because when it comes to company analysis, theory works well. Higher margins are better than lower margins, faster turnover is better than slower turnover, higher returns on capital are better than lower returns, and strong balance sheets are better than weak ones. We'll rely on well-established fundamental ratios such as these.

STAYING FOCUSED

The hardest part of the good-company tasks is keeping our focus. There's plenty of "noise" out there that can easily distract us from the task at hand.

The Doability Question

Notice what was not mentioned earlier in connection with identifying good companies: good management, strong technologies, barriers to entry by new rivals, efficient manufacturing systems, market leadership, productive employees, and so on. It's not that these things aren't important. They are crucial. The problem is a practical one: How can investors directly assess such issues?

Consider Dell Computer. How would we go about evaluating

management? If we could get in, we might start by meeting personally with Chief Executive Officer Michael Dell and/or Chief Financial Officer James Schneider. But how much would we really learn? Nowadays, the extent to which companies can communicate one-on-one with members of the investment community is more tightly regulated than ever. So we can be sure that they'll be very careful about what they tell us. Perhaps we can get a facilities tour. But how much of this would we comprehend? How many investors have the kind of operations training necessary to enable them to look at the activities and make credible judgments as to whether tasks are being handled as effectively as possible? And how can we determine that competitors are not managing their operations more effectively? As a matter of fact, how do we know we're even meeting with the right people? Professional investors usually speak to executives in charge of investor relations, to the chief executive, and to the chief financial officer. Often, though, day-to-day success depends on managers several layers lower in the organization, people whose names we don't even know.

If these questions seem challenging, bear in mind we're talking about Dell Computer. At least we know what Dell does. In fact, many of us use computers purchased from Dell. Suppose instead we move to a different participant in the industry, Sun Microsystems.

Most of us have heard of Sun and know it makes enterprise servers. But do those of us who are not information technology professionals *really* know much, if anything, about this kind of hardware? Are we equipped to independently assess the quality of information we might learn if we hear a presentation given by Chief Executive Officer Scott Mc-Nealy? Philip A. Fisher, in his investment classic *Common Stocks and Uncommon Profits* (John Wiley & Sons, 1996), recognizes that we may not be able to directly answer such questions. So he suggests we look to the business grapevine ("scuttlebutt") for help. But in truth, few of us have the resources or contacts to build a consistent investment program based on this approach.

Ideally, we'd like to be able to adopt a proprietor's perspective when assessing the quality of a company. This is pretty much what we'd have to do to implement the approach of Greenwald et al. described in Chapter 1. To properly value the company's assets, we would need to be able to come up with realistic assumptions about the valuations, which, for ongoing operations, will often be based on replacement cost. This can be very difficult for many investors, even experienced professional investors, to do. Similarly, many will find it hard to accurately judge the extent to which earnings are generated within the context of a "franchise." Unless we have a true workaday understanding of the business, we may find that we are disturbingly inaccurate in the judgments we make.

If you can make these kinds of judgments, by all means make them and use them. Another scenario is that you find yourself able to make them for some kinds of businesses but not others. For example, if you have a background in paper manufacturing, you may possess certain insights about production processes, market dynamics, and so on that most investors cannot replicate. In such situations, you certainly should use any special knowledge you might possess. But unless you're going to stick with paper companies only, you will eventually find yourself confronted with the need to make comparable judgments about businesses that are less familiar to you.

Some investors will be quite content to stay entirely within their fields of expertise. But over time, most will not want to limit themselves to such an extent. The desire to stray beyond one's own professional nest is reasonable and consistent with widely accepted principles relating to diversification. This may not sound so pressing if your expertise is in a field that has strong prospects, that is likely to stay strong for a prolonged period, and that has a sufficient number of pure-play publicly traded companies whose shares are priced at reasonable levels. But if your expertise lies in an area that is for one reason or another not attractive from an investment standpoint, you will have to either be willing to invest in other fields or avoid stocks altogether.

The avoidance option might well be the correct one if we really are unable to assess companies outside our own professions. But reality is not nearly that harsh. Good companies tend to leave good footprints, and bad companies tend to leave bad footprints. And even if we are unable to discourse at length about the details surrounding the company's technologies, its processes, its supplier relationships, its employee pool, and so forth, we can often view and analyze basic ratios that flow from the company's performance regarding such issues. Such knowledge isn't perfect, but it can be combined with common sense and a sound awareness of general business/economic conditions to support the sort of reasonable company-oriented judgments that lead to successful investment performance.

We will use these footprints of success to identify good companies. Going back to the Dell example, we may not be able to assess the efficiency of the company's operations from a facilities tour. But we can examine readily available fundamental data and see that while Dell has suffered from the technology slump that started in late 2000, it is faring far better than its rivals in a variety of important margin and return on capital criteria. And even those who are oblivious to the high-profile scuttlebutt that always seems to surround Dell would have to sit up and take notice of this company's trailing 12 months receivables turnover (12.75 versus a 6.86 industry average), inventory turnover (93.42 versus a 34.43 industry average), and asset turnover (2.38 versus a 1.45 industry average), as well as revenue and income per employee numbers that are nearly double the industry averages. Companies can't produce numbers like those unless management is doing something right. We may not know the details, but it's easy to look at data that embodies such footprints of success.

Examining such data relationships is the meat of Step 2 (Analyze). In Step 1 (Find), we can take a more activist approach. We can create company-oriented screening tests to call our attention to firms that leave demonstrably superior financial footprints.

The Earnings Game

Today, many investors view good companies and good earnings performance as synonymous. But that's not necessarily true. Today's condition of strength or weakness may not be sustainable over a prolonged period. (Even the best of companies have cold periods, and on the other side, every dog has its day.) It wouldn't matter one way or the other if the return on capital generated by the new business was far less than the cost of capital used by the enterprise, or if the risk associated with the activity was out of proportion to the return it produced. Still, unless we avoid all contact with other investors and the financial media, we will find ourselves continually barraged by rhetoric that equates "good" with short-term earnings performance.

This can be traced back several decades, when the investment community started to gravitate toward a custom whereby shares of companies with favorable near-term earnings momentum (usually defined with reference to year-to-year quarterly EPS comparisons) were favored, while shares of companies with lackluster momentum were held in lesser regard. At first, this approach was done on the basis of the most recently reported period. There was a generally accepted although unspoken presumption that companies that looked good in the latest period will continue to look good in future periods. And the presumption often worked in the real world. After all, economic conditions and company characteristics don't usually experience substantial change overnight. This sounds a bit like physics (a body in motion tends to stay in motion) and is how the word "momentum" became so firmly planted in the investment lexicon. Later on, as Wall Street research departments grew and became more capable, the analysis shifted toward a forward-looking approach. The distinction between successful and unsuccessful investing became increasingly tied to one's ability to accurately predict what would happen in the next quarter.

Since stocks were being bought on the basis of good earnings news, it was very easy for even sophisticated investors to overpay, sometimes by a lot. But as long as one was able to create or gain access to reasonable forecasts for the next quarter (or at least more reasonable than those used by other investors), one could achieve superior investment results.

Needless to say, theoreticians never liked this system. Since value was not part of the basic inquiry, even supposedly knowledgeable investors wound up buying very overpriced stocks and selling very undervalued issues. And to make matters worse, such errors did not damage their performance. In fact, this system became so prevalent that for many years those who did it right (paid attention to value) wound up suffering below-average performance. (The overpriced stocks they sold continued to get more and more overpriced, while the undervalued stocks they bought remained unappreciated and undervalued for prolonged periods.)

For many years, it looked as if the theoreticians were losing the battle. But as the 1990s progressed, the earnings momentum system gradually became victimized by its own success. Because it served so well for so many, more and more investors followed the approach with increasing fervor. Eventually, we wound up with a situation where too many investors did the same thing at the same time in response to the same item of information. That led to grotesquely large share price movements that created more and more opportunity for those who kept their attention anchored to the more basic qualities that make a company good or bad.

As of this writing, the earnings momentum style remains very much alive. But the extreme share price movements it sparks make it increasingly easy for value connection investors to identify quality companies whose shares have been beaten down out of proportion to any fundamental shortcoming. In these situations, the buyer need not wait years for the Street to recognize the company's merits. The stock may adjust in a matter of weeks or months; sometimes, all it takes is one announcement to the effect that earnings progress is back on track. On the other side of the coin, those who chase momentum stories higher and higher are more exposed than ever to rapid, punishing losses; one bad earnings report can offset a lengthy period of superior performance in a matter of hours.

This doesn't assure the value investor of victory. Momentum payers can continue to succeed if they find a better way to identify ebbs and flows of earnings progress and refine their trading rules to better adjust to the nature of the changes that are occurring. But it does mean the momentum players have to work harder than they did in the past. More importantly for our purposes, the value investor is back in the game. With stock prices adjusting so suddenly and so rapidly to shifts, or perceived shifts, in fundamentals, value investors now have just as good a chance as momentum investors to see their insights rewarded with superior share price performance within reasonable time frames.

SEARCHING FOR FOOTPRINTS OF SUCCESS

Let's now consider the fundamental concepts we can use to screen for good companies. We'll start by discussing how to define, for screening purposes, attractive metrics. The concepts are straightforward. Sample tests will refer to a generic "return" variable. All approaches can be implemented for any of the various good-company variables our screeners might offer.

We'll do our best to avoid using numeric tests because it's so hard to come up with a particular number that has a bearing on investment merit. One might suppose that for return on capital, we could use a reasonable threshold based on the prevailing risk-free rate plus a risk premium. But some companies and industries experience prolonged cold spells during which returns don't quite measure up. Things change, and we're trying to find companies that are best positioned for whatever the future may bring. Comparative testing can help us do this. For example, we might accept a company with a 4 percent return on capital if the industry average is, say, 1.5 percent and/or the company's 4 percent tally is an improvement over a 2 percent historical average. Either scenario would indicate that something special is occurring at this company. We don't yet know if this indication will continue to hold up as we progress through Step 2 (Analyze). But at least we know it's worth our while to look into the situation. That's what Step 1 (Find) is all about.

Hence, whenever we screen for quality, we should try to use comparative tests. Fortunately, more and more of today's screeners are letting us do that. If we can't, we have two choices.

1. **Defer to Step 2 (Analyze).** Screen for quality as best we can given the variables offered by the application, and pay special attention to comparative quality indications in Step 2 (Analyze).

2. **Use the application's auxiliary features.** Apply the techniques described in the appendix to Chapter 3 to estimate reasonable numeric targets or to establish priorities for Step 2 (Analyze) based on sorts of quality-oriented data items.

Assuming our application allows us to create comparative screening tests, here are variations of a theme worthy of being used often. (Remember, these examples apply not just to returns, but also to margins and turnover.)

Return > Industry Average Return

Relative Return > 60

Return in Top 25% within Industry

Creating tests such as these involves two important decisions.

1. **Which time period should we use?** It's standard for screeners to offer trailing 12 month (TTM) data, and this certainly can be used. But if our screener also offers data averaged over longer (usually three- or five-year) periods, consider using this in addition to or in place of TTM data. Company quality is an enduring concept. Hence it's useful to use a longer-term perspective. Several applications allow us to do this with returns and margins. But for the time being, turnover variables tend to be TTM only. Hopefully, that will change in the future.

2. **Which comparative benchmark should we use?** For screening applications that permit company-to-industry comparisons, I suggest that this be the first choice. Sector comparison should be the second choice, and a broader comparison such as the S&P 500 or the database average should be the backup option. The narrower the comparison, the easier it is to hone in on company-specific qualities. Table 5.1 provides an example using late 2002 data for Stanley Works.

   Stanley would be blocked by a test that compares companies to the S&P 500. But the industry comparison suggests Stanley is doing something right that its peers are not doing. Hence it would pass a test based on industry comparison. This is the kind of result we hope to achieve in Step 1 (Find).

We can also use time series comparisons.

TTM Return > 5 Year Return

ConAgra illustrates the benefit of time series comparison. Table 5.2 compares its late 2002 returns on investment to the average for the food processing industry.

TABLE 5.1 Late 2002 Return on Investment Comparison for Stanley Works

	Company	Appliance and Tool Industry	S&P 500
5-year average ROI (%)	10.01	6.69	12.81

TABLE 5.2 Late 2002 Return on Investment Comparison for ConAgra

	Company	Industry
TTM ROI	7.52	9.44
5-year average ROI	7.26	13.97

We see that ConAgra would fail any test based on company-to-industry comparison, since it falls short of the benchmark in both the TTM and five-year periods. But look at the time series trends. For the industry, the TTM ROI is significantly below the five-year average. Yet over those same periods, we see marginal improvement for ConAgra. The company is still below average, but it is picking up steam. It can be worthwhile to build screens that seek such situations. It's entirely possible that we may catch on to improvements like this before they are fully reflected in EPS trends and stock prices.

Those who use a screener that permits complex tests (such as Multex's premium application or Stock Investor Pro) can carry the concept a step further with a test like this:

(TTM Return/5 Year Return) > (TTM Industry Average Return/5 Year Industry Average Return)

This test starts out by computing a ratio based on time series comparative return for the company (the TTM period compared with the five-year period). It then does the same thing for the industry average. To pass this test, the company's ratio must be superior to that of the industry. The benefits of such a test are illustrated in Table 5.3 using late 2002 data for IBM.

At first glance, the company data looks unappealing. IBM is below the industry average for both time periods. Also, both the company and the industry have significantly deteriorated from the five-year period to the trailing 12 months. But our complex screening test catches something subtle. IBM's time series comparative ratio of 0.75 (10.91 divided by 14.52) is

TABLE 5.3 Late 2002 Return on Investment Comparison for IBM

	Company	Industry
TTM ROI	10.91	12.04
5-year average ROI	14.52	21.26

higher than the ratio for the industry, which is 0.56 (12.04 divided by 21.26). In other words, the company has suffered less from the technology slump. This may be a clue that there is something happening specifically at IBM that warrants our attention.

It bears repeating that even if your screener can't handle a test like this, you can easily assess the situation in Step 2 (Analyze). Tables 5.2 and 5.3 show the data just the way you'd see it on the MultexInvestor.com web site.

Let's now move beyond our generic examples where we screened for "return" and look more closely at the types of data items we can use in our screens.

RETURN ON CAPITAL

When it comes to judging the quality of a company, return on capital is the premier metric. That's because it aims directly at a company's very reason for being: its ability to generate a reasonable profit for its owners. The key is how we define "reasonable."

It's not a matter of size. We cannot infer that Company A, with annual profits of $35 million, is better than Company B, with annual profits of $5 million. Suppose Company A used $7 billion worth of capital to produce its $35 million profit. That's a return of only 0.5 percent. Even in late 2002, with interest rates at extremely low levels, we could still have earned a higher return had we invested in risk-free short-term U.S. government debt. Why would we accept a lesser return on a business venture, which is riskier than government obligations? A company whose return on capital is below its cost of capital is a losing proposition. It would be as if we pay 8 percent interest on money we borrow to invest in a bond that returns 5 percent. We'd be losing money on the deal and would have been better off bypassing the whole thing.

This doesn't mean that if we encounter a company whose returns are below the cost of capital we should attend the annual meeting and demand liquidation and distribution of proceeds to shareholders who, presumably, would reinvest more profitably. Perhaps the problem stems from a temporary cyclical downturn, and over the course of a full business cycle the company will cover its cost of capital with plenty of room to spare. But it does mean we should inquire to see if the problem is likely to be temporary or permanent. And don't completely dismiss the liquidation angle. A company that consistently fails to generate a reasonable return without justification (such as cyclical problems that cannot be avoided) may attract interest on the part of the takeover crowd. Maybe they really will consider liquidation. Or they may see an opportunity to acquire the firm on the cheap, reform the business, and benefit from stronger returns on capital in the future.

Suppose we also learn that Company B was able to produce its $5 million using only $25 million of capital. That's a 20 percent return. It's possible we could find companies that produce greater returns. But we'd have to look pretty hard. We certainly could not come close to that level with risk-free Treasuries.

If we were to further learn Company B is a chemicals manufacturer, we'd be even more impressed. As of this writing, the average return in that industry is about 4.5 percent. Now we're learning something exciting about Company B. It is not simply riding the coattails of a hot industry. Actually, its industry is pretty lackluster. The good returns are being generated by uniquely good things being done by Company B. I'm not necessarily pulling impressive numbers out of my head to support a theoretical point. Companies possessing such levels of superiority really do exist. At the time this is written, Cabot Microelectronics, a chemical company, has reported a return of 20.75 percent.

This may seem removed from day-to-day reality. But in truth, it is the engine that powers the events upon which the market obsesses. Consider the growth question. Which company seems better able to generate good earnings gains? (Assume that both companies maintain consistent returns and that neither company pays a dividend.)

- Company A enhanced its capital base by the $35 million in income it generated. If it again earns 0.5 percent on its capital (now $7.035 billion), next year's earnings will be $35.175 million (i.e., only 0.5 percent growth).
- Company B enhanced its capital base by the $5 million in income it generated, enabling it to work with $30 million in the new year. If it again earns a 20 percent return on $30 million, it will have a profit of $6 million, a 20 percent one-year rate of earnings growth.

Notice, in each case, that the earnings growth rate is equal to the return on capital. This is our starting point.

In the real world, we constantly see growth rates that do not equal return on capital. That's because our assumption that companies maintain consistent returns often fails to hold up. Business entities are not rigid. They continually change, sometimes getting better and other times turning sluggish. Trends in return on capital, reveal whether the company is changing for better or worse. They also help us evaluate the credibility of earnings forecasts. If analysts are predicting 12 percent growth for a company whose returns on capital have been in the 5 to 7 percent range, we are prompted to look more closely to see if the analysts present a convincing explanation of how the company will improve. Maybe they are expecting operational changes to stimulate higher returns in the future.

Measuring Return on Capital

There are several ways this vital metric can be measured, and most screeners offer at least some degree of choice. None are necessarily right or wrong. Each measure gives us a different message. This book will refer to the Multex definitions. Be sure to check the glossary in any other source you might use.

- **Return on Equity (ROE):** This is the capital owned by the shareholders. If I put up $50 million to start a business, my equity is $50 million. If the business earns an $8 million profit, return on equity is 16 percent ($8 million divided by $50 million).
- **Return on Investment (ROI):** Suppose I need more capital, but don't want to put in any more of my own money. I decide to borrow $25 million. Assume this is long-term debt. There is a maturity date, perhaps 10 years hence. But in truth, I don't intend to repay the debt. My goal is to operate with a mixture of capital, part equity and part debt. (When this $25 million obligation comes due, I'll refinance it.) Now I have $75 million to work with, $50 million of my money and $25 million in borrowings. The business activities still generate an annual return of 16 percent, so my profit is $12 million (16 percent of $75 million). ROI, which compares income to the entire $75 million capital base, is therefore 16 percent. If we were evaluating the business activity itself, we'd say it's a wash. I earn 16 percent whether I use only my own money or a combination of my money and borrowed money.

  But that's not the whole story. A company represents a mixture of two things—the day-to-day business and overall corporate strategies. My decision to work with borrowed money boosted profits to $12 million without my having to add to my own $50 million investment. Hence ROE, the return on owners' capital, was leveraged up to 24 percent ($12 million divided by $50 million). Of course, there is a trade-off: The higher ROE is accompanied by the higher risk that is inevitable when borrowed money enters the picture.
- **Return on Assets (ROA):** This measure is similar to ROI in that it takes a more comprehensive view of the capital base. It includes equity, long-term debt, and all other liabilities. For example, besides $50 million in equity and $25 million in long-term debt, I might maintain a revolving credit line in order to pay for raw materials. As I collect revenue from selling the finished goods, I pay down the debt. Assume, on

average, $5 million in this kind of short-term debt is outstanding. My total asset base is now $80 million. If I earn a $12 million profit, my ROA is 15 percent.

There is an important common flaw to all these measures. Calculating the amount of equity capital is subject to all the shortcomings discussed in Chapter 4 in connection with book value. Indeed, for most companies, equity and book value are one and the same. (This is another place where it's important to check glossaries; some providers include preferred stock in a comprehensive equity account; others separate preferred equity from common equity.) A seeming 20 percent ROE would lose a lot of luster if we had reason to believe the book value is only one-quarter of the true market value of the assets, in which case we might be tempted to use 5 percent as a more economically correct ROE.

But in this context, there are some subtleties that weren't present when we considered whether a share price is modest or high relative to book value per share. Let's go back to the example where I contribute $50 million to a business that uses this capital to generate $8 million in profit. Assume that for some reason, the value of the productive assets management purchases with my $50 million doubles. Hence the market value is $100 million, not $50 million. On one level, we could argue, as we did in connection with book value, that such distortions are likely to be similar among companies in similar businesses and that company-to-industry comparisons remain valid. But beyond that, nothing alters the fact that I contributed only $50 million. If we were to say economic ROE is only 8 percent rather than 16 percent, we'd be unjustifiably penalizing management. The fact remains that I put $50 million to work, not $100 million. And the company used the $50 million to produce $8 million in profit.

So in evaluating the quality of management's efforts, it is reasonable to use calculations based on conventional methods of accounting for equity. But we still ought not brush the book value-to-market value gap aside. As value connection investors, we are still comparing what we pay for the stock with some measure of the true value of what our stake in the company is worth. Presumably, if the market value of our assets has risen to $100 million, buyers of such assets believe $100 million to be reasonably representative of the present value of the cash flows they could receive through their ownership. If our managers are not fully exploiting all the benefits the assets can produce nowadays, somebody else may see an opportunity to make an acquisition bid, which we would accept if it is above what we could earn by holding on.

There is another metric that has come on the scene that helps us address situations like this.

- **Return on Enterprise Value (ROEV):** Enterprise value (EV) is the amount that would have to be paid by somebody who wants to purchase the entire company. To calculate this figure, we pretend that such a buyer would not pay any special premium above market price. (In reality, however, control is deemed to have value in and of itself, presumably because a controlling owner can make changes and squeeze more profit out of the assets while a passive shareholder cannot.) EV is calculated by multiplying share price by number of shares, adding in preferred equity and total debt, and then subtracting cash.

    This assumes the buyer is purchasing all outstanding stock at market prices, redeeming any preferred shares that might be outstanding, and paying off all outstanding debt. We subtract cash because the buyer could apply cash held by the company toward debt repayment, thereby reducing the amount one must come up with for this purpose. To calculate a return on EV, we would not use net income because it includes interest expense. We don't want to count this since EV assumes all debt is retired. We can recalculate income on our own estimating the interest savings. But many are content to simply use EBIT (earnings before interest and taxes). This excludes taxes in addition to interest expense, but that's all right. Acquisition analysis is usually done with respect to pretax income.

Screening for Return on Capital

My first-choice metric is ROI, because it gives me information about the performance of the business and is more readily available nowadays than ratios based on EV. Two companies whose business operations are performing equally well would have the same ROI even if their balance sheets were very different. Their ROEs would differ, since this ratio blends information about business performance with the impact of financing strategies. Both metrics are important. But when I use return on capital in the context of Step 1 (Find), I'd rather concentrate strictly on business performance. I can use separate balance sheet–related tests if I want to screen for financial strength. Most of the time, though, I defer consideration of financing issues to Step 2 (Analyze).

Some screeners don't offer variables for ROI. In that case, I'm content to substitute ROA. And if ROE is the only option, I'll use that. Return on capital is such an important concept, I'd rather put aside my reservations about ROE than omit the concept altogether.

All of the sample quality tests presented on pages 84 through 86 apply smoothly to ROE, ROI, and ROA. Here's another test we can create based on the theoretical ideal to the effect that a company's growth rate should be equal to its ROI.

5 Year EPS Growth > 5 Year ROI

This is a generally unstable situation. Eventually, the ROI should rise or the EPS growth rate should slow. We can seek companies likely to exhibit the former by pairing this test with one that seeks a pattern of accelerating growth.

5 Year EPS Growth > 5 Year ROI

3 Year EPS Growth > 5 Year EPS Growth AND TTM EPS Growth > 3 Year EPS Growth

Unfortunately, the state of screening technology is such that we cannot use enterprise value as readily as we can use the other return variables. Users of the Multex premium screener or Stock Investor Pro can use the definition on page 91 to create a user-defined variable for EV. Otherwise, for those willing to use EBITDA instead of EBIT, there's SmartMoneySelect.com, which has a built-in variable that allows us to create a test like this:

(Enterprise Value/EBITDA) in Bottom 50% within Industry

We can also use the techniques described in the appendix to Chapter 3 to work with EV. We can sort in order to prioritize our Step 2 (Analyze) efforts with a list created through a screen that doesn't use EV. Or we can do some legwork to help us devise a reasonable numeric test for our preferred EV comparison (i.e., EV-to-EBIT).

COMPONENTS OF RETURN ON CAPITAL

Since return on capital is the prime measure of company quality, it seems reasonable to assume we'd want to expand our understanding of why a company's returns are what they are. That leads us to the components of return on capital. There are many ways of calculating the return ratios (even beyond the three we have just considered). So it follows that there are also many ways of defining the components of return. The full range of detailed definitions is not germane to our discussion, since we are focusing on the data items that are readily available to us for use in Step 1 (Find) and Step 2 (Analyze).

For our purposes, it is sufficient to state that returns are based on three concepts: margin, turnover, and leverage (use of debt). We are not going to tie ourselves down to replicating the mathematics of calculating return based on these factors. But we will consider how we can use these components to identify opportunities that might not stick out if we focused only on the ultimate return numbers.

Margin

All else being equal, higher margin for a company equates to higher returns. We can say the same about turnover and leverage. But margin plays a distinct role in our efforts because it is so widely understood and followed in the investment community. Hence on many occasions stocks react directly to changes in margin.

On one level, the concept of margin is very straightforward. It's the percent of each sales dollar that is left over as profit after subtracting costs. Depending on which kinds of costs we wish to examine, we can work with a variety of margins. The most comprehensive is net margin, the percent of each sales dollar left over after *all* costs have been subtracted. This is the margin that is most often used in mathematical analysis of return on capital. But we aren't taking a math test here. Net margin is not always the one that is most useful to our efforts to find and analyze investment opportunities. We can often learn more by "drilling down" to the components of the income statement and working with data that shows us how the net margin got to be what it is.

As we saw with return on capital, seemingly simple concepts can come in different flavors that leave different tastes in our mouths. Some measures tell us about the company's day-to-day business. Others tell us about the corporate entity as a whole. And as is the case with return, most of today's screening applications allow us to screen for margins that address both views of the company.

Here are the kinds of margins we can usually choose from when we create screens.

- **Margins that address basic business performance.** This includes gross margin (sales minus direct costs, often referred to as cost of goods sold), operating margin (sales minus direct costs and overhead), and EBITDA (earnings before interest, taxes, depreciation, and amortization) margin. When using a screening program that has variables based on all three of these margins, I prefer operating margin. That's because there is room for discretion when companies decide whether certain types of costs should be considered direct or overhead. A recent noteworthy example involved Amazon.com's shipping costs. Different classification decisions can make it difficult to compare gross margins from one company to another. Firms that account for these borderline expenses as overhead (as Amazon.com originally did with shipping costs) will report higher gross margins (a fact loudly trumpeted by critics who contended Amazon's gross margins looked higher than they really should have been). Use of operating margin facilitates comparison, because this measure encompasses all business costs, whether the company accounts for them as direct or overhead.

Meanwhile, EBITDA margin is my lowest preference. As discussed in Chapter 4, I am not completely comfortable eliminating depreciation and amortization from my assessment of business performance, because it's often a proxy for routine plant-related expenditures that are classified as capital spending and therefore aren't recognized on the income statement. Note, though, that despite the limitations of gross and EBITDA margins, I'd be willing to work with them if my screener did not offer operating margin. The benefit of being able to isolate business performance is sufficiently important to warrant flexibility if I can't get my first-choice data item.

- **Margins that address performance of the company as a whole.** There are two margins in this category—pretax margin and net margin. For the most part, pretax margin is based on sales minus all expenses except taxes, while for net margin, we also subtract taxes. Those definitions should suffice for all practical purposes. For precise definitions, check glossaries accompanying whatever sources you use. For example, when Multex calculates net margin, it not only subtracts taxes from pretax income, but also subtracts equity income (the company's pro rata share of income generated by partially owned subsidiaries). For our purposes, the focus should be on the difference between operating margin and pretax margin. This is attributable to income and expense items that do not relate to the basic day-to-day business operations. Examples include interest expense, interest income, gains or losses from the sale of assets, and unusual charges for restructurings or plant closings.

For purposes of Step 1 (Find), I occasionally use pretax or net margin, but most of the time I prefer to use operating margin. My preference is based on the nature of our mission in Step 1 (Find), which is to identify companies worthy of further, more in-depth review. Generally I do not like to invest in companies that are experiencing sustained struggle in day-to-day operations. So if a company fares poorly in terms of operating margin (or gross or EBITDA margin if my screener does not offer operating margin), it's unlikely I'll want to learn more.

Margin-related screening tests can be constructed based on the examples provided at the beginning of this chapter. There is, however, an interesting wrinkle based on the ratio of operating margin (or gross or EBITDA margin) to pretax (or net) margin. The higher this ratio, the greater the degree to which the company's fortunes are being driven by factors that are separate from the running of the day-to-day business. The investment community prefers clarity and simplicity, a trend that has become magnified in the post-Enron era. So it is plausible that we might define a good company as one whose ratio of operating margin to pretax margin is low (an indication that nonoperating issues play only a modest role in the company's fortunes).

We might seek such companies using tests like these:

(TTM Operating Margin/TTM Pretax Margin) < (Industry Average TTM Operating Margin/Industry Average Pretax Margin)

(TTM Operating Margin/TTM Pretax Margin) < (5 Year Operating Margin/5 Year Pretax Margin)

If your screener cannot accommodate such tests, you can examine these data relationships in Step 2 (Analyze).

Note: These computations could be distorted by the inclusion of negative numbers. For example, a struggling company with a negative operating margin would pass the screen. You can weed these out in Step 2 (Analyze) or include additional screening tests requiring each of the referenced margins to be above zero.

Turnover

All else being equal, higher turnover equates to higher return. But in the real world, the status of turnover differs considerably from that of margin. While the latter is widely understood, the turnover concept is a hard one for many investors to grasp. This is not to say investors ignore it. High on the list of modern concerns that can send a stock lower are a slowdown in collection of receivables (falling receivables turnover) and undue inventory buildup (falling inventory turnover). But even when investors react to such problems, they don't often make the intellectual connection between the events and the link between turnover and return on capital.

Both of these are subsets of the main concept, asset turnover. This is defined as trailing 12 month (TTM) sales divided by average assets for that interval. Receivables turnover is TTM sales divided by average annual accounts receivable, and inventory turnover is TTM cost of goods sold divided by average annual inventory.

All three ratios are easy to calculate, but it's hard to grasp, in a real-world sense, what they tell us. Standard textbook-type explanations, such as statements to the effect that turnover tells us how quickly the company is converting its physical asset base into sales, usually don't help.

Perhaps the best way to approach this is to imagine we take $30 and use it to open a lemonade stand. Our capital is used to buy the materials we need to build the stand, the ingredients we need to make the drinks, and the cups and pitchers for serving them. Suppose we wind up bringing in $30 in revenue on the first day. We started with an asset base of $30 and wound up with exactly that, $30, in revenue. In other words, we got our asset investment back—no more, no less. That's what we learn when we calculate a 1.00 single-day asset turnover ratio.

Now, let's change the facts. Assume it's a very hot day and our revenue is $60. We put $30 into the business and got twice that, $60, back in revenue. We got our investment back twice. That's reflected in the 2.00 daily asset turnover ratio. If it were a cool day and revenue amounted to only $10, we might have gotten back only one-third of our investment that day. Hence our daily asset turnover ratio would have been much lower, 0.33.

Which scenario would make us feel most comfortable? Clearly, whenever an investment is made, there is always a sense of uncertainty as to what, if anything, we'll get back. So the sooner our money comes back, the more content we feel. The 1.00 turnover scenario, where we get our money back in one reporting period (a day in this case), leaves us feeling okay. The 2.00 turnover scenario that brings back double our money in one day leaves us feeling much happier. The 0.33 turnover scenario leaves us feeling least satisfied. In the latter case, a full day has passed and we still feel insecure; we're only one-third of the way to the feeling of relief we get once we recoup the money we laid out.

The receivables and inventory concepts are analogous.

- When we look at receivables turnover, we aren't counting the number of times we get our investment back. Instead, we count the number of times we're made whole after we let our customers run up a tab. Receivables turnover tells us how many times the tab gets repaid.
- When we look at inventory turnover, we count how many times over we recoup the money we spent in making or acquiring goods we hope we'll be able to sell.

As you can see, there is a real-world basis for the notion that high turnover is better than low turnover.

Now, let's look at Table 5.4, which provides an example of how high turnover can offset low margin to produce strong returns on investment.

We see that specialty retailer margins are below those customary in oil field services. But return on investment (ROI) is substantially higher due to a large edge in asset turnover. If you go into the oil field service business, you'll need more than a year to recoup your investment. But if you go

TABLE 5.4   Margin-Turnover Analysis Based on Late 2002 Data

Industry	TTM Turnover	TTM Net Margin	TTM Return on Investment
Oil field services	0.67	8.35	4.81
Specialty retail industry	2.10	5.77	10.61

into specialty retail, you can get your money back a bit more than two times over in the first year.

If a company decides to boost margins by raising prices, turnover will slow. But that might not be the end of the world. After all, ROI combines turnover and margin. Table 5.5 shows two different routes to an ROI that is above the specialty retail average.

99 Cents Only Stores went for the higher margin and was willing to sacrifice turnover. Dollar General went for faster turnover and was willing to accept a lower margin to move merchandise more quickly. But despite different margin-turnover strategies, both companies achieved ROIs that were substantially above the industry average.

We see, here, that companies with very low margins can have high returns on capital (and be considered excellent from a standpoint of company quality) if asset turnover is high. But many investors have a greater awareness of margin. Therefore, companies whose strengths are in the area of turnover may not be as appreciated as margin-oriented firms, and their stocks may be more modestly valued. This can present interesting opportunities. It's not as if we'd expect the world to someday wake up to the concept of turnover. The key is that fast turnover helps generate high returns on capital, and high returns indicate a capacity to generate good EPS growth in the future. That's something the market definitely notices.

So if your screener incorporates turnover variables, be willing to use them. Unfortunately, the range of tests that can be created is limited since today's applications generally offer TTM turnover only. Hence we cannot screen for time-series comparisons. But several applications do allow us to create turnover tests that compare companies to industries.

TABLE 5.5   Margin-Turnover Trade-Offs Based on Late 2002 Data

	TTM Turnover	TTM Net Margin	TTM Return on Investment
99 Cents Only Stores	1.85	8.23	16.38
Dollar General	2.35	4.05	15.11
Specialty retail industry	2.10	5.77	10.61

Leverage

If companies include debt in their capital structures, this will influence return, mainly through a higher ROE as we saw on page 89. Indeed, that's the upside management hopes to achieve when they borrow. The downside is higher risk, not just of bankruptcy but of increased earnings volatility. So when we screen for leverage, we're doing so as a matter of self-protection. We appreciate the higher ROE, but want to make sure risk is not unduly high.

The amount of debt a company can comfortably carry depends on the level and stability of cash flows. Different industries have different characteristics, so this is an area where it's especially important to use comparative testing. If your screener does not permit you to create cross-sectional (or at least time-series) comparisons, I suggest omitting this topic from your screens and confining your balance sheet assessment to Step 2 (Analyze).

Most screeners offer variables based on debt-to-equity ratios. A ratio of 1.00 means the company's debt and equity are equal. But be sensitive to details. Some screeners offer a debt-to-capital ratio. Capital is usually defined as debt plus equity. If debt and equity are equal, the debt-to-capital ratio is 0.50, since debt comprises 50 percent of total capital.

Also, stay alert to differences between long-term debt (due more than a year hence) and total debt. Screening applications usually offer variables based on long-term debt, since this is the part that is deemed a permanent part of the company's capital structure. But if you have access to total debt, you can gain interesting insights. Total debt ratios that are very large (based on cross-sectional or time-series comparisons) can serve as a warning sign. Perhaps inventories are accumulating. (That would mean the company isn't bringing in cash quickly enough to pay down temporary trade borrowings as promptly as it usually does.) If a company is struggling, it may have trouble raising badly needed permanent capital and wind up offsetting its cash drain by tapping preexisting lines of credit.

If you use a screener capable of structuring complex tests, such as the premium Multex application or Stock Investor Pro, you can create a test like the following to weed out companies that may be overly aggressive in their use of short-term debt. If you use a different screener, you can look at this data relationship when you go through Step 2 (Analyze).

> (Total Debt Ratio/Long-Term Debt Ratio)/(Industry Average Total Debt Ratio/Industry Average LT Debt Ratio) <= 1.25

This compares a company's total debt ratio to its long-term debt ratio, and then does likewise for industry averages. We allow the company ratio to exceed the industry ratio by as much as 25 percent to give companies some leeway. It is perfectly legitimate for firms in the same industry to employ varying financing strategies. A test such as this eliminates only those companies that go far out on a limb relative to what their peers are doing.

Some screeners include variables based on interest coverage ratios (TTM pretax income divided by TTM interest expense). A ratio of 1.25 means the company generated 25 percent more pretax income than it needed to cover its annual interest expense obligation. Use industry comparisons to determine what's acceptable for an individual company. Again, if your screener cannot accommodate such a test, you can defer consideration of the matter to Step 2 (Analyze).

While debt review is an important aspect of risk assessment, it's not the only approach, and arguably not even the best approach. Regardless of how much debt a company has, as long as it has or can quickly obtain cash, it can continue to survive. But once liquidity drains, survivability prospects diminish. The company would now depend entirely on an infusion of new capital, or creditors' willingness to relax or renegotiate debt service obligations. Current ratio (current assets divided by current liabilities) is the primary screening item dealing with liquidity and the one that's most likely to be present in any screener you use. Some applications include the more stringent quick ratio (cash and short-term investments divided by current liabilities). As with debt capacity, each industry is different in terms of acceptable liquidity characteristics. Some even have cash flow patterns that permit current ratios to fall below 1.00. So it is best to screen based on company-industry comparisons. If your screener cannot accommodate this, it's preferable to confine your liquidity analysis to Step 2 (Analyze).

PROPRIETARY ANALYTICS

Two screening applications include proprietary analytics that zero in on the good-company theme.

- **Morningstar Premium Stock Selector:** This application offers two grades that are directly relevant. The Profitability grade is based on three factors that are weighted according to a proprietary formula: Raw Profitability (five-year average returns on capital), Trend (a formula that rewards companies whose returns are trending upward), and Consistency (a formula that rewards companies with stable return trends). There's also a Financial Health grade that is based on Morningstar's weighting of two factors: Raw Financial Health (an assessment based on the latest quarter's cash, cash flow, free cash flow, and the assets-to-equity ratio) and Trend (an assessment of whether financial health is improving or deteriorating). The grades range from "A" (best) to "F" (worst) and are based on how companies measure up against others in the same sector. Morningstar gives the worst 10 percent grades of "F." The other grades are equally divided. The web site provides, for each company, data tables showing trends (over five full years and the latest year-to-date) in key data items used in the grades. The information in these tables is not sufficient to enable us to replicate Morningstar's grades, but a visual scan can give us a general sense of why the grades are what they are.

- **ProSearch:** This application offers a Fundamental Rank based on current ratio, long-term debt-to-equity ratio, interest coverage, the five-year rate of cash flow growth, and the ratio of the share price to cash and cash equivalents (i.e., marketable securities). Strictly speaking, this rank is more attuned to measuring financial risk than it is to company quality, since it does not include measures of return on capital, margin, or turnover. But as a measure of financial risk, it is fairly comprehensive.

The MSN Money StockScouter rank also includes a Fundamental grade. But the site's explanation clearly shows the factors to be based on earnings trends. So this rating would not be suitable for a good-company screening theme as defined in the context of the value connection. The Morningstar and ProSearch grades/ranks are most suitable for use as secondary themes in screens whose primary tests are aimed at a good-stock approach.

## CHAPTER 6

Expanding Our Horizons

G enerally speaking, value investors are a patient group, willing to wait more than a day, a week, or even a quarter for an investment to pay off. Indeed, patience is a virtue, but only if not carried to extreme. This chapter, which discusses ways to expand our strategic perspective, addresses one oft-repeated criticism of value—that practitioners tend to be exorbitantly patient. (Chapter 5 addressed the other main criticism, the one that charges value investors with being insufficiently attentive to company quality.)

We'll turn our attention now to various alternative themes that can be incorporated into our value connection screens. For the most part, they help us narrow our focus to value opportunities that are likely to come to fruition within a reasonable period of time.

At this point, if you have any reservation or uncertainty about the role of alternative screening themes, I suggest going back the Chapter 3 to review the concept. To many, the idea of utilizing investment approaches that are unrelated and possibly even antagonistic to our goals seems almost unthinkable. It's unfortunate that so much investment literature reflects that point of view. In fact, alternative themes often make the difference between a run-of-the-mill screen and one that runs way ahead of the market.

Two screens I maintain on MultexInvestor.com based on value-connection principles demonstrate this point. Both have fared very well under monthly performance testing during the 2000–2002 bear market (the tests assumed equal stakes in each stock in the screen and one-month holding periods, after which the screens were rerun and the hypothetical portfolios reconstituted for another month).

- **Relative Value:** As of this writing, this screen's primary value-oriented tests reduced a database of about 9,177 stocks down to 489. Two alternative themes, growth and price momentum, were used to reduce the final list to 28 stocks.
- **Growth at a Reasonable Price:** As of this writing, this screen's primary value-oriented tests produced a list of 356 stocks. The same two alternative themes, growth and price momentum, brought the final list down to 18 stocks.

In the Relative Value screen, the primary good-stock tests eliminated 94.7 percent of the total database, and in the Growth at a Reasonable Price screen, they weeded out 96.1 percent of the full group. So in both cases, our final lists will bear very strong value stamps. The question is how we go about winnowing our way down to lists that are more manageably sized. We could make the good-stock tests more stringent. But there's just so much improvement we can get if we cause investors in one style camp, value, to describe the stocks as ultra super-duper, instead of merely super-duper.

In a world where share price strength occurs only if demand for shares overwhelms supply, we can gain more advantage if we create a list that will cause a wider number of investors (pursuing a more varied repertoire of styles) to like the stocks. Indeed, inclusion of tests that appealed to a wider audience probably enhanced the performance records of the Relative Value and Growth at a Reasonable Price screens. During the course of the three-year testing period, the Relative Value screen beat the S&P 500 by approximately 120 percentage points, and the Growth at a Reasonable Price screen outperformed the blue-chip index by about 70 percentage points. (Both screens are detailed in the appendix to Chapter 7.)

Hence the alternative tests should not be treated as cosmetic items. They can be instrumental in making a screen work.

Here, now, are the alternative themes we can use when implementing the value connection.

TOP-DOWN

Top-down alternative themes can be used if we know, ahead of time, that we have distinct preferences relating to company size, industry, or sector.

For example, if we know at the outset that we do not want technology stocks, our alternative test would look like this.

Sector <> Technology

If we want to confine our inquiry to consumer stocks, we might create a test that looks like this.

Sector = Consumer Cyclical AND Consumer Noncyclical

Note, though, that not all screeners will allow us to specify more than one industry or sector for inclusion or exclusion.

The other key top-down theme relates to company size. We can address this with an alternative test that looks like this.

Market Capitalization > $1 Billion AND Market Capitalization < $5 Billion

If we have access to enterprise value as a screening variable, we could use that in place of market capitalization.

Top-down testing can help if you have a particular reason to prefer or avoid a theme. But I rarely use the top-down approach in Step 1 (Find). I can more than adequately address any preferences I might have by eye-balling the results of a screen and letting my preferences influence which stocks I emphasize or avoid when I move to Step 2 (Analyze). This approach helps us get around the restrictiveness of screeners that cannot specify more than one industry or sector for inclusion or exclusion. And in some instances, the eyeballing approach spares us the burden of delineating precise category boundaries, say between mid-cap and small-cap. Even if we usually think of the boundary in terms of a $1 billion market capitalization and prefer to be above the line, we may appreciate having the leeway to accept a stock with a $970 million market cap if it looks appealing in other respects.

GROWTH

Growth, a key variable in our valuation methods, is conspicuously present in just about any screener. Even though we know the past isn't necessarily predictive of what's likely to occur in the future, it is acceptable to use historic data as a starting point. Note that most of the discussion and examples in this section focus on EPS growth. You can create similar tests using sales growth and, if permitted by your screener, net income growth, cash flow growth, and so on.

Within growth, there are three subthemes: life cycle, peer comparison, and line item.

Life Cycle

It's perfectly normal for businesses to exhibit different growth characteristics depending on where, within their respective corporate life cycles, they are. Generally, very young companies experience very rapid rates of growth. As companies progress toward maturity and get bigger, growth decelerates toward a level that is, presumably, more sustainable over a longer period. The final stage involves decline, where growth decelerates markedly and earnings may even turn sustainably lower.

Those who are inclined toward the more aggressive end of the value spectrum may wish to use a set of acceleration-oriented tests such as this.

TTM EPS Growth >= 3 Year EPS Growth
3 Year EPS Growth >= 5 Year EPS Growth

We might even wish to add a minimum requirement, such as a test requiring the five-year rate to be at least 20 percent. But if you adopt this approach, stay on your guard when you get to Step 2 (Analyze).

The more acceleration oriented our screens are, the more vigilant we must be in Step 2 (Analyze) about the company's life cycle position when assessing the sustainability of rapid growth. If we see a company with a 30 percent rate of EPS growth, it is prudent to start with an assumption that the growth will slow dramatically as time passes. We'd expect the same of a company with a 15 percent growth rate, but we could assume the latter may decelerate at a much slower pace. In any case, when we see a company experiencing very rapid growth, we should impose a burden of proof on anyone who wishes to argue that the company will continue to accelerate or stabilize at the very high rate.

Peer Comparison

This is the approach to growth I use most often. Peer comparison tends to be more stable than acceleration. While we have to expect a company with a 30 percent growth rate to decelerate as it ages, there's no reason to presume a company that beats industry averages will eventually become a laggard. In fact, we might even go the other way and presume companies with track records of industry leadership will retain that status. After all, they probably achieved their prior superiority through skillful management, productive employees, efficient production and distribution, brand leadership, and so on. There's no guarantee any such attributes will persist indefinitely. But since companies do not usually turn on a dime overnight, we can at least enter Step 2 (Analyze) with an innocent-until-proven-guilty preconception.

Not every screener is equally adept at handling peer comparisons, but the programs are gradually getting better. The Multex premium application, Stock Investor Pro, and SmartMoneySelect.com all offer considerable opportunity to create comparative tests. The latter two offer flexibility in how we can define the peer group. Where possible, I recommend sticking with comparisons to industry averages, which is the approach used in the Multex screener. This is the best way to isolate companies achieving excellence based on company-specific factors. Suppose, for example, that retail is weak right now, and its average rate of year-to-year EPS growth for the last quarter was a mere 2 percent, versus 14 percent for the S&P 500. If retailer ABC Company had a growth rate of 11 percent, that would be impressive, especially if the stock has fallen in sympathy with other retail issues. ABC would pass a screening test comparing company to industry, but it would fail a test comparing company to S&P 500.

Line Item

When we consider growth, most of us focus on EPS growth. And when we extend our consideration to sales growth, many of us almost instinctively prefer to see EPS growth outpace sales growth. That's fine if the company is benefiting from economies of scale that spread fixed costs over an increasingly large product base. That reduces the per-unit cost, causing margins to rise and EPS to grow faster than sales. Often, however, the situation is unsustainable. An example would be a company that is consolidating plants and laying off employees to cut costs. This sort of thing can persist for just so long. Eventually, EPS growth will slow, or perhaps reverse into a decline, unless the company can find a way to boost sales.

Hence if your screener permits, you might wish to consider a test like this:

3 Year Sales Growth >= (3 Year EPS Growth) * .9

If your screener cannot handle a flexible test like this, you may wish to omit line item comparisons from Step 1 (Find) and rely on Step 2 (Analyze) to narrow the group down to firms whose sales really are more or less keeping pace with EPS growth.

ANALYST SENTIMENT

Analyst information, more specifically estimate revision and ratings, is an especially fertile ground for alternative tests that can be included in value connection screens. That's because they are flexible enough to identify stocks that are attractive for reasons we cannot envision and quantify ahead of time.

Consider a simple estimate revision test such as this:

Current Year Consensus Estimate >= Current Year Consensus Est.
4 Weeks Ago

Here's a more aggressive variation on the theme.

Current Year Consensus Est. > Current Year Consensus Est. 4 Weeks
Ago
Current Year Consensus Est. 4 Weeks Ago > Current Year Consensus
Est. 8 Weeks Ago
Current Year Consensus Est. 8 Weeks Ago > Current Year Consensus
Est. 13 Weeks Ago

This is an excellent bridge between the general philosophical considerations that point us toward the good-company and good-stock approaches, and day-to-day market realities. They tune us in to the stocks the general investing public likes best, shares of companies with favorable earnings trends. Chasing earnings trends for their own sake is antithetical to value connection investing; any dog of a company with an overpriced stock can produce good earnings news from time to time. But the combination of good earnings news (which appeals to the short-term focus of the Wall Street herd) and value connection principles is hard to beat. It's a great way to hone in on stocks that deserve better valuations and have a visible catalyst that may bring such improvement about sooner rather than later.

Analyst ratings, also referred to as recommendations, are another interesting data point. Lately, analyst ratings have been the subject of considerable negative publicity. To the extent that analysts may have adjusted their stated opinions based on their firms' quest for getting or retaining investment banking business, the negativity is clearly warranted. Fortunately, as of this writing, there is considerable momentum for reform. The impetus reflects a combination of self-improvement, as firms work to separate research from investment banking, and attention from the Securities and Exchange Commission (SEC) and state attorneys general.

There's also much talk of analysts' reluctance to offer "sell" recommendations. This criticism is not so clearly justified. It is true that "sell" has traditionally been treated as a four-letter word in the Wall Street community. But analysts and their clients have long been accustomed to ignoring a rating's label and paying close attention to where it stands on a best-to-worst scale. Traditionally, this has been a five-part scale. Each firm and data provider supplies its own labels; at the present time, Multex identifies the ratings as buy, outperform, hold, underperform, and sell. Regardless of terminology, one thing is obvious if you look at ratings for a variety of stocks. Analysts routinely utilize the top three ratings. So it's easy to see which stocks analysts like (a preponderance of ratings toward the top of the scale) and which they shun (more ratings toward the middle of the scale).

Unfortunately, the research community failed to properly communicate this jargon to those outside the narrow circle of institutional investors it was accustomed to dealing with. This shortcoming, and the resulting public disdain, is having an impact. Some firms are making greater efforts to use the full five-part scale, including the two lowest categories. Others are simply going to a three-part scale of buy, hold, and sell.

Either way, we can easily use rating information to help us screen for analyst sentiment. For example, SmartMoneySelect.com allows us to create tests based on the percent of ratings that are bullish. This is done via the relative strength comparisons. Here's a screen that finds stocks that are more strongly favored than others in their own industry. (*Note:* Under SmartMoneySelect.com terminology, the five ratings are identified as Strong Buy, Buy, Hold, Sell, and Strong Sell).

% Strong Buy in Top 25% within Industry
% Buy in Top 25% within Industry
% Hold in Bottom 25% within Industry
% Sell = 0
% Strong Sell = 0

Recognizing that it is sometimes difficult to decide if one rating profile is more bullish than another, some data providers translate each configuration to a single numeric score. On Multex, this is known as the average or mean rating. The best possible score would be 1.00 (where every analyst covering the stock rates it a buy), and the worst possible score would be 5.00. Realistically, most average ratings would fall between 1.00 and 3.00.

Table 6.1 demonstrates how Multex calculates the average rating.

This score of 2.29 is a bit worse than the midpoint of the informal scale typically used consisting of the top three ratings. It therefore shows

TABLE 6.1 Sample Mean Rating Calculation—Stock A

Category Name	Category Score	×	# Ratings in Category	=	Category Total
Top (e.g., buy)	1	×	3	=	3
Second (e.g., outperform)	2	×	4	=	8
Middle (e.g., hold)	3	×	7	=	21
Fourth (e.g., underperform)	4	×	0	=	0
Worst (e.g., sell)	5	×	0	=	0
Total			14		32
Average rating = 32 divided by 14 = 2.29					

us that analysts are cool toward the stock. We see this despite the fact that no analyst actually said "sell."

Average rating can be very effective in screening tests. Here's one example.

Average Rating Current < 1.50

This would identify stocks for which analysts are, on the whole, bullish. Table 6.2 demonstrates a rating profile that would pass this test.

Notice that use of the numeric average rating score enables us to conclude that analysts are more bullish on Stock B even though one analyst departed from the usual three-part scale and published a rating in the fourth category, something that did not happen with Stock A.

Remembering that lower mean ratings are more bullish, we can easily screen for changes in analyst sentiment. Here's an example.

Average Rating Current < Average Rating 4 Weeks Ago

TABLE 6.2 Sample Mean Rating Calculation—Stock B

Category Name	Category Score	×	# Ratings in Category	=	Category Total
Top (e.g., buy)	1	×	8	=	8
Second (e.g., outperform)	2	×	2	=	4
Middle (e.g., hold)	3	×	0	=	0
Fourth (e.g., underperform)	4	×	1	=	4
Worst (e.g., sell)	5	×	0	=	0
Total			11		16
Average rating = 16 divided by 11 = 1.45					

If we want to be more aggressive, we can consider something like the following requirement that the average rating improve by more than 10 percent.

Average Rating Current < Average Rating 4 Weeks Ago * .9

Here's an example of a screen introduced on MultexInvestor.com in early 2003 based on average ratings. (Lines 4 through 6 are examples of secondary and alternative screening themes referred to earlier on pages 60–61. Such strategies will be explored more thoroughly in Chapter 7.)

1. Average Rating Current <= 1.75
2. Average Rating Current < Average Rating 4 Weeks Ago
3. Average Rating 4 Weeks Ago < Average Rating 13 Weeks Ago
4. # of Analysts Issuing Long-Term EPS Growth Forecasts > 0
5. PEG Ratio <= 2
6. Short Interest as % Float <3) OR (Short Interest as % Float Now < Short Interest as % Float 1 Month Ago)

Even if you are skeptical about the quality of analyst work product, as many are nowadays, I still encourage you to consider using estimate revision and/or ratings to conduct alternative value connection screens. Tests conducted on the preceding screen using old data showed that it would have produced a price gain of 38 percent in the three-year period from February 1, 2000, through January 31, 2003. Over that same span, the S&P 500 fell 37 percent.

The preceding screen uses analyst sentiment as a primary theme and value as an alternative theme. Another screen introduced on Multex Investor in early 2003 is known as Favored Value Plays. This screen, reproduced on pages 132–133, makes value the primary theme and relegates analyst data to alternative status. Tests using old data show it would have produced a price gain of 63 percent from February 1, 2000, through January 31, 2003.

So for better or worse, despite the negative publicity, stocks still respond, often vigorously, to estimate and rating revision. Hence, this data contains information that can help you determine which among the value connection stocks we already identified through our primary and secondary tests are most likely to appeal to the herd whose decisions cause stocks to move.

GENERAL SENTIMENT

Analysts are not the only investment community constituency whose actions can be worth noting. We can create behavioral tests that tune us in to the thoughts of the analysts' main client group, institutional investors, as well as corporate insiders and short sellers.

Institutions

According to some, the opinions of institutional investors should be respected because of the extensive effort they devote to research. Others criticize institutional investing as being too short-term oriented. Either way, because of their size, institutional investors tend to move markets. Hence it's important that we be cognizant of their opinions whether we agree with them or not.

The following sample tests would be of interest to someone who wishes to follow the lead of institutions.

Institutional Share Purchases (Net of Sales) Latest Quarter > 0

% Institutional Ownership Latest Quarter > % Institutional Ownership Prior Quarter

\# Institutional Shareholders Latest Quarter > \# Institutional Shareholders Prior Quarter

The last test can be especially interesting when dealing with smaller-capitalization issues. It focuses on the number of institutional decision makers who have turned bullish on a stock, regardless of how many shares they are buying. And since we're considering such data from a behavioral standpoint, the number of decision makers is especially telling.

Obviously, if we want to take a contrary position, we can reverse the tests to seek net institutional selling or a decrease in the number of institutional holders. A reversal of the percent ownership test can be very useful in value connection screening even beyond the contrarian angle. A shift from underownership to normal or preferably overownership is a scenario that is very attractive to value investors. But timing is highly uncertain. If we use such a test, we may want to combine it with other alternative tests designed to ferret out situations where a move may be imminent.

Insiders

Insider ownership is important to value investors. It can have a bearing on the likelihood of a company being taken over. High levels of ownership obviously preclude a hostile buyout. But it could set up a situation where a friendly buyout becomes a viable scenario. This might be the case in a family-owned business with no clear succession to the next generation. This is a matter that can be investigated in Step 2 (Analyze).

An increase in insider ownership might serve as behavioral evidence in support of an investment case for a stock. After all, insiders presumably know the company better than anyone else. Hence it can be worthwhile to screen for insider buying. And if our screener allows, we should focus on the number of insider buy transactions. Each is a decision, which is a better gauge of sentiment than the number of shares, which also incorporates information about the personal wealth of the decision maker.

The reverse is not necessarily so. Insider selling might reflect worries about the future, but we have no way of knowing if that's the case. Insider selling is often motivated by key employees wishing to convert part of their compensation (stock options) to cash, and to diversify their stock holdings.

Short Interest

The Multex screeners, and to a much more limited degree, ProSearch and SmartMoneySelect.com, allow us to screen based on short interest. Those investors who use other screeners can examine short interest data as part of Step 2 (Analyze).

We start with the notion that short sellers who sell now and buy later (at what they hope will be lower prices) act because they expect prices to fall. But this is not always so. Many short sales are made pursuant to broader hedging strategies. So if we screen based on short interest, we should focus mainly on big numbers—that is, short interest (stocks sold short as a percent of the total common outstanding) above 3 percent. Once we are above that threshold, it can be useful to screen for changes in short interest. Here are two examples.

Short Interest Current Month < Short Interest Prior Month

Change in Short Interest Past Month < 0

Such tests stand can stand as behavioral evidence of improving sentiment. This can be especially potent if combined with other analyst or general indicators.

PRICE/VOLUME/TECHNICAL

Technical analysis (the study of share price and volume trends) can serve as a powerful alternative theme in a value connection screen. The idea is to view this information as a window into the conclusions reached by others who have studied company fundamentals. As with the general and analyst sentiment categories just discussed, this one can make a big difference in finding stocks that ought to attain a well-deserved higher valuation sooner rather than later.

Of the screening applications described in Chapter 3, all have at least some capacity to address technical analysis. But aside from ProSearch, the programs focus primarily on fundamental analysis. Hence those who wish to have price and volume trends play a major role in their Step 1 (Find) efforts will have to use the ProSearch application, or defer consideration of the matter to Step 2 (Analyze).

Price Range

Alternative tests that examine where a stock stands relative to recent trading activity can be illuminating to upscale or downscale value connection screening. The upscale value shopper would seek stocks trading near their highs, as per the following example.

Price/52-Week High >= 0.9

The downscale screener would seek stocks trading near their lows. The following pair of tests accomplishes that.

Price/52-Week Low <= 1.2
Price/52-Week High <= 0.5

The first test seeks stocks priced no higher than 20 percent above the 52-week low. If the low is 20, the price can be no higher than 24. But suppose the 52-week high is 30. A price of 24 could hardly be described as sufficiently depressed to be of interest to downscale investors. Hence we need the second test. A stock currently trading at 24 would not pass unless the 52-week high was at least 48.

Another way to screen based on highs and lows is via the FYI Advisor category of the MSN Money screener. There, we can find a general variable that helps us locate stocks that hit a new 52-week high or low within a time period we specify.

Those who are especially proficient in technical analysis can use ProSearch to screen based on the stochastic oscillator, which measures a stock's position within its trading range based on the following formula:

(Current Price – Low Price for the Period)/(High Price for the Period – Low Price for the Period)

A stock with a range of 20 to 30 and a current price of 24 would have a stochastic value of .40. A price of 24 within a 20–48 range yields a stochastic value of .14. According to ProSearch, scores below .25 suggest oversold stocks, while scores above .75 suggest the shares may be overbought.

ProSearch also offers an interesting variable that lets you measure stocks based on how near or far they are from a more-or-less central trend within the high-low range known as the "least squares" line. (Least squares is the name of the mathematical technique used to calculate the trend line's exact position within a price graph.) ProSearch allows you to screen for stocks whose prices are above or below the line (positive or negative least squares deviations respectively).

Price Trend

It's one thing to say a stock is near the upper or lower end of a trading range. But it's another thing to differentiate whether it is moving toward or away from a boundary of the range. It's also worthwhile to know if that movement is rapid or gradual. Obviously, we can study price charts as part of Step 2 (Analyze). But we can also create screening tests that will help steer us toward the kinds of charts we hope to see.

One simple approach is to compare price performances over differing time periods. Here's a pair of tests an upscale value shopper can implement with several programs.

Price % Change Last 4 Weeks > Price % Change Last 13 Weeks
Price % Change Last 13 Weeks > 0

The first test seeks stocks that have gained more ground as a percentage of price in the past four weeks than they did in the past 13. The second test assures that the stocks have been going up. Without it, we may find stocks that declined less over the past four weeks than over the 13-week period.

Here's a variation involving some price acceleration.

Price % Change Last 13 Weeks > 0
Price % Change Last 26 Weeks > 0

Price % Change Last 4 Weeks > Price % Change Last 13 Weeks
Price % Change Last 4 Weeks > Price % Change Last 26 Weeks

On some applications, you can create the same sort of tests using relative strength.

A contrarian investor could reverse the approach.

Price % Change Last 4 Weeks < Price % Change Last 13 Weeks
Price % Change Last 13 Weeks < 0

Another approach involves use of moving averages. Suppose today is Monday and it's the 10th of the month. A 5-day moving average would be the average closing price from last Monday (the 3rd of the month) through the most recent Friday (the 7th of the month). Tomorrow, on Tuesday the 11th, we would redo the calculation based on a new five-day sample starting on Tuesday the 4th and continuing through Monday the 10th. This is called a "moving" average because the time period used in the calculation shifts every day. We can screen based on this concept by creating tests that identify stocks whose moving average for a short period is higher than or jumped above a moving average for a longer period. This can be done with the ProSearch or MSN Money screeners.

Relative Comparison

Here is one of my favorite price-related tests based on the Multex premium screener.

Share Price % Change Last 4 Weeks > Industry Average Share Price %
Change Last 4 Weeks

Using Morningstar's Premium Stock Selector, we would express the same idea this way:

1 Month % Rank Industry < 50

The latter test compares a stock's total return (share price performance plus dividends, if any) to its industry average. A percentile score of 1 means the stock is in the top 1 percent of its industry (i.e., it outperformed 99 percent of its industry peers). The above example seeks stocks in the upper half of their industry comparisons.

Other applications reverse the definition and use the term "relative strength." For example, in Stock Investor Pro, a score of 99 means the stock outperformed 99 percent of all others. Hence in the latter application our test would look like this:

Relative Strength 4 Weeks > Industry Relative Strength 4 Weeks

This situation represents one more example of why it is so important to check glossaries.

These relative comparison tests allow us to filter out stocks that are strong solely because of good market conditions and hone in on shares that do well because of good things that are happening to the individual companies.

Suppose construction equipment is in a slump, and share prices in that industry declined an average of 8 percent in the prior month. Assume, too, that shares of one company in that group, ABC Inc., rose 12 percent. This implies that something interesting is happening at ABC that is not occurring at its peers. And if ABC also passed a series of primary good-stock or good-company tests, the fact that it is standing out from its peers becomes especially enticing. This kind of test is included in both the Multex Investor value connection screens mentioned at the beginning of this chapter (Relative Value and Growth at a Reasonable Price).

If the program you use doesn't offer industry-oriented price variables, you may be able to compare stock prices to a broader universe. Here are two examples.

Price % Change Last 4 Weeks > S&P 500 % Change Last 4 Weeks

Relative Strength Past 4 Weeks > 50

Volume

Heavy or rising volume means investors are more definitive in their opinions, whether positive or negative. So screening tests based on volume should be accompanied by other tests seeking positive or negative price performance, depending on whether you're pursuing the upscale or downscale approach.

In ProSearch, you can measure volume directly through the "Volume Ratio" variables that allow you to specify that volume over a recent period, say five days, be at least a certain percentage above a longer-term (usually 30-day) average. The Multex screeners and Stock Investor Pro allow for creation of a similar test by combining variables relating to different periods. Here's an example from Multex.

10 Day Average Volume >= (3 Month Average Volume/20) * 1.5

Notice that the 10-day variable is a per-day average, while the three-month variable is a monthly average, so to use them together, we divide the three-month variable by 20 (a ballpark estimate of the number of trading days in a month) to get an approximation of a daily number. Now it's easy to see that the test seeks stocks whose average daily volume is up at least 50 percent over the past 10 days compared with the past three months.

## CHAPTER 7

Strategic Screening

C hapters 4, 5, and 6 presented a lot of ideas that can be used to screen for value connection stocks. But we certainly can't use all of them in the same screen. No individual opportunity can be expected to offer everything we might hope to see, so if a screen contains too many tests, we will probably wind up with too few or even zero passing stocks.

We can never be sure how many stocks will appear in a screen. Much depends on market conditions. One of my favorite value screens lists five or fewer names during bull markets, but more than 80 when the market is weak. Ideally, we'd like to see our lists have between 15 and 50 names. This leaves a cushion that makes it likely we'll have a reasonable number of choices even after we eliminate stocks that don't make the cut in Step 2 (Analyze). Many investors won't have the time to analyze even 15 stocks (much less 50). But at this size range, the workload is tolerable considering that some names will be already familiar because they were in the screen the last time it was run. Also, we can use our sorting techniques to prioritize our efforts.

As of this writing, there were 1,806 stocks in the Multex database with P/Es at least 25 percent below the industry average. When I added a requirement that the five-year ROI be at least 25 percent above the industry average, the number of passing companies dropped to a still burdensome 500. Adding another test requiring the five-year EPS growth rate to exceed the industry average by at least 25 percent brought the list down to 261, which is still too many. Notice, though, that I already departed from the basic good-stock and good-company concepts and introduced an alternative theme, growth. Yet the list is still too big. Should we add tests for TTM ROI and EPS growth (to supplement the existing tests that measure five-year performance)? Should we add a test based on the PEG ratio? Perhaps we should add another alternative theme such as one based on insider buying.

This is not an optimal way to approach the screening process. We're just grabbing any tests that come to mind in an effort to get our list down to a manageable size. Trial and error is not by any means a bad thing. But like anything else, it works best in the right context. The way we're doing it here, meandering in an unfocused manner through a huge list of choices, is more likely to lead to frustration than to worthwhile investment ideas.

That's why it's so helpful to adopt a strategic approach to screening. A screening strategy won't eliminate trial and error, but on each occasion when we do experiment, we'll be using a more comfortable sized array of choices, and the selection process will be enhanced by our knowing exactly what we are trying to accomplish with each part of the screen.

STRATEGIC BLUEPRINTS

The building blocks of any screening strategy are based on the themes we introduced in Chapter 3. The primary theme constitutes our main investment goal. A secondary theme is an investment approach that differs from but is generally supportive of our primary theme. An alternative theme is an approach that is unrelated, and possibly even antagonistic to, our primary theme. Each screen should have a clearly identifiable primary theme and at least one additional theme.

This enables us to establish some very clear strategic blueprints. There are six approaches that are relevant to the value connection style.

We'll identify each blueprint by listing the primary theme first. In all cases, the primary theme will be either good stock (based on the concepts discussed in Chapter 4) or good company (based on the concepts discussed in Chapter 5). If we choose to use both good stock and good company in the same screen, the one listed first is the primary theme; the other is the secondary theme. This makes a big difference because we'll be using fewer and/or more lenient tests in the secondary theme. Finally, we'll state whether we're using an alternative theme.

Here are our six blueprints.

Stock-Company (S-C)
- Establish a primary theme based on good stock concepts.
- Add a secondary theme based on good company principles.

Stock-Company-Alternative (S-C-A)

- Establish a primary theme based on good stock concepts.
- Add a secondary theme based on good company principles.
- Add an alternative theme.

Stock-Alternative (S-A)

- Establish a primary theme based on good stock concepts.
- Add an alternative theme.

Company-Stock (C-S)

- Establish a primary theme based on good company concepts.
- Add a secondary theme based on good stock principles.

Company-Stock-Alternative (C-S-A)

- Establish a primary theme based on good company concepts.
- Add a secondary theme based on good stock principles.
- Add an alternative theme.

Company-Alternative (C-A)

- Establish a primary theme based on good company concepts.
- Add an alternative theme.

IMPLEMENTING THE STRATEGIES

Selecting a blueprint is not by any means a random thing. In the Introduction, when we described value investing as getting our money's worth, we saw that this style goes well beyond a quest for lowball prices, or to be more precise, low stock valuation metrics. It also involves consideration of the merchandise being bought. Anytime we shop, whether for cars, clothing, home electronics, food, or stocks, good-quality merchandise should be valued more richly than low-grade offerings. Some value investors shop in the high-rent district. Others browse the bargain counters. Both seek share prices that are reasonable relative to the merchandise they are getting. We'll see that different shopping preferences will influence our choice of a screening blueprint.

Upscale Screening

In this approach, we start out seeking great companies, recognizing that we may have to pay up to get them. The difference between this kind of value investing and other styles that pay no attention at all to value is that as willing as we are to pay up, we will not be oblivious to how high a price we will pay. In other words, there is nothing here that even vaguely resembles the sort of growth-at-any-price strategies that led so many astray during the late 1990s.

The best way to pursue an upscale value connection screening strategy is to use the C-A (Company-Alternative) blueprint. In articulating specific tests, we stick with the conventional approach in which we seek stocks that are superior under whatever criteria we consider. In other words, we seek high returns on capital, high margins, fast turnover, modest debt, rapid growth, insider or institutional buying, upward revision in earnings estimates, and so forth. We won't necessarily get all of them in one screen, but regardless of which variables we use to build our tests, we proceed under the impression that higher is better than lower (except in cases where data definitions make lower numbers better, such as debt ratios). We do likewise for alternative themes such as growth (higher rates are better) and sentiment (bullish behaviors such as insider or institutional buying or upward estimate revisions are better).

I'm willing to completely omit good-stock concepts from upscale Step 1 (Find) screens and defer the matter to Step 2 (Analyze). We'll see, in Chapter 8, that Step 2 (Analyze) is divided into three phases, two of which focus heavily on the reasonableness of the stock price. Those activities will be more than adequate to protect us from the growth-at-any-price trap.

Upscale investors who really want to address good-stock principles in Step 1 (Find) can use the C-S (Company-Stock) and C-S-A (Company-Stock-Alternative) blueprints. But it's important to recognize that the good-stock secondary value theme must be handled with care. When we're shopping in the high-rent district, we understand that we're probably going to have to accept stock valuation metrics above, possibly even far above, those commonly associated with value investing. The easiest tests are those that relate P/E to growth. That will automatically allow for high P/Es on shares of companies that are growing rapidly.

A third approach to upscale screening is to use the S-A (Stock-Alternative) strategy in a way that turns the good-stock tests upside down and places them in a behavioral context. An example of this is the High P/E Ratios screen I maintain on the MultexInvestor.com web site. It uses the following tests.

1. TTM P/E > Industry Average TTM P/E
2. TTM P/E > Prior 12 Month P/E
3. TTM P/E < 200

4. PYQ % EPS Growth > Industry Average PYQ % EPS Growth

5. 3 Year % EPS Growth > Industry Average 3 Year % EPS Growth

6. PYQ % EPS Growth > 3 Year % EPS Growth

7. # Analysts Publishing EPS Estimates for Next Qtr. > 3

8. Short Interest 1 Month % Change < 0

The first three tests express a primary theme that seeks high P/E ratios (subject to a ceiling, set at 200, to prevent the ratio from getting completely out of hand). The idea, here, is that nowadays, with so much information so readily available, P/Es could not go that high unless a great number of investors examined the company and found things to their liking. The other alternative-theme tests confirm this by seeking indications that there really are positive things to be found at the companies. They seek a combination of above-average EPS growth (for the PYQ and three-year periods), growth acceleration from the three-year to the PYQ period, the fact that at least some analysts are following the company and hence are aware of what's going on, and the fact that short interest is declining (suggesting that market participants see positive things). The alternative tests, by themselves, don't necessarily prove the company possesses sufficient merit to warrant the P/E ratios we see. But they do provide some buffer against the growth-at-any-price trap. And the fact that the screen beat the S&P 500 by almost 30 percentage points in the past three years suggests that we are getting a good head start for Step 2 (Analyze).

I offer one important caveat to the behavioral approach. If we're going to use good-stock concepts in this manner and combine them with sentiment-based tests, which also tend to be behavioral, we need to be careful. Such an approach might pull us away from the value connection discipline. Consider the following variation.

1. TTM P/E > Industry Average TTM P/E

2. TTM P/E > Prior 12 Month P/E

3. TTM P/E < 200

4. Share Price Change Last 4 Weeks > Industry Average 4 Week Share Price Change

5. Net Institutional Share Purchases > 0

6. Short Interest 1 Month % Change < 0

There's nothing necessarily wrong with this screen. It's just a matter of philosophy. Rather than being consistent with the value connection philosophy, a disciplined approach to getting our money's worth, this screen aims entirely at stocks that are popular. The first example, the one that included growth tests, is preferable because it included anchors (the growth tests) that address the issue of whether or not the stock's popularity is appropriately deserved.

Here is a summary of the screening strategies most suitable for the upscale approach.

- **Company-Alternative (C-A).** This is my first-choice upscale strategy. It offers the most flexibility in creating ways to identify superior companies. Consideration of good-stock principles can be done in Step 1 (Find) by using valuation metrics as a basis to sort the results of a C-A screen, or it can be deferred to Step 2 (Find).
- **Company-Stock (C-S) or Company-Stock-Alternative (C-S-A).** If either of these approaches is used, make sure the good-stock tests are sufficiently lenient to accommodate the fact that we must expect to pay up for the best companies.
- **Stock-Alternative (S-A).** Use high valuation metrics in a behavioral context (as evidence that observers are favorably impressed with the quality of the company). Make sure the alternative tests are at least somewhat tied to some aspect of company performance to show the companies deserve high stock valuation metrics.

Middle-Market (Balanced) Screening

This is as close as we get to conventional value investing. Generally speaking, we seek low share price valuation metrics. But we don't carry this quest so far that we are willing to accept low-grade companies.

For this approach, our screens should always have primary themes based on good-stock tests. This means we can use the S-C (Stock-Company), S-A (Stock-Alternative), or S-C-A (Stock-Company-Alternative) formats.

In each such screen, the primary good-stock theme should include at least one test aimed at the relationship between the stock price and the corporate earnings (or dividend) stream. This rule is based on the nature of middle-market screening. We can see that if we consider the kinds of situations that would tempt us to omit reference to the price-to-earnings anchor.

One would involve an exceptional company whose share price is based on expected rapid earnings growth over a very long time. In such a case, the P/E ratio would probably be so high as to not be meaningful. And we could almost count on the fact that the company would not be paying a dividend. This scenario probably sounds familiar. William Miller's investment in Amazon.com is a good example. And as we discussed, this is not a situation where we could be said to be shopping in the middle-market district. We would, instead, be in the upscale district and we would be building our screens consistent with those principles.

The other situation is where the company is struggling. Again, we would not screen based on dividend income. Either the company would not be paying a dividend or, if there is a dividend, it would be especially vulnerable to reduction or elimination. And P/E ratios would not be meaningful because the company is losing money, in which case databases would not provide P/E ratios and would instead contain codes indicating that such data is not available (NA) or not meaningful (NM). P/E ratios would also be not meaningful if the company was only nominally profitable (i.e., mathematically, a stock price of $7 and an EPS of $0.02 would produce a P/E of 350, which would be logged in most databases with an NM code). The struggling-company scenario likewise takes us out of the middle-market district. If we want to find these companies, we'll visit the funky neighborhood and apply vulture screening techniques, which will be discussed in the next subsection.

Here are the four ways a middle-market investor can address the relationship of share prices and earnings streams.

1. **Comparative:** Create a P/E test based on comparison to a peer group. For example:

   P/E < Industry Average P/E

   P/E < S&P 500 P/E

   P/E Relative Strength > 65

2. **PEG:** Create a P/E test based on the price/earnings-to-growth ratio. For example:

   (P/E/Projected Long-Term Growth) <= 1.25

3. **Numeric:** Compare the P/E ratio to a specific numeric threshold. For example:

   P/E <= 15

4. **Income:** Compare the stock price, not to EPS, but to that portion of the earnings that are actually paid out as dividends. For example:

   Dividend Yield > 3.0

We can supplement this with consideration of other price ratios (sales, cash flow, book value, etc.). But this is optional. We can also utilize liquid asset metrics. But if this is done, I recommend using the sorting approach described in the appendix to Chapter 3. In the middle-market district, it's unlikely screening tests aimed at specific liquidity thresholds will produce enough results to be considered productive.

Income screens should always include at least one test that addresses the issue of a company's capacity to maintain or grow its dividend. Since these tests come from the good company group, we'll assume that those who stress dividend income will use either the S-C or S-C-A format. If we're not emphasizing income we can use any of the good stock formats: S-C, S-C-A, or S-A. Our main concern beyond the primary theme is to seek some indication that the company deserves the respect of the investment community (presumably, more respect than it has received to date).

Downscale (Vulture) Screening

On one level, vulture screening approaches are pretty self-evident. We seek low valuation metrics. This points us to the S-C (Stock-Company), S-A (Stock-Alternative), or S-C-A (Stock-Company-Alternative) formats we examined in connection with middle-market screening. The S-A approach, with alternative tests that are behavioral in nature, is usually my favorite way to probe the bargain basement.

Be careful about supposedly obvious applications of the S-C or S-C-A approaches. Consider the following S-C-A example.

1. P/E/Growth <= .5
2. P/E <= Industry Average P/E * .5
3. 3 Year EPS Growth < Industry Average 3 Year EPS Growth
4. 5 Year EPS Growth < Industry Average 5 Year EPS Growth
5. 5 Year ROI < Industry Average 5 Year ROI

Strictly speaking, the screen, which turned the secondary and alternative themes upside down and sought underachieving companies, works. It identifies firms whose share prices may be unduly depressed because investors believe the companies are weaker than they actually are. Or we might find interesting opportunities where the market fails to appreciate that formerly troubled companies are starting to experience better times. (Notice that the screen does not have a company-oriented test based on the TTM period, thereby leaving open the possibility that things have been getting better recently.)

But there may be a problem of overkill. The first two tests, the ones that addressed relative P/E and the P/E-to-growth ratio, can, by themselves, accomplish pretty much everything we seek: identification of companies that are unappreciated by the market. The other three tests suggest reasons why the market might be negative toward the stocks. But we may be omitting too many worthy opportunities if we limit ourselves to stocks that are unappreciated for one set of particular reasons as opposed to all the other possible causes. For example, our list is not enhanced by excluding stocks that are beaten down because the company's problems manifested in the TTM period rather than in the three- or five-year time frames.

I suggest that we refrain from prejudging why a stock has fallen into the vulture category. Step 2 (Analyze) will afford us ample opportunity to address the full range of reasons why the company is in Wall Street's doghouse. In Step 1 (Find), we're better off simply identifying the down-and-outs and setting priorities for the analysis phase. We do this through screens whose primary themes are based on very low valuation metrics. As to the liquid assets ratios that aren't easily screenable, this is where it can be useful to create numeric tests using the procedure described in the appendix to Chapter 3 (where we do some preliminary investigation to help us identify reasonable numeric thresholds).

As noted earlier, vulture screening works best when the primary good-stock theme is supplemented with alternative themes comprised of behavioral tests (the S-A blueprint). There are two ways we can approach this.

In the negative approach, we use alternative tests to confirm the Street's disdain for the companies. Consider the following example.

1. P/E/Growth <= .5
2. P/E <= (Industry Average P/E) * .5
3. Share Price Change Last 4 Weeks < Industry Average 4 Week Share Price Change
4. Short Interest > 3% AND Short Interest > Short Interest 1 Month Ago

At first glance, the third and fourth tests may seem superfluous in that they confirm what the P/E tests already tell us: that the stocks are out of favor. But in fact, these tests add an additional dimension to the screen. The P/E tests do not differentiate between stocks that are out of favor because the Street has simply lost interest in the companies, as happens from time to time, versus situations where investors are actively thinking about the companies and reacting negatively to what they perceive. The short interest test is especially poignant here; it helps tune us in to stocks that received the spotlight and are being actively shoved off the stage because the audience does not like what it sees.

The other, positive, approach is to use alternative tests to identify situations where others are becoming intrigued by potentially interesting bargain merchandise. One way we could do this is by simply reversing the last two tests in the preceding example.

1. P/E/Growth <= .5
2. P/E <= (Industry Average P/E) * .5
3. Share Price Change Last 4 Weeks > Industry Average 4 Week Share Price Change
4. Short Interest < 3% AND Short Interest < Short Interest 1 Month Ago

This screen seeks deep-discount vulture situations that may possess a catalyst that can cause so-called hidden values to be realized reasonably soon. It may be something structural such as a takeover or a major reorganization. It may simply be a matter of the market tuning in to the fact that the stock is too modestly valued. Either way, the result is potentially favorable; we get an opportunity to buy low and sell high.

We can also turn the C-A approach upside down (analogous to our previously discussed upscale S-A screen) and seek a state of dissonance where strong good-company indicators are matched with an alternative theme seeking negative share price performance. The Contrarian Opportunities screen I maintain on MultexInvestor.com is an interesting example.

Here are the tests.

1. 5 Year Operating Margin > Industry Average 5 Year Operating Margin
2. 5 Year ROE > Industry Average 5 Year ROE
3. 5 Year ROI > Industry Average 5 Year ROI
4. 3 Year % EPS Growth > Industry Average 3 Year % EPS Growth
5. 5 Year % EPS Growth > Industry Average 5 Year % EPS Growth
6. Share Price % Change Last 4 Weeks < Industry Average Share Price % Change Last 4 Weeks
7. Share Price % Change Last 4 Weeks < –15

The first five tests seek good companies. But the last two tests, which constitute an alternative theme seeking poor share price performance, seem inconsistent.

In truth, it's easy to envision reasons for such dissonance. More likely than not, the companies encountered problems in a more recent (quarterly or trailing 12 month) period. Hence in Step 2 (Analyze) we'll be focusing on whether the problems are likely to be temporary or sustained. But we go into that process with the law of probabilities in our favor. Over the past three years, this screen outperformed the S&P 500 by about 170 percentage points.

Here's a summary of the recommended vulture screening approaches.

- **Standard Vulture Screens:** Establish a primary S-A theme based on very low valuation metrics, and use liquidity-oriented valuation ratios to sort and thereby establish priorities for Step 2 (Analyze).

  Negative alternative theme: Use alternative behavioral tests designed to confirm that investment community disdain was implied by the low valuation ratios.

  Positive alternative theme: Use alternative behavioral tests designed to identify situations containing a potential catalyst that might spark near-term improvement in the stock price.

- **Dissonance:** Establish a primary C–A theme based on positive good-company factors and then switch gears by pairing these with negative alternative (behavioral) themes.

Whichever vulture approach we take, sorting based on the liquidity-based valuation ratios can help us set our Step 2 (Analyze) priorities. For instance, let's go back to the example of the negative alternative theme (stocks that are underperforming their industry peers and for which short interest is rising). As of this writing, the screen lists 84 stocks. I choose to sort based on the ratio of share price to net cash per share, with net cash defined, here, as cash minus total debt. This allows me to immediately push 62 stocks to the side because for them the ratio is negative (meaning that the companies have more debt than cash).

> *Among the 22 stocks that remain, the "top" company (the lowest price-to-net cash ratio) is W. R. Grace, which is at present in bankruptcy (a filing that was made in response to prospective asbestos-related liabilities). Its ratio is a mere 0.39. Still, this situation isn't for everybody. But if there ever was a classic vulture situation (for better or worse), this is it.*

Two other names among the "top" 10 I recognize right away.

> *One is JAKKS Pacific (price-to-net cash ratio: 2.608), a toy company that has actually done a nice job acquiring its way into niche markets not aggressively pursued by major toy companies like Hasbro and Mattel. But the Street has been negative toward JAKKS because of sluggish earnings performance, and more importantly from a vulture context, corporate governance issues:*

cash-heavy compensation packages for senior management, the repricing of underwater employee stock options, the granting of bonuses based on pretax profit rather than something like return on capital, and the use of an auditor not well known in the investment community. Again, this situation is not for everybody. But it is a classic vulture situation—a case where share value might be unlocked, so to speak, through some sort of change in corporate governance.

The other is TTI Team Telecomm (price-to-net cash ratio: 1.105), a good-quality manufacturer of network monitoring equipment that got hammered after severe weakness in end markets caused the company to state that estimates would have to be significantly reduced. But the company's competitive position has been improving during hard times and, as indicated by the net cash position, its balance sheet is strong. One also has to wonder about the extent to which the market is reacting negatively to the fact that the company is headquartered in Israel. As of this writing, tensions in the Middle East are higher than they have been in many years. Once again, we have a company that probably would not qualify as a mainstream value situation, but the situation definitely is worthy of the attention of the vulture audience.

We see that this simple example of the negative alternative theme has helped us find the three main kinds of vulture investment ideas: a company near or in bankruptcy, a decent company whose share price performance is being restrained by corporate issues, and another decent company whose shares are deeply depressed due to severe external problems.

APPENDIX TO CHAPTER 7

Sample Value Connection Screens

Here are sample screens that apply the techniques described in this chapter. The tests are expressed in a generic "language" that's broadly similar to the one used in the Multex applications. (In cases where a multiplication factor is used together with a "greater than" comparison involving a number that might be negative, the actual screen includes the adjustments explained on page 42–43.) The following abbreviations are used throughout this appendix:

MRQ	Most recent quarter
PYQ	Prior year quarter (the same quarter a year ago)
TTM	Trailing 12 months
Indy. Avg.	Industry average
ROA	Return on assets
ROE	Return on equity
ROI	Return on investment
EPS	Earnings per share
CurrYr Est	Consensus estimate of EPS for the company's current fiscal year
CurrQtr Est	Consensus estimate of EPS for the company's current fiscal quarter
NextYr Est	Consensus estimate of EPS for the company's next fiscal year
ProjPE NextYr	P/E calculated using estimate of EPS for the next fiscal year
LT Growth	Consensus projection of long-term (three- to five-year) EPS growth

STOCK-COMPANY (S-C) STRATEGY

Basic Income

Shopping District: Middle-market (balanced)
Primary Good-Stock Tests: Lines 1–4
Secondary Good-Company Tests: Lines 5–7

1. Yield (%) >= 2
2. 3 Year Dividend Growth > 0
3. 3 Year Div. Growth >= Indy. Avg. 3 Year Div. Growth
4. 5 Year Payout Ratio <= (Indy. Avg. 5 Year Payout Ratio) * 1.25
5. 5 Year Capital Spending Growth > 0
6. 5 Year Capital Spending Growth > (Indy. Avg. 5 Year Capital Spending Growth) * .9
7. TTM Interest Coverage < Indy. Avg. TTM Interest Coverage

Note: Lines 5–6 guard against pent-up capital spending needs.

STOCK-COMPANY-ALTERNATIVE (S-C-A) STRATEGY

Value Connection Plus

Shopping District: Middle-market (balanced)
Primary Good-Stock Tests: Lines 1–2
Secondary Good-Company Tests: Lines 3–4
Alternative Tests: Lines 5–6 (growth)
Alternative Test: Line 7 (sentiment)

1. ProjPE NextYr/LT Growth <= 2
2. TTM Price/Sales <= (Indy. Avg. TTM Price/Sales) * 1.5
3. (5 Year ROE >= Indy. Avg. 5 Year ROE) OR (5 Year ROI >= Indy. Avg. 5 Year ROI) OR (5 Year ROA >= Indy. Avg. 5 Year ROA)
4. MRQ Long-Term Debt to Equity < Indy. Avg. MRQ LT Debt to Equity
5. PYQ Sales Growth >= Indy. Avg. PYQ Sales Growth
6. PYQ EPS Growth >= Indy. Avg. PYQ EPS Growth
7. Short Interest as % Float < Prior Month Short Interest as % Float

Yield with Price Spark

Shopping District: Middle-market (balanced)
Primary Good-Stock Tests: Lines 1–4
Secondary Good-Company Test: Line 5
Alternative Test: Line 6 (price)

1. Yield (%) >= 2
2. 3 Year Dividend Growth > 0
3. 3 Year Div. Growth >= (Indy. Avg. 3 Year Div. Growth) * 1.10
4. (Yield/Indy. Avg. Yield) <= (5 Year Yield/Indy. Avg.e 5 Year Yield) * 1.10
5. 5 Year ROE >= Indy. Avg. 5 Year ROE
6. Share Price % Change Last 4 Weeks > Indy. Avg. Share Price % Change Last 4 Weeks

Note: Line 4 guards against too great a time series increase in relative yield.

Growth at a Reasonable Price (from MultexInvestor.com)

Shopping District: Middle-market (balanced)
Primary Good-Stock Tests: Lines 1–2
Secondary Good-Company Tests: Lines 3–4
Alternative Tests: Lines 5–7 (growth)
Alternative Test: Line 8 (price)

1. ProjPE NextYr/LT Growth <= 1
2. TTM P/E <= 3 Year % EPS Growth
3. Tax Rate >= 25
4. 5 Year ROE/5 Year ROI <= 1.2 OR (5 Year ROE/5 Year ROI) <= (Indy. Avg. 5 Year ROE/Indy. Avg. 5 Year ROI)
5. LT Growth >= 20
6. 3 Year % EPS Growth >= Indy. Avg. 3 Year % EPS Growth
7. 3 Year % EPS Growth > 5 Year % EPS Growth
8. Share Price % Change Last 4 Weeks > Indy. Avg. Share Price % Change Last 4 Weeks OR Share Price % Change Last 4 Weeks > 0

Quality Bargains

Shopping District: Downscale (vulture)
Primary Good-Stock Tests: Lines 1–2
Secondary Good-Company Tests: Line 3–4
Alternative Test: Line 5 (price)

1. MRQ Price/Net Cash > 0 AND MRQ Price/Net Cash < 7
2. TTM Price/Sales <= Indy. Avg. TTM Price/Sales
3. 5 Year Operating Margin > Indy. Avg. 5 Year Operating Margin OR 5 Year ROI >= Indy. Avg. 5 Year ROI
4. (5 Year Operating Margin/5 Year Pretax Margin) < (Indy. Avg. 5 Year Operating Margin/Indy. Avg. 5 Year Pretax Margin)
5. Share Price % Change Last 4 Weeks > Indy. Avg. Share Price % Change Last 4 Weeks

Note: In this screen, net cash is defined as cash minus all liabilities.

STOCK-ALTERNATIVE (S-A) STRATEGY

Relative Value (from MultexInvestor.com)

Shopping District: Middle-market (balanced)
Primary Good-Stock Tests: Lines 1–4
Alternative Tests: Lines 5–6 (growth)
Alternative Test: Line 7 (price)

1. TTM P/E <= (Indy. Avg. TTM P/E) * 1.1
2. TTM Price/Sales <= (Indy. Avg. TTM Price/Sales) * 1.1
3. TTM Price/Free Cash Flow <= (Indy. Avg. TTM Price/Free Cash Flow) * 1.1
4. ProjPE NextYr <= (LT Growth) * 2
5. TTM % EPS Growth >= (Indy. Avg. TTM % EPS Growth) * 1.25
6. 3 Year % EPS Growth >= (Indy. Avg. 3 Year % EPS Growth) * 1.25
7. Share Price % Change Last 4 Weeks > Indy. Avg. Share Price % Change Last 4 Weeks

High P/E Ratios (from MultexInvestor.com)

Shopping District: Upscale
Primary (behavioral) Good-Stock Tests: Lines 1–3
Alternative Tests: Lines 4–6 (growth)
Alternative Test: Line 7 (analyst aentiment)
Alternative Test: Line 8 (general sentiment)

1. TTM P/E > Indy. Avg. TTM P/E
2. TTM P/E > Prior 12 Month P/E
3. TTM P/E < 200
4. PYQ % EPS Growth > Indy. Avg. PYQ % EPS Growth
5. 3 Year % EPS Growth > Indy. Avg. 3 Year % EPS Growth
6. PYQ % EPS Growth > 3 Year % EPS Growth
7. # Analysts Publishing EPS Estimates for Next Quarter > 3
8. Short Interest 1 Month % Change < 0

Bottom Fishing

Shopping District: Downscale (vulture)
Primary Good-Stock Tests: Lines 1–3

Alternative Tests: Lines 4–5 (sentiment)
Alternative Test: Line 6 (price)

1. MRQ Price/Net Cash > 0 AND MRQ Price/Net Cash < 10
2. TTM Price/Sales <= Indy. Avg. TTM Price/Sales
3. MRQ Price/Book <= Indy. Avg. MRQ Price/Book
4. # Insider Buy Transactions > 0
5. Short Interest as % Float < Prior Month Short Interest as % Float
6. Share Price/52 Week High Price <= .6 AND Share Price/52 Week Low Price <= 1.2

Note: In this screen, net cash is defined as cash minus total debt.

Favored Value Plays (from MultexInvestor.com)

Shopping District: Middle-market (balanced)
Primary Good-Stock Tests: Lines 1–3
Alternative Tests: Lines 4–5 (analyst sentiment)
Alternative Test: Line 6 (analyst estimates)

1. TTM P/E <= Indy. Avg. TTM P/E
2. ProjPE NextYr/LT Growth <= 2
3. TTM Price/Sales <= Indy. Avg. TTM Price/Sales
4. Average Recommendation <= Average Recommendation 4 Weeks Ago
5. Average Recommendation < 2
6. CurrQtr Est Now >= CurrQtr Est 4 Weeks Ago

COMPANY-STOCK (C-S) STRATEGY

Basic Value Connection

Shopping District: Middle-market (balanced)
Primary Good-Company Tests: Lines 1–6
Secondary Good-Stock Tests: Lines 7–8

1. TTM Operating Margin > Indy. Avg. TTM Operating Margin
2. TTM ROI > Indy. Avg. TTM ROI
3. 5 Year ROI > Indy. Avg. 5 Year ROI

4. MRQ Current Ratio > Indy. Avg. MRQ Current Ratio
5. MRQ Long-Term Debt to Equity < Indy. Avg. MRQ LT Debt to Equity
6. TTM Asset Turnover > Indy. Avg. TTM Asset Turnover
7. ProjPE NextYr/LT Growth <= 1.75

8. TTM P/E <= (Indy. Avg. TTM P/E) * 1.1

COMPANY-STOCK-ALTERNATIVE (C-S-A) STRATEGY

Justifiably Appreciated

Shopping District: Upscale
Primary Good-Company Tests: Lines 1–4
Secondary Good-Stock Test: Line 5
Alternative Test: Line 6 (analyst sentiment)

1. TTM ROI > Indy. Avg. TTM ROI
2. TTM ROI > 5 Yr. ROI
3. TTM Operating Margin > Indy. Avg. Operating Margin
4. TTM Operating Margin > 5 Year Operating Margin
5. (ProjPE NextYr/LT Growth >= 1.5) AND (ProjPE NextYr/LT Growth <= 3.0)
6. Average Recommendation <= 2

COMPANY-ALTERNATIVE (C-A) STRATEGY

Strong Returns on Investment (from MultexInvestor.com)

Shopping District: Middle-market (balanced)
Primary Good-Company Tests: Lines 1–4
Alternative Test: Line 5 (analyst sentiment)
Alternative Test: Line 6 (general sentiment)

1. TTM ROI > (5 Year ROI) * 1.2
2. TTM ROI > (Indy. Avg. TTM ROI) * 1.2
3. 5 Year ROI > (Indy. Avg. 5 Year ROI) * 1.2

4. (TTM ROI/Indy. Avg. TTM ROI) > (5 Year ROI/Indy. Avg. 5 Year ROI) * 1.2

5. CurrYr Est Now >= CurrYr Est 8 Weeks Ago

6. Institutional (Net) Shares Purchased Latest Quarter > 0

Strong Operating Margins
(from MultexInvestor.com)

Shopping District: Middle-market (balanced)
Primary Good-Company Tests: Lines 1–4
Alternative Test: Line 5 (growth)
Alternative Test: Line 6 (analyst estimates/analyst sentiment)

1. TTM Operating Margin > Indy. Avg. TTM Operating Margin

2. 5 Year Operating Margin > Indy. Avg. 5 Year Operating Margin

3. TTM Operating Margin > (Indy. Avg. 5 Year Operating Margin * 1.25

4. (5 Year ROE >Indy. Avg. 5 Year ROE) OR (5 Year ROI > Indy. Avg. 5 Year ROI) OR (5 Year ROA > Indy. Avg. 5 Year ROA)

5. TTM % EPS Growth > Indy. Avg. TTM % EPS Growth

6. CurrQtr Est Now > Curr Qtr Est 4 Weeks Ago OR Average Rating Current < Average Rating 4 Weeks Ago

Fastest Turnover
(from MultexInvestor.com)

Shopping District: Middle-market (balanced)
Primary Good-Company Tests: Lines 1–4
Alternative Test: Line 5 (analyst estimates)

1. TTM Asset Turnover > (Indy. Avg. TTM Asset Turnover) * 1.25

2. TTM Inventory Turnover > (Indy. Avg. TTM Inventory Turnover) * 1.25

3. TTM Receivables Turnover > (Indy. Avg. TTM Receivables Turnover) * 1.25

4. 5 Year ROI >= Indy. Avg. 5 Year ROI

5. CurrYr Est Now >= CurrYr Est 8 Weeks Ago

Contrarian Opportunities
(from MultexInvestor.com)

Shopping District: Downscale (vulture)
Primary Good-Company Tests: Lines 1–3
Alternative Tests: Lines 4–5 (growth)
Alternative Tests: Lines 6–7 (price)

1. 5 Year Operating Margin > Indy. Avg. 5 Year Operating Margin
2. 5 Year ROE > Indy. Avg. 5 Year ROE
3. 5 Year ROI > Indy. Avg. 5 Year ROI
4. 3 Year % EPS Growth > Indy. Avg. 3 Year % EPS Growth
5. 5 Year % EPS Growth > Indy. Avg. 5 Year % EPS Growth
6. Share Price % Change Last 4 Weeks < Indy. Avg. Share Price % Change Last 4 Weeks
7. Share Price % Change Last 4 Weeks < –15

Analyze . . . Specific Ideas to See If the Value Connection Is Sound

## CHAPTER 8

The Value Connection Story

Thus far, we've consistently defined value in terms of getting our money's worth on the stocks we buy, whether they carry high, low, or midlevel price tickets. Sticking with the shopping analogy, we can describe Step 1 (Find) as the process of sifting through various shopping malls, stores, and departments culminating in our winding up in front of the bin, rack, or aisle that is most likely to have the kind of merchandise we seek. Now we shift to Step 2 (Analyze). This is where we examine individual merchandise items (stocks).

Some shoppers start by looking at the goods first, assessing their attributes, and then looking at the price tags. Others reverse the procedure and check the price tags first. It's a matter of taste. Ultimately, both will have the same information in hand before making a decision to purchase or pass it by.

For the sake of convenience, we will present a Step 2 (Analyze) framework based on the assumption that we first check the price tag, then examine the merchandise, and wind up by deciding if we would truly be getting our money's worth if we were to buy. Accordingly, we'll use the following format.

- **Check the price.** We start by examining and understanding the stock's valuation metrics. Obviously, this alone can't tell us whether the stock is attractive, since we haven't yet examined the company (the merchandise). But it shows us what others think (a richly valued stock is, presumably, well regarded within the investment community) and gives us a standard by which we'll judge the company-specific information we'll examine. And, of course, this information can confirm that we're looking at the kind of merchandise we seek. In other words, we'll quickly learn if an upscale item somehow found its way onto the bargain table.

- **Assess the merchandise.** Next, we'll turn our attention to the good-company theme. This is implemented by reviewing descriptive information, historical data, and information regarding analyst expectations for the future. For convenience, our efforts will be organized as follows:

  Getting acquainted: Get a sense of what the company does and what key events are occurring.

  Exploring the fundamentals: Dig into the data to determine how good the company is.

  Finishing touches: Make sure nothing important fell through the cracks.

- **Determine whether we are getting our money's worth.** By now, we have a sense of what the company is capable of accomplishing and what analysts and investors expect it to accomplish. At this point, we determine if the current stock price reflects a rational reconciliation between accomplishment and expectation. If so, it is probable that we can get our money's worth from a purchase of the stock. If accomplishments and expectations are unaligned, we are on notice that the merchandise, however good the quality may be, is probably not properly priced.

As noted, the sequence of the first two tasks is a matter of convenience. One could easily assess the merchandise first and the price second. What's most important is that we recognize the distinctiveness and importance of each of the three tasks. If we do this, we will find ourselves easily able to organize what may strike others as an overwhelming amount of information, and we'll feel secure in the knowledge that we have not missed important issues.

CHECKING THE PRICE

In the context of stock market investing, when we say price, we're really referring to valuation metrics relating to the share price. A stock priced at $10 with a P/E ratio of 30 could be far more expensive than a stock priced at $85 with a P/E ratio of 16. Ultimately, we'd have to compare the merchandise (the companies) to see if this is really so. But until we learn more, we'd start with an assumption that the $85 stock is lower-priced (a better value) than the $10 stock.

The valuation metrics we'll review here are pretty much the same as the ones we discussed in Chapter 4. A simplistic approach would involve little more than glancing at all the available price-related ratios. For many (sadly, for too many), that would be more than they've been accustomed to doing. So in a sense, I could simply present a checklist of the ratios and move on to the next topic.

I will, in fact, present a set of checklists in Appendix A of this chapter. We divide the overall metrics collection into five categories: (1) P/E, (2) P/E alternatives, (3) income, (4) general assets, and (5) liquid assets.

As we saw in other chapters, especially Chapter 7, value investing comes in a variety of flavors, and different categories are best suited for different kinds of approaches. So it's highly unlikely that any single investor will find the entire checklist relevant. We will therefore consider each style of shopping/investing (upscale, middle-market, and downscale) and discuss in each case which metrics ought to be considered and the level of importance that should be attached to the preferred metrics.

When you look at Appendix A, you will quickly notice that whichever research source you use, it is likely that some of these ratios will be missing. Fortunately, though, you should easily be able to find the underlying data you'll need to calculate the ratios on your own. That could get very burdensome if you try to do it for every missing ratio for every stock you examine. I suggest the do-it-yourself approach only for those missing ratios that are deemed highly relevant to your chosen style.

Let's now consider the metrics that are appropriate for each style of value investing.

Upscale Style

In this approach, we seek great companies. We won't carry this quest so far as to ignore the price tag. But we understand that those who see value in terms of popular stereotypes will wince at how much we will be willing to pay.

For upscale investing, we can eliminate three categories of valuation metrics right up front. We'll skip income because the stocks we'll probably be examining are likely to have zero or nominal yields. We'll also eliminate the two asset-oriented categories, general assets (e.g., book value) and liquid assets. This kind of valuation is very much tied to what the companies are all about in the here and now. On the other hand, the companies most likely to be of interest to upscale investors are those with promising futures, those that are expected to become far more than what can be seen through a conventional here-and-now appraisal. This leaves us with two categories, P/E and P/E alternatives. We'll use them both.

Here are the appropriate upscale valuation metrics in order of importance.

P/E Growth Comparison   This, of course, is the PEG ratio. Use the forward-looking variation (see Table 8A.1 in Appendix A). PEG ratios of 1.50 to 2.00 are, often, mathematically reasonable, so we consider it a significant plus if the stock we're analyzing is valued in that range. For the most part, though, we'll have to tolerate PEG ratios above 2.00. Ratios at or above 3.00 are somewhat delicate. Several big-name new economy stocks had such valuations before the plunge, so the market's collective experience in this level of the stratosphere is not good. But we need not adopt a rigid 3.00 ceiling, since the expectation assessment we'll do in the last part of Step 2 (Analyze) will caution us about excessive valuations. But a PEG ratio at or above 3.00 should at least serve as a red flag alerting us to be exceptionally diligent about the assumptions we plug into our expectation analysis.

P/E Peer Comparison   Here, we're comparing a company P/E to an appropriate benchmark, preferably an industry average. (If the company is a one-of-a-kind operation that doesn't seem to blend comfortably in any industry classification, compare the company P/E to a broader benchmark such as the S&P 500 average.) Note, too, whether the company-to-peer comparisons using the five-year high and low P/Es are materially different from the one based on TTM P/E. The less variation there is, the more comfortable we can be with an assumption that today's company-to-peer relationship is near a "normal" level. If the stock's P/E is less than the peer average, that's a plus. Above-average P/Es are not necessarily negative. Indeed, we'll often see them in upscale situations. But they do warn us that we need to be cautious. We can accept them if (1) they top the averages by modest amounts (say, up to 30 percent above the average), (2) the PEG ratio is reasonable, or (3) the stock passes the expectation assessment.

Price/Sales   Use this the same way we use the P/E peer comparison. Generally, price/sales can help us confirm a conclusion we reached using the former or raise a red flag requiring us to be especially attentive about the assumptions we use in the expectations assessment. Price/sales can also be a helpful substitute where a P/E cannot be computed because the company is losing money, or it is earning only a nominal level of profit, as often happens with great companies while they are very early in their life cycles.

Price/EBIT   This can fulfill the same confirmation and/or substitution functions as price/sales.

Price/Free Cash Flow   This, too, can fulfill the confirmation and/or substitution functions, but it may be less effective in doing so because free cash flow can fluctuate widely from one year to the next in ways that are unrelated to the company's underlying economic prowess. An example would be a large capital-spending program that is ramping up or winding down.

Price/EBITDA and Price/Cash Flow   These ratios can also be used in the roles of confirmation and/or substitution. But they are the least effective because, as explained in Chapter 4, the EBITDA and cash flow numbers do not adequately account for costs associated with fixed assets.

It's apparent from the foregoing that one way or another, P/E is the key metric and that within that category, the P/E growth comparison is of primary importance.

Middle-Market (Balanced) Style

This is what most observers would describe as mainstream value investing. This style uses all categories of valuation metrics except P/E alternatives. But the asset-oriented categories, especially liquid assets, are of lesser importance.

It's tempting to assume that P/E alternatives might be fruitful in the event that usable P/E ratios are temporarily unavailable. That could happen if a normally profitable company loses money in a particular year, or even posts a big enough single-quarter loss to pull overall TTM results below breakeven. In such situations, we might glance at price/sales out of the corner of our eye, but on the whole we ought to still be able to use forward P/E ratios. The consensus estimates on which these are based do not typically include losses from nonrecurring sources. And analysts generally assume that business conditions will be sufficiently normal to keep the bottom line in the black. If we encounter a situation where this is not so, we'd have to question why the stock is being analyzed pursuant to the middle-market style. If earnings problems are likely to be prolonged, perhaps we should be applying downscale approaches. If losses are occurring because the company is still in a very young, start-up phase of its life cycle, we probably should be testing the stock against upscale standards.

Here's a more specific rundown of the mainstream approach.

P/E Growth Comparison   As noted earlier in connection with the upscale style, PEG ratios of 1.50 to 2.00 often turn out to be consistent with the mathematical valuation models we introduced in Chapter 1. So as a general rule, a middle-market value investor can deem any such ratio to be adequate. Obviously, ratios below that signify attractive share pricing, while ratios above 2.00 suggest caution, or at least challenge us to consider switching to the upscale camp and assessing company quality on that basis.

P/E Peer Comparison   Here, again, we're comparing a company P/E to an appropriate benchmark, preferably an industry average (or for one-of-a-kind companies, a broader benchmark such as the S&P 500 average). And once again, we'll examine company-to-peer comparisons, seeing whether the five-year high and low P/Es are materially different from the one based on TTM P/E in order to assess whether the TTM comparisons can be deemed normal. For middle-market investing, our goal is to seek P/Es that are less than the peer average. Such a ceiling need not be rigid, but if we do accept an above-average P/E, at least seek below-average readings in some of the P/E alternatives, or a lower PEG ratio.

Income   Although as of this writing, dividends are deservedly regaining some popularity, we aren't yet far enough along this path to draw negative conclusions from the absence of a dividend. So from the standpoint of this category, the only conclusions we should expect to draw are positive or neutral. When assessing this component of value, add up the current yield and the dividend growth rate and compare the total to generally prevailing fixed income rates. Draw favorable conclusions if yield plus dividend growth is at least equal to the rate on five-year Treasuries plus a 4-to-5 percent equity risk premium. (If you want to go full out, multiply the equity risk premium by the stock's beta before adding it to the risk-free rate.) Strictly speaking, the payout ratio is a quality/risk indicator, not a valuation metric. But in this context, it can provide a clue as to the importance management places on the dividend. High payout ratios (so long as they are not so high as to raise red flags on company quality issues) should prompt us to give extra attention to the income component of our valuation inquiry.

Asset-Based Metrics   Generally, middle-market value investors are not overly attached to the company's here-and-now position, so asset-oriented metrics ought not be foremost in our minds. But in contrast to the upscale approach, mainstream value is less likely to pursue high-flying companies. So we might encounter instances where an asset-oriented metric can serve as an eye-opener. Middle-market investors should understand up front that asset metrics will prove fruitless more often than not. But under the principle of "you never know," we should take the trouble to make themselves aware of the following ratios.

Price/Book Value   Look for situations where company ratios are substantially below peer averages.

Price/Net Working Capital and Price/Net Cash   Most of the time, these ratios will be negative numbers (total liabilities will exceed current assets, or debt will exceed cash). Ratios that are above zero and below 10 should be considered noteworthy.

When that's the case with the price/net cash ratio, it might be worthwhile to get a sense of what P/E the market is assigning to the business alone (without the cash). Here's how a quick back-of-the-envelope calculation can be made, using as an example Mueller Industries, which, as of this writing, had a share price of $29.03, EPS of 1.90, price-to-net cash ratio of 5.966, and P/E of 15.25.

1. Divide the share price by the price/net cash ratio, which gives us net cash per share. (For Mueller: 29.03/5.966 = 4.87.)

2. Estimate pretax per-share interest income generated by the net cash. Let's assume the company earns 5 percent annually on the money. (For Mueller: 4.87 × .05 = 0.24.)

3. Estimate after-tax per-share interest income. I suggest using a standard 35 percent rate. Hence we'd multiply the pretax figure by 0.65, the percent left over after allocating for taxes. (For Mueller: 0.24 × 0.65 = 0.16.)

4. Reduce the actual EPS by the estimated per-share after-tax interest income. (For Mueller: 1.90 − 0.16 = 1.74.)

5. Adjust the share price to eliminate the net cash per share. (For Mueller: 29.03 − 4.87 = 24.16.)

6. Compute the operations-only P/E by dividing the adjusted share price by the adjusted EPS. (For Mueller: 24.16/1.74 = 13.89.)

We can now compare Mueller's adjusted 13.89 P/E to the peer average and to Mueller's growth rates.

Note, though, that this is a very rough back-of-the-envelope calculation. If the difference between the actual P/E and adjusted P/E appears large, it would be prudent to look directly at the financial statements and make more detailed adjustments. To do that, make more precise estimates of the income earned on the net cash and the applicable tax rate.

Return on Enterprise Value (ROEV)   This metric was presented in Chapter 5 as a good-company (rather than good-stock) indicator since it measures the return on the market value (as opposed to book value) of capital. But it's a metric that straddles the good-stock and good-company areas. In the context of assessing the reasonableness of the stock price (which plays an important role in determining enterprise value), ROEV provides an indication of how appealing the company might be as a buyout candidate. The greater the extent to which ROEV exceeds cost of capital, the more acquirable the company is. In the middle market, there's a chance we may see something that catches our eye in this regard. But most of these firms are being analyzed by the investment community as going concerns. Hence many will show unexciting ROEV.

We see from the foregoing that in middle-market value investing P/E is the primary category. But in contrast to the upscale approach, we're making much more substantive use of non-P/E categories. Income is a category that can shoulder the good-stock load entirely on its own. And our quest for interesting surprises among the asset metrics is not merely a ritual. Attractive situations will appear from time to time.

Downscale (Vulture) Style

In downscale stock analysis, the status of P/E moves from prime importance to good-if-we-can-use-it status. If the company is sufficiently profitable to allow us to compute meaningful P/E ratios, we'll use the growth and peer comparisons as we did earlier except that we'll work with lower thresholds. PEG ratios should be below 1.00, and preferably by a substantial margin. And P/Es should be below, preferably well below, peer averages.

If, as is often likely to be the case, P/Es cannot be computed or are not meaningful (because the company is losing money or is only nominally profitable), look for below-peer-average comparisons in the P/E alternatives. Among these, price/sales is the prime measure. Beyond that, in descending order of importance, consider price/EBIT, price/free cash flow, price/EBITDA, and price/cash flow.

Income is not usually part of this inquiry because companies in this category either don't pay dividends or are likely to eliminate any dividends that they may be paying up to this point. If you think you see a dividend-paying vulture candidate that doesn't fit either of those scenarios, it might be a rare gem. More likely, though, it's a cue that the stock should be assessed under middle-market, rather than vulture, criteria.

Asset-oriented valuation metrics are of greater import because in this instance, we are concerned with the here-and-now situation (perhaps even in a literal way, if we see the company as a liquidation or buyout candidate). So obviously, we should pay attention to the price/book value ratio as compared to peer averages (the lower the better). And this is the one situation where I may feel comfortable checking the comparison with the price/tangible book value ratio. As noted in Chapter 4, modern accounting techniques do not fully account for the value of often crucial intangible assets. But it may be reasonable to presume that if a company is in the vulture category, the intangibles may not be carrying their full weight (i.e., patents may not be all that valuable or the company may not be appropriately commercializing them, brand image may have deteriorated, etc.).

We should also take note of the return on enterprise value (ROEV). In the downscale category, we are more likely to encounter situations where ROEV is high.

The liquid asset metrics should be calculated. In the vulture category, we're more likely to see at least one variation that looks attractive. As we review these, we should give priority to the most stringent tests, since these are the ones that have the least distortion between a theoretical liquidation/buyout windfall and a real one that might occur.

Here is a proposed order of stringency/priority.

1. Price to net cash (second alternative computation: cash minus total liabilities).
2. Price to net cash (standard computation: cash minus total debt).
3. Price to net cash (first alternative computation: cash minus current liabilities).
4. Price to cash.
5. Price to net working capital.
6. Price to working capital.

Don't be reluctant to check the lower-priority items. As we saw in Chapter 1, valuation is never an exact science. That's especially so in the vulture category. What we're really looking for, here, is a degree of comfort, a sense that there are enough liquid assets to help support the share price.

ASSESSING THE MERCHANDISE

In this context, the merchandise is the company itself. That's what we own when we buy stock. The better the company, the higher the price (measured by valuation metrics) we should expect to pay for its stock.

When it comes to evaluating companies, there is no precise universally accepted definition of "good." But generally speaking, the idea of growth is never far from center stage. We see that when we look at the world around us, as investors and commentators almost universally praise stocks accompanied by strong company growth stories and dismiss those without. We also saw in the classic valuation approaches we examined in Chapter 1 that G, the variable that stood for growth, was the one that separated stocks from bonds. Absent growth, there's no reason why stocks should not trade at a level that produces a consistent spread between dividend yields and bond yields.

But acting on the growth standard is easier said than done, since the growth that really counts, future growth, cannot be known until after it's too late. Therefore, we examine clues that help us form reasonable assumptions about future growth.

Our analytic process is based on the system spelled out in detail in *Screening the Market*. One important difference is that here, we expanded upon the stock-oriented tasks and placed them in the separate section just presented. Another is that we supplement our assessment of the credibility of analyst projections with a more comprehensive expectation assessment (to be covered starting on page 157.)

Historic growth data plays a role. Past performance does not necessarily determine future outcomes, but since companies don't usually change character every day, a thoughtful assessment of the track record serves as a worthwhile starting point. We'll go further and also consider analyst expectations about the future (including an assessment of the credibility of those expectations). But rather than accepting the assumptions passively, we'll double-check by considering the opinions of other investment community constituencies. We'll also review fundamental ratios that provide clues as to a company's capacity to generate growth, and stay alert for potential aberrations that may cause the company to perform other than as the track record suggests it should.

But let's not put the cart before the horse. Step 1 (Find) will have brought to our attention many interesting companies we may not have previously heard of. So we'll get our analysis off to a solid start by figuring out who and what the company is. Let's turn now to step-by-step company analysis.

Getting Acquainted

We ought not get so wrapped up in ratios and trends that we miss one of our most important tasks, knowing what the company does and what's going on. Diligence at this stage will help us see, quickly, if a particular firm is one we'd like to study in further detail. More importantly, from the standpoint of time management, we will also see companies that don't appeal to us. If, indeed, we develop a negative toward a company at this stage, there's no point in going further. Drop it from the list immediately.

Descriptive Information   There are several sources that provide information on the company's business. And several sites, including Multex-Investor.com, provide longer versions for those who would like to go beyond the bare-bones basics. It's also easy to find links to company home pages. Don't be shy about using these. Undoubtedly, the material here will contain a pro-company slant. But if we recognize this up front, we'll find that there's plenty of in-depth information on many of these sites. The premier business description is, of course, the one contained in 10-K documents filed annually by companies with the SEC. In the old days, these were exercises in dry legalese. That's still the case with many companies. But many more are working a lot harder than in the past to improve readability and add substance. This trend may be related to Regulation FD, which limits the ability of corporate executives to communicate one-on-one with investors. It puts pressure on management to make publicly accessible written descriptions shoulder more of the communication burden than in the past. And an increasingly litigious investment community encourages corporate executives to be prudent about the amount of self-serving spin, as opposed to substance, they present.

Stock Price Chart   After getting a sense of what the company does, we should next turn our attention to the stock price. We're not necessarily going to become chartists. But price trends, resulting from trends in supply and demand for shares, give us an instant view of the collective opinions of others. We're free to disagree, but if we at least know how the herd feels, it can set the context for the rest of our analysis. For example, the presence of highly favorable ratios combined with a downward price trend puts us on notice that we have to keep digging. We may think the herd's reasons for acting are silly or shortsighted, but such reasons are rarely, if ever, nonexistent.

What's Happening   It's easy nowadays to stay current on important events impacting companies. News links are standard fare on financial web sites. MultexInvestor.com goes a step further with its "Significant Developments" feature—short summaries created by Multex for especially important developments. The actual text of company announcements can also be found on their own web sites. In many cases, links to upcoming or archived investment community conference calls are also offered.

Important Details   MultexInvestor.com offers two seldom noticed items that can have a big impact on our investment decisions. The item referred to as "Equity Information" indicates the presence of major shareholders with controlling ownership blocks, multiple classes of common stock (with different classes having different voting power), convertible debt, or preferred issues. For downscale investing, the presence of such items can prove important in that they may indicate a greater degree of difficulty in executing hostile buyouts. Another item, "Footnotes," describes things like stock splits, major acquisitions, divestitures, or changes in accounting practices. In ascertaining a good-company investment case, such items can signal us when historic data might have unusually low predictive value about the future due to basic changes in the corporation itself.

Exploring the Fundamentals

This is the heart of the good-company inquiry. Some of the tasks, the direct part of our inquiry, will involve study of ratios drawn directly from fundamental data. The other, indirect, part will be based on the opinions of others—analysts, insiders, institutional investors, and short sellers.

Don't underestimate the importance of indirect sources. Presumably, the individuals whose behavior gives rise to such information acted based on a broader range of information than is provided by the numbers alone. This is a way for us to tap into qualitative factors impacting share price performance.

I suggest addressing the fundamentals through the following sequence.

Analyst Expectations   Start with the analysts. Many large institutional investors consider and act on their advice, and for better or worse, that has a major impact on near-term share price movement. Hence even if we prefer not to follow analyst recommendations, this is a group that should not be ignored. Making an informed decision to go our own way will give us the perspective we'll need to react rationally, rather than emotionally, if the stock doesn't go our way from the outset.

- **Evaluate the credibility of the long-term growth forecasts.** Start by noting the number of analysts issuing the forecast and the range of expectations. Broad ranges and/or a small number of analysts make forecasts more iffy than usual. Then, compare the long-term growth forecast to historic rates of growth. (Since EPS numbers are always prone to unusual items that can temporarily distort growth trends, look, too, at sales growth.) Decide whether this seems consistent with the company's position within its life cycle. If analysts are forecasting future growth rates above what has been achieved in the past, we should expect to see an early-stage company. The other usual justification for such a forecast would be a situation where the firm is recovering from a cyclical downturn in its markets. Aside from that, seek some evidence that the company is, indeed, a special situation.

- **Evaluate the credibility of the near-term estimates.** As with the long-term projections, get a handle on the solidity of the consensus numbers by checking the range of expectations and the number of analysts. Note, though, that companies tend to give more detailed guidance on the near term. That means we have more latitude to accept as credible a consensus that is based on a smaller number of analysts. On the other hand, we should be less tolerant of broader ranges. Then, assess how the near-term estimates mesh with recent quarterly growth trends. The forecasting process is such that analysts typically anticipate that past trends will persist unless they see a good reason to assume otherwise. The greater the extent to which estimates represent a break from recent trends, the greater our need to focus on specific explanations (usually contained in company news releases, archived conference call replays, or analyst research reports).
- **Assess the extent to which analysts have a handle on the situation.** Estimates are continually being changed. Usually, stocks perform well when analysts are compelled to chase reality upward by raising their estimates. Conversely, stocks tend to perform poorly when analysts are reducing estimates in an effort to chase reality downward. Look again at the stock price chart, and determine whether you believe the market's reaction to the most recent revisions is reasonable.
- **Note the distribution and trend of analyst recommendations.** As discussed in Chapter 6 ("Analyst Sentiment" section), low average or mean rating scores are bullish. Another bullish setting is an improving trend in analyst ratings. Note, though, that attractive buying opportunities can occur when analysts are bearish. This is because analysts gear their recommendations toward institutional clients who are often highly sensitive to near-term corporate earnings trends. Hence value connection practitioners need not necessarily draw negative conclusions from bearish recommendation profiles.

General Sentiment   We use general sentiment data in a context similar to that applicable to analyst data. It helps us understand why the stock is behaving as it is. We are, therefore, better equipped to make rational, rather than emotional, decisions to ride with the herd or stand against it. General sentiment data could be deemed at least as credible as analyst data, if not more so. It reflects actual investment activity, not just expressions of opinion. It also reflects a larger and often more diverse group of decision makers.

- **Get a sense of whether the stock is generally in or out of favor compared to key benchmarks.** Never underestimate the power of a general bull market to reward many not-so-meritorious stocks (the rising-tide-lifts-all-boats phenomenon). The "Price Performance" table on MultexInvestor.com shows percentile ranks (with 0 being worst and 99 being best) indicating how the stocks in an industry have performed over various time periods compared with all other industries, and another rank showing how this stock has fared relative to others in its own industry. Discrepancies in these ranks can be especially interesting. A low industry rank coupled with a high stock rank, a hot stock in a cold industry, may point us toward better-quality companies, those whose shares might be especially rewarding at a later time when the industry as a whole moves into favor. The reverse, a cold stock in a hot industry, is also noteworthy. This scenario involves the rising-tide-lifts-all-boats phenomenon.

- **Note institutional presence and trading activity.** Low levels of institutional ownership can present opportunities—the proverbial undiscovered gem. But if institutional presence is too low, double-check other company-quality data to make sure you didn't miss one or more important negatives that may be causing institutions to avoid the stock. Meanwhile, it's always worthwhile to know what institutions are doing, whether or not we are inclined to follow them, simply because they are so big. In the short term, stocks will perform well if institutions are buying, and poorly if they are selling.

- **Note insider presence and trading activity.** Large insider share ownership percentages are often seen as positive in that they supposedly align the interests of corporate managers with those of shareholders. The downside is that less capable managers can more easily become entrenched. Hence when we see large insider stakes, we should interpret them in light of the footprints of success we'll discuss in the next subsection. We can also come to different opinions on the takeover angle. Large insider stakes certainly preclude a hostile buyout, but could enhance the probability of a friendly deal. Meanwhile, as noted in Chapter 6, insider buying can be interpreted as a bullish signal. Insider selling is harder to assess. It certainly could be a reflection of bearish sentiment. But it's hard for us to determine whether that's really the case. There are many other legitimate reasons why insiders might be selling (diversify personal holdings, raise cash for personal expenditures, etc.).

- **Take note of significant levels of and changes in short interest.** As with institutional trading data, we may be called upon to make thoughtful decisions as to whether we'll go with the flow or stand apart. In other words, we may allow ourselves to be put off if we see large and/or growing short interest. Or we may take a contrarian stance and anticipate a positive development that will prompt shorts to buy shares to cover their positions. One way or the other, we should make sure our choices are knowledgeable.

Footprints of Success   Here, we revisit the good-company concepts discussed at length in Chapter 5. The difference is that in this stage, we are not bound by the limitations of the screening process (the capabilities of the applications we use and/or the fact that there are just so many tests that can be fit into any one screen). Now, we can and should review all aspects of a company's fundamental position.

Review Data Relating to Growth Rates, Margin, and Returns on Capital In doing so, we should ask ourselves the following questions.

- For each data item (EPS growth rate, pretax margin, return on equity, etc.) in each time period (most recent quarter, trailing 12 months, five-year average, etc.), is the company better than the peer benchmark? If possible, compare the company growth rates to industry averages.
- For each data item, are the company's more recent tallies better than the company's own long-term averages? (For example, is the most recent quarterly sales growth rate better than the trailing 12-month growth rate? Is the trailing 12-month growth rate better than the five-year average?)
- Is the company's relative performance improving or deteriorating? For example, is the company's relative trailing 12-month return on equity (company return divided by peer group return) better or worse than the relative five-year return on equity?
- With regard to growth rates, has the company's capital spending growth kept pace with sales growth? With the peer group? (Negative responses here may signify a need for catch-up spending in the future.)
- With regard to margin, is the company's tax rate generally in line with peer averages? (A substantially below-average company tax rate may portend a future drag on EPS. Double-check to determine the sustainability of those factors that are allowing for a low rate.)
- With regard to margin, assess the nonoperating component of corporate performance by comparing operating margin to pretax margin. Is the company's nonoperating component greater or less than the peer average? Over time, is the company's nonoperating component growing or shrinking? How does this time-series trend compare with the peer average?
- With regard to return on capital, assess financial aggressiveness by comparing return on equity to return on investment (or assets). Is

the company's financial aggressiveness greater or less than the peer average? Over time, is the company's financial aggressiveness growing or shrinking? How does this time-series trend compare with the peer average?

No company can be expected to fare well under all these questions. In Chapter 10, we'll see examples of how Step 3 (Buy) helps us weigh and balance the pros and cons.

Review Data Relating to Management Efficiency   In doing so, we should ask ourselves the following questions.

- Is there reason to expect the company's labor efficiency data to be at least in line with peer averages? If so, is the company above the peer average in terms of revenue and net income per employee?
- Are the company's turnover ratios (receivables turnover, inventory turnover, asset turnover) above the peer averages?

Again, we cannot expect a company to be above par in all respects. In Chapter 10, we'll see examples of how Step 3 (Buy) helps us weigh and balance the pros and cons.

Review Data Relating to Financial Strength   In doing so, we should ask ourselves the following questions.

- Are the company's liquidity ratios (quick ratio, current ratio) above the peer averages?
- Are the company's debt ratios (total debt to equity, long-term debt to equity) lower than the peer averages?
- Is the company's reliance on short-term debt (total debt to equity divided by long-term debt to equity) less than the peer average?
- Is the company's interest coverage ratio above the peer average?

Not every company will look good from all angles. In Chapter 10, we'll see examples of how Step 3 (Buy) helps us weigh and balance the pros and cons.

Finishing Touches

No matter how thoroughly we review fundamental ratios, there's always a chance that something unique about a particular situation may slip through the cracks. We guard against this by examining the following types of information.

Financial Statements   Thus far, we haven't considered what so many others regard as the staple of investment analysis, the financial statements. Instead, we examined data extracted from the raw statements and re-presented it in more usable formats. So by now, we already know most of the important information that can be gleaned from the financials. Still, every investment story is unique and it's always possible something important wasn't captured by the main data presentation. Therefore, we should check the statements, which are presented by major financial web sites. We use these as safety valves to see if there's anything important the data tables missed. Here are the main things we should be examining.

- **Sequential Trends:** We've already looked at data presentations showing long-term (usually over three or five years) averages. But we don't know if the year-by-year trends are smooth or choppy (the latter pattern would be more risky). We can check this by looking at the financial statements themselves. We can also look beyond an erratic trend in EPS, for example, and examine each line of the income statement to see exactly why that's occurring. Such an effort can help us make thoughtful assumptions as to whether the volatility is likely to persist in the future.
- **Unusual Income/Expenses:** Unusual income statement items can impact the fundamental ratios in a substantial way. Examination of the financial statements is useful in two respects. First, obviously, we can see if unusual items are present. Secondly, and some might say more important, we can see how often unusuals find their way onto the income statement. Sadly, for some companies, unusual items are anything but unusual. Upscale value connection investors, and even some who focus on the middle-market, should think carefully about investing in companies that are too habitual in their reporting of unusuals. This may indicated erratic and/or ineffective management strategies. On the other hand, downscale/vulture investors may find this appealing, if they have reason to believe that the problems can be corrected by a buyout or a major reorganization.
- **Nonoperating Income/Assets:** As is the case with the unusuals discussed above, these items are unrelated to the company's main business. But they differ in that they tend to be present year in and year out. We are looking directly at the income statement and/or balance sheet to see how big they are in relation to the entire company. Many see large nonoperating income/assets as negative, a possible indication of lackluster strategic focus. That's not always the case. But it should prompt us to dig deeper into the documents (i.e., the footnotes of the annual SEC 10-K filing) in order that we may know, rather than

guess at, what's going on. But a satisfactory answer here may not be sufficient. Many are troubled by the burden of having to understand and become comfortable with matters whose essence is not immediately visible and whose impact may be hard to predict. The latter concern might be alleviated somewhat if the financial statements show stable period-to-period trends in nonoperating items.

- **Cash Generation:** Typically, a steady pattern of positive cash generation is deemed favorable. But we should look critically. Unless the company pays out a significant portion of surplus cash flow as dividends, we should check the return on capital trends. There's no virtue in reinvesting increasingly large sums of cash into activities that generate a pattern of deteriorating returns (such as ill-conceived acquisitions). Vulture investors may see opportunity in such companies. In any case, much can be learned by drilling down to the three components of cash flow: operations, financing, and investment. Positive cash flow from the operating component should be viewed favorably, since that relates most directly to the core business operations. In the investment category, it's perfectly normal to see a net outflow, since it includes capital spending. But it's important that we note whether outflows are also occurring because of acquisitions. Investment inflows usually come from funds generated by asset divestitures. Many look askance at companies if acquisitions and divestitures are very prominent. We should also be attentive to the financing category (issuance or retiring of debt or equity). Positive cash generation is not bullish if the company relies too heavily on infusion of capital from outside sources.

Wall Street Research Reports   Earlier, we suggested that the credibility of estimates be measured by the extent to which forecasted growth seems consistent with the company's life-cycle status. That's a good rule of thumb. But we have to understand that this rule, like all others, is often broken. Analyst reports are most useful when they shed light on factors that allow us to comfortably assume the company will break the mold, for better or worse. We won't accept all the conclusions at face value. We should act as if we're sitting in a jury box and the analyst is an attorney delivering a summation. We'll apply skeptical common sense and consider whether or not the analyst cites sufficient evidence in support of his or her contentions. Our main challenge is to gain access to reports. Some are available only to institutional clients. But many nowadays can be purchased individually on MultexInvestor.com and affiliated sites such as Yahoo! Finance. Most reports sell for $25.00 or less.

Independent Research Reports   Sell-side analysts (those who work for brokerage firms) are not the only research providers. There are also independent firms. Among these, Standard & Poor's and Morningstar work especially hard to make their reports widely accessible. They can be purchased via annual subscription or on a pay-per-view basis (costing $5.00 per report for S&P and $10.00 for Morningstar) on MultexInvestor.com and affiliated sites (such as Yahoo! Finance). Such commentary isn't as lengthy or deep as are some sell-side reports. But the independents are objective and easy to understand.

The Executive Suite   Some sites, such as MultexInvestor.com, present data about the company's officers and directors. Because it contains vital information about important individuals in the corporation, it's must reading for any investment case based on expectations of reorganization or buyout. The information on MultexInvestor.com consists of brief biographies, information on compensation (salary, bonus, fringe benefits, etc.), and information about stock options. I suggest resisting tendencies in the media that imply compensation ought to relate to short-term earnings or share price trends. Corporate executives cannot control many relevant factors (such as business or market cycles), and companies understand they will not be able to attract and retain talented executives if they start slashing compensation every time there's a stock market correction. The best way to look at this data is by comparing a company to others in the same general business and of the same general size. When compensation viewed this way seems excessive, that might be a red flag, especially if insider share control is heavy.

GETTING OUR MONEY'S WORTH

Now it's time to pull together everything we've done up till this point in Step 2 (Analyze). Some of us looked at the price tag first and then examined the merchandise. Others looked at the merchandise first and then checked the price tag. Either way, however, we have not yet judged what we saw. For example, we are still open to the possibility that a P/E of 50 may prove reasonable, or that a P/E of 12 may turn out to be excessive. The task now at hand will change that. We are about to combine what we know about the price and the merchandise and determine whether what we'd pay is reasonable in relation to what we'd get for our money.

We're going to do this through a mathematical process that is based on the classic ivory tower principles discussed in Chapter 1. But we're going to introduce an important twist that will minimize the role of the hardest-to-answer questions and direct our focus to the inquiries that are most answerable.

I make no claim to having a crystal ball that can show us the future. At the end of the process, we will still wind up acting on the basis of assumptions about the future that, by necessity, are imperfect. But some issues more readily lend themselves to the process of making rational assumptions than others. Our goal is to enhance our probability of success by emphasizing the most doable assumptions.

Rewriting the Equations

Most mathematical approaches are designed to compute a fair price for a stock. Harking back to the language of high school algebra, we could say that these equations "solve for P." Recall the Dividend Discount Model presented in Chapter 1.

$$P = D/(R - G)$$

where P = stock price
    D = dividend
    R = required rate of annual return
    G = projected dividend growth rate

We solve for P by starting with the dividend and dividing by a number we compute by subtracting the projected growth rate from the required rate of return. Let's consider the degree of difficulty involved in establishing each element of the equation.

- P is a here-and-now item we can easily locate.
- D is another here-and-now item we can easily locate.
- We must make assumptions about R. The process is not perfect, but it is very manageable compared with other things investors must do. We compute R based on three things.

  1. We use the risk-free interest rate. There is no single universally correct data point, but we can make reasonable assumptions based on known government securities rates.

  2. We use the equity risk premium. Again, there is no single universally correct data point, but the investment community can draw on considerable historic experience to make plausible assumptions.

  3. We use a stock's beta. We can easily calculate beta based on historic price data. The past does not necessarily predict the future, but in this regard, the historic number can give us a workable assumption for R.

- G is almost impossible to predict.

Notice the flaw in the model. Why bother using the math to compute P, the stock price? We already know what the price is. But to perform the calculation, we are forced to make a specific assumption about something that is almost impossible to predict, G. In other words, we're pretending we can predict something that is extremely unpredictable (G) in order to compute something we already know (P).

Practitioners would say we're really not asking the equation to tell us what P is. Instead, we're determining what P ought to be. But that should not make us feel better. If a crucial input to the calculation, G, is extremely unreliable, how can we confidently use the procedure to say P should be such and such?

Let's rearrange the equation so that it does what equations like this should do—use information that is known (or that can be plausibly assumed) to calculate the item we are least capable of knowing. We'll move P, the known data item, to the right side of the equation and bring the unknowable G to the left side. Algebraically speaking, we're going to "solve for G."

Skipping all the algebraic machinations, we wind up with the following equation.

$$G = R - (D/P)$$

The D/P (dividend divided by price) expression should look familiar. It's the dividend yield. So we can rewrite the equation as:

$$G = R - Y$$

where G = projected dividend growth rate
           R = required rate of annual return
           Y = current dividend yield

This equation is much more practical than the basic DDM. We can plausibly estimate R. We know Y. Hence we can easily calculate what dividend growth rate we would have to expect in order to justify buying the stock at the current price. Now, we have a much more palatable question. Instead of being forced to predict the rate at which dividends would grow, all we need do is look at the target growth expectation and say whether or not we're comfortable with an assumption that dividends can grow at least that quickly.

Suppose R is 11 percent and the yield is 2 percent. Under our reconfigured model, we can say the stock is buyable if we're willing to assume future dividend growth will be at least 9 percent per year. And if we say "yes," we can buy the stock whether the growth rate really should be 9 percent, 11 percent, 15 percent, or 40 percent. If we're uncomfortable with the

9 percent threshold, we avoid the stock. We need not take the trouble to defend an assumption that G will be 8 percent, 6 percent, and so on.

In determining whether we're comfortable with a 9 percent growth forecast, we're not left to read tea leaves or tarot cards. The company has a history, including a historic dividend growth rate. We can use that as a starting point. If the historic rate is 8 percent, our inquiry turns to whether business prospects are such that the company is likely to be able to achieve a dividend growth rate that is modestly better than what it has delivered to date. If the historic rate is 4 percent, we fall back on the proposition that companies do not usually change character overnight. We know to avoid the stock unless we can somehow meet the burden of proving that this situation will be special.

We saw on page 11 in connection with the DDM that if $R - G$ turns out negative, so, too, would the price of the stock. The fact that such an illogical result could ensue is one reason why the DDM is often unworkable in the real world. But here we don't have to worry about numbers that turn out negative. If R is 12 percent and Y is 15 percent, we'd say the stock is buyable if the dividend shrinks 3 percent per year. If the decline is milder, or if the dividend actually holds steady or grows, so much the better. Realistically, it's hard to imagine getting excited about the prospect of dividend declines. But the real point is that at least we can debate the merits of such a situation. (For example, if we expect the dividend to remain steady we could be bullish on the stock.)

As you can see, we have not eliminated the need to predict. But to the greatest extent possible, we have simplified the most difficult aspect of the forecasting process. The classic DDM tells us to specifically predict the dividend growth rate. The approach we introduce here asks us to develop a general sense of whether the company can, in the future, do better or worse than in the past.

Solving for *G* in the Real World

Although our revised equation is much more usable than the classic DDM, it still bears some of that model's burdensome ivory tower legacy. It's tied to assumptions about infinite growth, and it fails to account for the fact that EPS and P/E have supplanted dividend and yield as the main ingredients in stock valuation.

This is not a problem. All we need do is apply our solve-for-*G* philosophy to a new task. Instead of determining how much dividend growth is needed to justify the current stock price, we'll focus on EPS growth. Accordingly, we'll determine how fast EPS must grow in order to make the stock price attractive, and we'll decide whether we're comfortable assuming the company can grow at least that quickly.

This ties together the work we've done thus far in Step 2 (Analyze). This part of the analysis is more likely to produce favorable answers if valuation metrics are well aligned with company quality. The lower a stock's valuation metrics, the less of a growth rate expectation we'll need to see to justify purchase. And the better a company is from a quality standpoint, the more growth it will be capable of producing.

Table 8.1 illustrates the type of output we can expect to see from this analysis. Among the hypothetical situations depicted in the table, we're likely to find the lowest valuation metrics for shares of Company D. That's because the most modest amount of future EPS growth, only 5.1 percent per year, would be sufficient to justify the current stock price. But as little as we pay, we wind up getting the least for our money. Company D's capacity for growth is also the lowest.

The most "expensive" stock, based on pure good-stock principles, is likely to be C. The current price would be excessive unless the company could deliver a future EPS growth rate of 18.6 percent. But its capacity for growth is well above that. By comparing what we pay with what we get, Company C seems like the best deal for the money.

Now, let's proceed step-by-step and see how the art and science of Step 2 (Analyze) combine to produce a single numeric result that indicates the extent to which we either get or don't get our money's worth on our stock purchases.

Estimating the Growth Expectation

An eight-step procedure will be presented here for calculating the EPS growth expectation that's implied by today's stock price. Then, we'll consider data that can be used to support a growth capacity assumption. Fi-

TABLE 8.1 Expectation Analysis

	Company A	Company B	Company C	Company D
Company's capacity for EPS growth (based on historic data)	8.6%	13.4%	22.4%	4.2%
EPS growth expectation implied by current stock price	9.0%	12.5%	18.6%	5.1%
Expectation index (ratio of capacity for growth to expected growth)	0.96	1.07	1.20	0.82

nally, we'll see how to combine them and evaluate the result. The basic tasks will be presented and we'll explore opportunities where you can opt for simplicity or complexity (a matter of personal preference).

All this may look cumbersome the first time you read it. But in truth, it's really pretty easy. After the procedure is presented in detail, a brief summary of the tasks will be provided. Also, Appendix B to this chapter will give instructions for building a spreadsheet template to aid in the calculations.

As we go along, we'll calculate the index for Wal-Mart, based on data posted on MultexInvestor.com in mid-November 2002.

Task 1: Select a Time Horizon   I recommend a five-year period. That will help us filter out any unusual developments (noise) that may be temporarily impacting present-day trends, and focus, instead, on the more underlying and sustainable aspects of a company's character. Don't worry about the length of the period. We're not going to try to pinpoint a five-year growth rate. All we seek is a general sense of whether a company seems likely to do at least as well as a target rate.

Task 2: Determine the Required Annual Return   How much annual return is needed to justify investment? I suggest using the capital asset pricing model discussed in Chapter 1. Here, again, is the equation.

$$R = RF + (RP \times B)$$

where R = required return
RF = risk-free rate of return
RP = risk premium
B = beta assigned to the individual stock being examined

For the Wal-Mart example, I'll assume a risk-free rate of 5 percent, an equity risk premium of 4.5 percent (in the middle of the historic 4 percent to 5 percent range), and use Wal-Mart's beta of 0.94. Here's the computation.

$$R = .05 + (.045 \times 0.94)$$
$$= .0923$$

Hence, in order to buy Wal-Mart stock, I have to be willing to accept annual gains averaging 9.23 percent over the next five years.

Opportunities for Adjustment

- I could note that Wal-Mart stock has a 0.54 percent dividend yield and reduce the required stock price gains accordingly. For purposes of this example, I will not do that.
- Some stocks have betas that, if used strictly, may produce results that seem contrary to common sense. For example, as of this writing, Procter & Gamble has a beta of 0.07. If we were to use that, we'd come up with a required annual return of 5.3 percent, barely above the risk-free rate. Few investors would be comfortable with such an assumption. Since use of historical data to calculate beta is a best-we-can-do assumption, feel free to disregard it or adjust it subjectively if common sense so requires. When in doubt, set the beta equal to 1.00 (the market beta).

Task 3: Calculate the Predicted Price Five Years Hence   Here's the long way. (P_1 is price one year hence.)

$$P_1 = \text{Current Price} \times (1 + R)$$

$$P_2 = P_1 \times (1 + R)$$

$$P_3 = P_2 \times (1 + R)$$

$$P_4 = P_3 \times (1 + R)$$

$$P_5 = P_4 \times (1 + R)$$

Here are the calculations for Wal-Mart (WMT).

$$P_1 = 55.49 \times 1.0923 = 60.61$$

$$P_2 = 60.61 \times 1.0923 = 66.20$$

$$P_3 = 66.20 \times 1.0923 = 72.31$$

$$P_4 = 72.31 \times 1.0923 = 78.98$$

$$P_5 = 78.98 \times 1.0923 = 86.27$$

This means that purchase of the stock today at $55.49 is justified if we believe the stock can trade for at least $86.27 five years hence.

Here's a shortcut that can easily be implemented using a spreadsheet or a decent handheld calculator.

$$P_N = \text{Current Price} \times (1 + R)^N$$

where N = number of years

Here's the shortcut applied to Wal-Mart.

$$P_5 = 55.49 \times 1.0923^5$$
$$= 55.49 \times 1.5549$$
$$= 86.28$$

Don't worry about the minor discrepancy between the long and short methods. That's simply due to the way decimals are rounded.

Task 4: Establish the Future P/E for the Market   This is an area calling for human judgment. I use the S&P 500 as a proxy for the market, and I use the Fed model to estimate the S&P 500 P/E. Simply, the Fed model, based on the work of three researchers at the Federal Reserve initially released in 1996, suggests that a normal P/E for the index should be the reciprocal of the risk-free rate. In other words, we'd use the following formula.

Future Market P/E = $1/RF$

Since I assumed 5 percent for RF, I'll calculate the future S&P 500 P/E as follows.

S&P 500 P/E = $1/.05 = 20$

Opportunities for Adjustment
- Use of the Fed model is not mandatory. In fact, the model does not even purport to predict what the S&P 500 P/E will always be. It acknowledges that the market P/E is usually above or below this supposedly fair level. So feel free to use a higher or lower number depending on whether you predict the market as a whole will become more overvalued or undervalued. Along the same lines, you don't have to use the interest rate on 30-year government bonds (the maturity used in the initial Fed research project). Feel free to substitute another maturity, such as the one that matches your chosen time horizon.
- If analyzing shares of a company that consistently loses money and is likely to continue doing so in the foreseeable future, we'll have to work with sales. In that case, estimate a future price/sales ratio for the S&P 500. Do that by estimating the future P/E, as just described, and then assuming the same price/sales relationship to P/E for the future as we observe for the TTM period. Table 8.2 shows that for the S&P 500, the P/E is 25.58 and the price/sales ratio is 3.09. The P/S-to-P/E re-

lationship is .121 (3.09 divided by 25.58). Assume then that this same relationship will apply five years hence. That makes the predicted market price/sales ratio 2.42.

Task 5: Establish the Future P/E for the Stock   This is another area that calls for discretion. The key is to determine the relationship between the stock's P/E and the S&P 500 P/E. Examination of present and historic data can help.

Table 8.2 shows data (from the MultexInvestor.com Ratio Comparison report) that can help us formulate an assumption for Wal-Mart.

In Table 8.3, we compute ratios that show the relationships between company, industry, and S&P 500 metrics.

The last column, the one that contains the ratios of company metrics to market metrics, is the key. For TTM P/E, for example, the ratio of 1.26 is the company P/E (32.13) divided by the market P/E (25.58). Use this relationship as the starting point for the valuation analysis.

Eyeball the other rows in the last column to see if the company-to-market TTM P/E ratio is an aberration. (The last two rows, dealing with price/sales and price/book value, are of tangential relevance and should be considered only as a general guide in case there is no usable P/E data.) If so, make an appropriate discretionary adjustment.

TABLE 8.2   Predicting Relative P/E—Raw Data

	Company	Industry	S&P 500
P/E—TTM	32.13	29.64	25.58
P/E—5-year high	59.13	55.60	49.52
P/E—5-year low	26.98	25.10	16.64
Price/sales	1.03	1.05	3.09
Price/book	6.64	5.89	4.51

TABLE 8.3   Predicting Relative P/E—Relevant Ratios

	Company to Industry	Industry to S&P 500	Company to S&P 500
P/E—TTM	1.08	1.16	1.26
P/E—5-year high	1.06	1.12	1.19
P/E—5-year low	1.07	1.51	1.62
Price/sales	0.98	0.34	0.33
Price/book	1.13	1.31	1.47

The first two columns are redundant. Mathematically, the company-to-industry ratio multiplied by the industry-to-market ratio will be equal to the company-to-market ratio. Accordingly, the first two columns are for informational purposes only. Use them to spot aberrations that may justify manual modification of the primary company-to-industry 1.26 ratio.

In the case of Wal-Mart, there does not appear to be any reason to depart from the basic 1.26 company-to-market ratio. Accordingly, the predicted P/E for Wal-Mart stock five years hence is calculated as follows.

$$\text{WMT P/E} = \text{S\&P 500 P/E} \times \text{Company-to-Market Ratio}$$
$$= 20.0 \times 1.26 = 25.2$$

Opportunity for Adjustment

- If we're dealing with unprofitable companies, calculate a predicted price/sales ratio using, as a strong guide, the relationship between current P/S and S&P 500 P/S.

Task 6: Compute the Required EPS   What level of EPS will the company have to show to justify the future stock price? This is a simple straightforward computation. Divide the future price by the P/E that is predicted for the stock. Here's the calculation for Wal-Mart.

$$\text{WMT Future EPS} = \text{Future Price/Future P/E}$$
$$= 86.28/25.2 = 3.42$$

Opportunity for Adjustment

- If we're dealing with unprofitable companies, we'll be calculating future sales per share.

Task 7: Choose a Present or Near-Term Base Level of EPS
Since we're using the present-day stock price as a starting point for the growth expectation, it seems reasonable to use the consensus estimate of current-year EPS as a starting point. For Wal-Mart, the consensus EPS estimate at this time is 1.79.

Opportunities for Adjustment

- If you believe the estimate for current-year EPS is not reasonably representative of the company's underlying earnings power, you can use the actual result from the prior year, or use the consensus estimate for next year's EPS. Note, though, that if you use an EPS figure tied to the prior or current year, it's necessary to adjust the time period that will be used in the growth rate computation. (So if you started with a five-year time horizon and decide to use the estimate of next year's results as your EPS base, compute the growth rate over a four-year period. If you use the prior year's EPS, compute the growth rate over a six-year period.)

- Also, feel free to adjust the base EPS if you disagree with the consensus estimate.
- There's no rule that says you have to use only one base. You can use several different base scenarios and then average the growth rates that result from each.
- If we're dealing with unprofitable companies, use TTM sales per share as the base.

Task 8: Compute the Expected Growth Rate This is a basic growth rate calculation that can easily be handled using a spreadsheet or many handheld calculators.

Here's the mathematical growth rate formula.

$$G = (FV/PV)^{1/N} - 1$$

where G = growth rate
FV = future value
PV = present value
N = number of time periods

Here's the expected growth rate for Wal-Mart:

$$G = (3.42/1.79)^{1/5} - 1$$
$$= 1.911^{1/5} - 1$$
$$= 1.1382 - 1$$
$$= .1382$$

Opportunities for Adjustment

- In task 7, I suggested that we could use alternative base scenarios. We might, therefore, speculate that prolonged economic weakness (a debatable topic as this is written) will cause the current-year estimate to be reduced. If we use 1.60 as an alternative current-year estimate, we'd wind up with a growth expectation of 16.40 percent. If we average this figure with our core 13.82 percent expectation, we'd wind up with an adjusted expectation of 15.11 percent.
- If we're dealing with unprofitable companies, we'll be calculating a sales (per share) growth expectation.

We see that in mid-November 2002, when Wal-Mart stock sold for $55.49, purchase could be justified if an investor believed the company could experience an annual EPS growth rate of at least 13.82 percent over the next five years.

Estimating Growth Capacity

The purpose of the growth capacity estimate is to help us assess the doability of the growth expectation. To implement the capacity estimate, we'll look at pertinent data from the MultexInvestor.com Ratio Comparison report.

Tables 8.4 and 8.5 show sales and EPS growth rates for Wal-Mart over various periods. The five-year rates are of interest because they show prolonged time periods. But we'll also want to look at the more recent intervals, to get a sense if—and if so, to what extent—the company is improving or deteriorating from the long-term trend.

EPS is, of course, our area of direct concern. But these tallies can be boosted by cost cutting, an activity that is certainly laudable, but not sustainable forever. Hence we should also keep an eye on sales growth rates.

We see in Tables 8.4 and 8.5 that Wal-Mart's EPS growth has been accelerating while its sales growth has been slowing. The latter pattern raises doubts about use of the EPS growth rates as proxies for future growth capacity.

Table 8.6 shows return on capital data for Wal-Mart.

TABLE 8.4   Sales Growth Data Used in Expectation Analysis

Sales Growth	
Most recent quarter	11.49%
Trailing 12 months	13.03%
5-year rate	15.67%

TABLE 8.5   EPS Growth Data Used in Expectation Analysis

EPS Growth	
Most recent quarter	23.87%
Trailing 12 months	19.27%
5-year rate	17.46%

Return on capital is, of course, a key indicator of growth capacity. Return on investment is the core measure of business performance. But return on equity shows that Wal-Mart has been skillful in using debt leverage to boost returns. Meanwhile, the lower return on assets figures shows the extent to which the company's business requires it to tie up capital in less productive short-term uses (a fact of life in Wal-Mart's industry).

From this point, we have considerable flexibility in deciding how to combine these numbers into a growth capacity measure. At one extreme, we can simply eyeball the figures and use discretion to determine growth capacity. At the other extreme, we can adopt a rigid always-followed policy of mathematically combining them. We might, for example, average all the data items. Or we might take a weighted average giving greater emphasis to certain data points.

For purposes of this example, I'll adopt an in-between approach. I'll drop the EPS growth figures. Because they are so much higher than the sales growth record, I do not feel comfortable in assuming EPS can continue to indefinitely grow at the pace seen in recent years. Then, I'll compute the average of all the other numbers (sales growth and return on capital). That gives me a growth capacity measure of 14.32 percent.

Combining Growth Expectation and Growth Capacity

Table 8.7 contains our first answer to the expectation analysis. For all practical purposes, the price we pay for Wal-Mart shares seems in balance with what we get for our money. The expectation index of 1.04 is marginally better than the exact 1.00 point of neutrality.

Let's now push ahead for a more definitive answer.

TABLE 8.6 Return on Capital Data Used in Expectation Analysis

Return on Capital	
Return on assets—TTM	9.10%
Return on assets—5-year average	8.96%
Return on investment—TTM	13.87%
Return on investment—5-year average	13.58%
Return on equity—TTM	21.66%
Return on equity—5-year average	21.60%

TABLE 8.7 Expectation Index and Basic Components

Growth capacity	14.32
Growth expectation	13.82
Expectation Index	1.04

Recall, first, the impact of an earnings estimate cut, to $1.60 per share. It would change the growth expectation to 16.40 percent, well above the growth capacity. Even if we average the expectation numbers produced by the base case $1.79 earnings estimate (13.82 percent) and the conservative $1.60 a share estimate (16.40), we'd still wind up with an answer (15.11 percent) above the capacity assumption. We see that we do not have much of a margin for error regarding growth expectation.

Now, let's look more closely at growth capacity. We can start by checking the consensus long-term EPS growth forecast, which in the case of Wal-Mart is 13.84 percent. That's very close to the 13.82 number we calculated. So what we did initially is in line with the conclusions being reached by analysts.

Moving on, let's review Tables 8.3, 8.4, and 8.5. We understand that some of the sales growth deceleration we see is based on the economic weakness we were experiencing in late 2002. But remember, Wal-Mart is a big company. We have to consider that some deceleration may be resulting from life cycle issues. Note, too, the extent to which our initial calculation was impacted by returns on equity that were very high, not so much because of business performance but by use of debt financing. It's very easy for me to eyeball the data and adjust the growth capacity assumption to 13 percent, 12 percent, or even 11 percent. Table 8.8 shows the original and some alternative scenarios.

Frankly, I'm finding it way too easy to push the expectation index below the 1.00 threshold. And I haven't come up with comfortable alternative assumptions that bring the index above 1.04. So all things considered, I'm going to say Wal-Mart does not pass muster under the expectation analysis.

Summary Here's a simple summary of the procedure for calculating the growth expectation.

TABLE 8.8 Alternative Expectation Index Scenarios

	Original Scenario	Alternative Scenarios				
Growth capacity	14.32	14.32	14.32	13.00	12.00	11.00	12.00
Growth expectation	13.82	16.40	15.11	13.82	13.82	13.82	16.40
Expectation Index	1.04	0.87	0.95	0.94	0.87	0.80	0.73

1. *Select a time horizon.* A simple decision—I suggest five years.

2. *Determine how much annual return is needed to justify investment.* Set *RF* equal to a Treasury rate, set *RP* equal to .045, and use the current beta if reasonable (if not, set beta equal to 1.00).

3. *Calculate the predicted price five years hence.* This is a simple mathematical calculation.

4. *Establish the future P/E for the market.* Compute as 1 divided by *RF*.

5. *Establish the future P/E for the stock.* Eyeball based on current data, using the ratio of company TTM P/E to S&P 500 TTM P/E as a starting point.

6. *Compute the level of EPS the company will have to show to justify the future stock price.* This is a simple mathematical calculation.

7. *Choose a present or near-term base level of EPS to use as a starting point for the growth expectation.* Consider using the consensus estimate of current-year EPS.

8. *Compute the expected growth rate.* This is a simple mathematical calculation.

Next, estimate the growth capacity. You can make this as simple (eyeballing data) or complex (computing weighted averages) as you wish.

Combine growth expectation and growth capacity to calculate the expectation index. This is a simple division calculation: growth capacity divided by growth expectation.

Finally, evaluate the result. An index above 1.00 is bullish. An index below 1.00 is bearish. If the index is very close to 1.00, evaluate the margin for error and how confident you are in your assumptions.

Appendix B to this chapter will simplify the task even further by showing you how to build an expectations index spreadsheet template.

APPENDIX A TO CHAPTER 8

Comprehensive Listings of Useful Share Price Valuation Metrics

These are the valuation metrics likely to be most readily available on well-known financial Internet sites. As always, be sure to double-check the glossaries provided by whatever data source(s) you use, since in many instances there is more than one reasonable way to calculate a ratio. The definitions provided here are based on the Multex approach.

The "Availability" columns in Tables 8A.1 through 8A.6 provide a general

TABLE 8A.1   Price/Earnings Metrics

		Availability	
Metric	**Formula for Calculation**	**# Item**	**Comp.**
P/E TTM	Share price divided by TTM EPS	✔	✔
Forward P/E	Share price divided by estimate of EPS for current or next fiscal year	✔	
P/E 5-year high	Highest of the last 50 monthly TTM P/E calculations	✔	✔
P/E 5-year low	Lowest of the last 50 monthly TTM P/E calculations	✔	✔
Forward PEG	Forward P/E divided by projected growth rate	✔	
Historic PEG	TTM P/E divided by historic (TTM, 3-year, or 5-year) EPS growth rate	✔	
Mixed PEG	TTM P/E divided by projected EPS growth rate	✔	

TABLE 8A.2   P/E Alternatives

		Availability	
Metric	**Formula for Calculation**	**# Item**	**Comp.**
P/Sales TTM	Share price divided by TTM sales per share	✔	✔
P/EBIT TTM	Share price divided by per-share TTM earnings before interest and taxes		
P/EBITDA TTM	Share price divided by per-share TTM earnings before interest, taxes, depreciation, and amortization		
P/cash flow TTM	Share price divided by TTM cash flow (net income plus depreciation and amortization minus preferred dividends) per share	✔	✔
P/free cash flow TTM	Share price divided by TTM free cash flow (cash from operations minus dividends and capital spending) per share	✔	✔

TABLE 8A.3   Income

		Availability	
Metric	**Formula for Calculation**	**# Item**	**Comp.**
Yield	Dividend per share divided by share price	✔	✔
Dividend growth rate	Average annual growth rate of dividend per share, usually over past three or five years	✔	✔
Payout ratio	Dividend paid divided by net income; usually a TTM figure but can sometimes be presented as a multiyear average	✔	✔

TABLE 8A.4 General Assets

Metric	Formula for Calculation	Availability	
		# Item	Comp.
P/book value	MRQ book value (common equity; the full shareholder equity account minus preferred equity) divided by number of shares	✔	✔
P/tangible book value	MRQ tangible book value (book value minus goodwill and other intangible assets) divided by the number of shares	✔	✔

TABLE 8A.5 Liquid Assets

Metric	Formula for Calculation	Availability	
		# Item	Comp.
P/working capital	Share price divided by per-share working capital (MRQ current assets minus MRQ current liabilities)		
P/net working capital	Share price divided by per-share net working capital (MRQ current assets minus MRQ total liabilities)		
P/cash	Share price divided by per-share MRQ cash (including cash equivalents)		
P/net cash	Share price divided by per-share MRQ net cash (cash and equivalents minus total debt)		
P/net cash: first alternative	Share price divided by per-share first alternative net cash (MRQ cash and equivalents minus MRQ total liabilities)		
P/net cash: second alternative	Share price divided by per-share second alternative net cash (MRQ cash and equivalents minus MRQ current liabilities)		

TABLE 8A.6 Return on Enterprise Value

Metric	Formula for Calculation	Availability	
		# Item	Comp.
Return on enterprise value	Income measure divided by enterprise value *Income measures*: Operating profit, EBIT, or EBITDA *Enterprise value:* Market capitalization of common stock (price times number of shares) plus preferred equity plus total debt minus cash and cash equivalents		

sense of how accessible the information is likely to be as of this writing. However, Internet sites are constantly changing, so it is possible that your experience may be different (and hopefully, better, as many site revisions tend to be improvements over what was available before).

- If the "# Item" column is checked, it means the item is likely to be widely available as a precalculated numeric ratio.
- If the "Comp." column is checked, it means the item is likely to be widely available along with comparisons to relevant benchmarks such as industry, sector, and/or market averages.
- If neither column is checked, it means you will most likely have to calculate the ratio on your own based on readily available data.

Note: In all tables, TTM means trailing 12 months, and MRQ refers to most recent quarter.

APPENDIX B TO CHAPTER 8

An Expectation Analysis Spreadsheet Template

This template consists of two separate sheets, both of which can be held in the same Excel file. (Check the Excel help features for instructions on using more than one spreadsheet in the same file.)

The first sheet, illustrated in the first three figures, calculates the expectation index the conventional way, based on an estimate of how much future EPS growth is needed to justify the current stock price.

An alternative method is provided in the second sheet, illustrated in the last three figures. It is designed for use with companies that are losing money or whose levels of profitability are too skimpy to allow for calculation of meaningful P/E ratios.

In all cases except for the expectation index itself at the top of the spreadsheet, boldface type signifies a need for the user to input a number. Regular typeface is for labels and cells that contain formulas.

Each sheet/version consists of five parts.

1. A header (rows 1 and 2) providing reference information (ticker, date of analysis) and the value of the expectation index as calculated in the spreadsheet. I suggest you set this area off in such a way that it is always visible regardless of how far down the spreadsheet you scroll. Do this by placing the cursor in Cell A3 and making the following menu choices:

Windows → Freeze Panes

2. An area labeled "General Expectations" where you input your assumptions about market rates of return, risk premium, beta, the current stock price, and your starting point for EPS or sales per share.

3. An area labeled "Interim Calculations" which makes visible to you the results of some of your assumptions. If any of these strike you as unreasonable, you can go back to other areas of the spreadsheet and revise pertinent inputs. In each spreadsheet, one cell contains an arrow indicator spotlighting the most crucial interim calculation—the EPS or sales per share growth rate estimated by the spreadsheet as being required to justify the current stock price. Make especially sure you check this number to see if it passes the common-sense test.

4. A work area to help you create a growth capacity estimate.

5. A work area to help you predict a future relative (to the market) P/E or price/sales ratio.

USING EPS TO CALCULATE THE EXPECTATION INDEX

This set of calculations is done on the worksheet named "Exp. Index based on EPS." The sheet starts with Figure 8B.1.

The Header

As shown in Figure 8B.1, Cells A1 and A2 contain the ticker and date, respectively. These are strictly for your convenience.

The expectation index itself is in Cell D2. It uses the following formula:

$$=(D20/D27)$$

We will see that D20 houses the growth capacity estimate and D27 holds the expected annual EPS growth rate.

General Expectations

As illustrated in Figure 8B.1, key components of this section are contained in Column D.

Cell D5 Here, you input the time period (number of years from the present) you wish to use for your analysis.

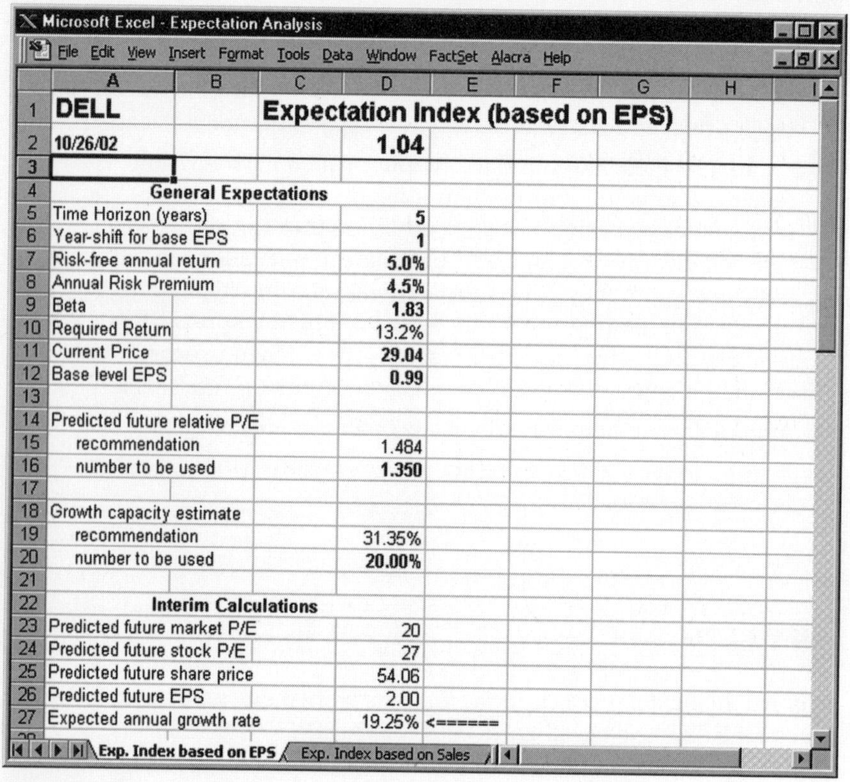

	A	B	C	D	E
1	DELL		Expectation Index (based on EPS)		
2	10/26/02			1.04	
3					
4	General Expectations				
5	Time Horizon (years)			5	
6	Year-shift for base EPS			1	
7	Risk-free annual return			5.0%	
8	Annual Risk Premium			4.5%	
9	Beta			1.83	
10	Required Return			13.2%	
11	Current Price			29.04	
12	Base level EPS			0.99	
13					
14	Predicted future relative P/E				
15	recommendation			1.484	
16	number to be used			1.350	
17					
18	Growth capacity estimate				
19	recommendation			31.35%	
20	number to be used			20.00%	
21					
22	Interim Calculations				
23	Predicted future market P/E			20	
24	Predicted future stock P/E			27	
25	Predicted future share price			54.06	
26	Predicted future EPS			2.00	
27	Expected annual growth rate			19.25%	<======

FIGURE 8B.1 The Header, General Expectations, and Interim Calculations Sections of the Expectation Index (Based on EPS) Spreadsheet

Cell D6 In this cell, you indicate adjustments based on whether you use for base EPS an estimate of the current year's results (in which case the year shift would be "0"), an estimate of the next year's results (in which case the year shift would be "1"), or even the trailing 12 month results (in which case the year shift would be "–1"). If there are unusual developments that cause you to believe none of these results are representative of the company's normal earning power, you might want to use as your base EPS from two years ago, in which case the year shift would be "–2."

You have some discretion here. If the trailing 12 month data ends with the third quarter of the company's fiscal year, you might use an adjustment of "–2" for the last completed annual period, and "–3" if you want to go back two years. Such softness in counting would displease academicians, but let's remember what we're doing: looking into the future. "False precision" is not a virtue!

Cell D7   Input your assumption of the risk-free annual rate of return, usually a rate on a U.S. government security.

Cell D8   Input your assumption for annual risk premium (the excess return stocks in general must show in order to make it worthwhile to switch out of risk-free securities).

Cell D9   Input the stock's beta. If the historical number, the only thing you'll find, seems inconsistent with common sense, feel free to modify the assumption. If in doubt, use 1.00 (an assumption that the stock will be as volatile as the overall market).

Cell D10   A formula giving you the return you require to make this stock worthwhile. It is calculated based on the capital asset pricing model using the following spreadsheet formula:

$$=D7+(D8*D9)$$

Cell D11   Input the current price of the stock.

Cell D12   Input the base EPS, the starting point for your growth calculation. This is a matter of taste. I usually prefer to use the consensus estimate for the next fiscal year. (Hence I usually place a "1" value in Cell D6.)

Cell D15   This is a recommended number you can use as a predicted relative future P/E. It is picked up from one of the spreadsheet's work areas using the following formula:

$$=G62$$

Cell D16   Input your prediction for what the stock's relative (to the market) P/E will be in the future. Often, you will choose to simply copy the number that appears in Cell D15. But this is not mandatory.

Cell D19   This is a recommended number you can use as a growth capacity estimate. It is picked up from one of the spreadsheet's work areas using the following formula:

$$=B52$$

Cell D20   Input your estimate of growth capacity. Often, you will choose to simply copy the number that appears in Cell D19. But this is not mandatory.

Interim Calculations

As illustrated in Figure 8B.1, key components of this section are contained in Column D. This entire area consists of numbers calculated from data elsewhere on the spreadsheet. Here are the formulas.

Cell D23   This is an estimate of the future (based on the number of years you specify in Cell D5) P/E for the overall market. It is the reciprocal of the risk-free rate. Here is the formula.

$$=1/D7$$

Needless to say, you are free to change this should you so desire.

Cell D24   This is the predicted future P/E for the stock, based on the predicted market P/E and the prediction you made of what the stock's relative P/E will be. Here is the formula.

$$=D23*D16$$

Cell D25   This is the predicted future price of the stock based on the following formula:

$$=((1+(D7+(D8*D9)))\wedge(D5))*D11$$

It is based on the required annual return, as estimated through the capital asset pricing model and the number of years you specified in Cell D5. ($\wedge$ means "to the power of.")

Cell D26   This is the level of future EPS that is required to justify the predicted future stock price. Here is the formula.

$$=D25/D24$$

This is the core of our method, where we turned the math around. We don't plug our assumption of earnings into the model. We determined how much share price growth we required and made an assumption about P/E (as per the work area of the spreadsheet). Then, we divide predicted share price by predicted P/E to calculate the level of EPS that must be achieved.

Cell D27   This is the annual rate of growth from the base EPS to predicted future EPS. Here is the formula.

$$=((D26/D12)\wedge(1/(D5-D6)))-1$$

Note the time period portion of the formula: D5 minus D6. If you use a five-year time horizon and estimated current EPS as the base, the time period will be five years (5 minus 0). If you use the estimate of next year's EPS as a base, the growth rate will cover four (5 minus 1) years. If you use EPS from two years ago as a base, you'll wind up with a seven (5 minus –2) year growth rate.

Growth Capacity Estimate

This section of the spreadsheet is illustrated in Figure 8B.2.

Most of your inputs are to Columns C and D. The data for Column C, and for the lone input to Column G, can be found on MultexInvestor.com and other web sites.

	A	B	C	D	E	F	G	H
1	**DELL**		**Expectation Index (based on EPS)**					
2	10/26/02			**1.04**				
29		Growth Capacity Estimate						
30			Actual	Weight	Weighted Value			
31	Sales Growth							
32		MRQ	11.14%	0	0			
33		TTM	-1.61%	0	0			
34		5 Yr. Avg.	32.06%	1	0.3206			
35	EPS Growth							
36		MRQ	0.00%	0	0			
37		TTM	29.38%	1	0.2938			
38		5 Yr. Avg.	21.87%	1	0.2187			
39	Return on Assets						Payout Ratio	
40		TTM	13.69%	0	0		0.00%	
41		5 Yr. Avg.	19.46%	0	0			
42							Retention Rate	
43	Return on Investment						100.00%	
44		TTM	30.46%	1	0.3046			
45		5 Yr. Avg.	42.98%	1	0.4298		REMINDER	
46							Multiply raw	
47	Return on Equity						Returns on	
48		TTM	39.19%	0	0		Capital by	
49		5 Yr. Avg.	55.90%	0	0		Retention Rate	
50								
51	Total			5	1.5675			
52	Raw Result	31.35%						

FIGURE 8B.2 The Growth Capacity Estimate Section of the Expectation Index (Based on EPS) Spreadsheet

Cell C32   Input the company's year-to-year percentage sales growth achieved in the most recent quarter (MRQ).

Cell D32   Input the degree of importance (the weight) the MRQ sales growth should have in your estimate of growth capacity.

What we seek, here, is a weighted average. Conventionally, you would calculate the average of 12, 13, and 16 by adding the numbers (getting a total of 41) and then dividing by 3 (to get an average of 13.67). Strictly speaking, this is equivalent to a weighted average with each value being weighted equally. To compute a weighted average, (1) multiply each value by its numeric weight, (2) add up all the resulting "weighted values," (3) add up the sum of the weights, and (4) divide the total of all weighted values by the total of all weights.

Table 8B.1 shows how we would use this method to compute the average of 12, 13, and 16.

Compared to the conventional method (add 12, 13, and 16 and divide by 3), Table 8B.1 seems a bit convoluted. But it's a lot more flexible. It allows you to say some numbers are more important and should be counted more heavily than others. Table 8B.2 shows an alternative where the number 12 is given eight times the standard level of importance, while 13 is given half the standard weight.

TABLE 8B.1   Sample Weighted Average Calculation

Number	×	Weight	=	Product
12	×	1	=	12
13	×	1	=	13
16	×	1	=	16
Total		3		41

Weighted average: 41/3 = 13.67

TABLE 8B.2   Sample Weighted Average Calculation

Number	×	Weight	=	Product
12	×	8	=	96
13	×	0.5	=	6.5
16	×	1	=	16
Total		9.5		118.5

Weighted Average: 118.5/9.5 = 12.47

We will use this weighted average technique to estimate growth capacity and predicted relative P/E.

Cell E32   This is the formula:

$$=D32*C32$$

It is the weighted values based on Cell C32 (MRQ sales growth) times Cell D32 (the weight assigned to MRQ sales growth). Notice, in this example, that we assign a zero weight to MRQ Dell's MRQ sales growth. That's because I believe it is diminished by temporary cyclical factors and, hence, not reflective of the company's underlying long-term growth capacity.

Rows 33 through 49   The other boldface cells in Column C hold other data relevant to estimating the company's growth capacity. The boldface cells in Column D hold the weights we assign to each of those other data items. The formulas in Column E are similar to the one in Cell E32; for each row, we multiply the data item in Column D by the data item in Column C.

Cell G40   In this cell, input the company's divident payout ratio.

Cell G43   This is the formula:

$$=1-G40$$

It's the retention rate, the percentage of earnings retained by the corporation after payment of dividends to shareholders. Strictly speaking, the return on capital numbers input into Column C, rows 39 through 49 ought to be multiplied by the retention rate. In other words, if a company has a 12 percent TTM return on equity and pays out 30 percent of its earnings as dividends, enter 8.4 percent (12 percent × 30 percent) into Cell C48.

If you'd like, you can enter the raw return on capital figures elsewhere on the spreadsheet, say in Column I, and establish formulas to automatically adjust the returns in Column C. In other words, you might input TTM return on equity in Cell I48. In that case, you'd put the following formula in Cell C48:

$$=I48*G43$$

However, I prefer to refrain from carrying spreadsheet automation this far. Dividend payout ratios are highly discretionary. Hence I'd rather make thoughtful choices about how to adjust returns on capital to take them into account. For example, I might choose to assume the company will let the payout ratio fall in the future in order to retain more profit for reinvestment. So going back to the previous example, even though the historic payout ratio was 30 percent, I might opt to assume a 20 percent payout ratio in the future. In this case, the 12 percent TTM return on equity would be multiplied by a higher 80 percent retention rate. Admittedly, that would not reflect actual historic experience (where the retention rate was 70 percent). But multiplying by 80 percent would produce a return (9.6 percent) that better reflects the likely growth of the capital base and, hence, is more relevant to our need to assess forward-looking EPS growth capacity.

Cell D51   This is the formula:

$$=SUM(D32:D49)$$

It's where we add all the weights that will be used to compute the weighted average.

Cell E51   This is the formula:

$$=SUM(E32:E49)$$

It's where we add all the weighted values that will be used to compute the weighted average.

Cell B52   This is the formula:

$$=E51/D51$$

We divide the sum of the weighted values (E51) by the sum of the weights (D51) and wind up with the weighted average. This is the number picked up in Cell D19 as the recommended growth capacity estimate. We can accept it (and copy it into Cell D20) or modify it as we wish.

Predicted Relative P/E

This section of the spreadsheet is illustrated in Figure 8B.3.

Cell C56   Input your estimate of the stock's PEG ratio. You can choose to use a forward-looking or historic calculation.

	A	B	C	D	E	F	G	H	I

Microsoft Excel - Expectation Analysis

File Edit View Insert Format Tools Data Window FactSet Alacra Help

	A	B	C	D	E	F	G	H	I
1	**DELL**			**Expectation Index (based on EPS)**					
2	10/26/02			**1.04**					
53									
54				Predicted Relative P/E					
55			Company	S&P 500	Ratio	Weight	Weighted Value		
56	PEG Ratio		1.708	1.243	1.374	2	2.748		
57	P/E TTM		42.27	24.79	1.705	1	1.705		
58	P/E 5 Yr. High		105.71	49.26	2.146	0	0.000		
59	P/E 5 Yr Low		45.3	16.83	2.692	0	0.000		
60									
61					Totals	3	4.453		
62					Raw Result		1.484		
63									

Exp. Index based on EPS / Exp. Index based on Sales

FIGURE 8B.3 The Predicted Relative P/E Section of the Expectation Index (Based on EPS) Spreadsheet

Cell D56 Input an estimate of the S&P 500 PEG ratio. Use the same forward-looking or historic calculation method you use for the stock. Sometimes, you'll have to calculate the S&P 500 ratio on your own. You can do this using the Multex screeners. Create the following one-test screen:

SP500 = True

Create a report showing, for all S&P 500 companies, market capitalization as well as the P/E and growth rates you'd like to use. Download to Excel and then create a PEG ratio column consisting of P/E divided by growth rate. Then, compute a weighted average of all PEG ratios using as weights each company's market capitalization. Note, of course, that this is a rough approximation (some companies will have no meaningful PEG ratios, and not all companies will tabulate earnings estimates for the exact same fiscal periods).

If you'd rather not bother calculating a PEG ratio for the S&P 500, you can leave Cells C56 and D56 blank, and put a zero in Cell F56.

Cell E56 This is the relative (company to S&P 500) PEG ratio. It is calculated using the following formula.

=C56/D56

Cell F56   Input the weight you would like to assign to the relative PEG ratio.

Cell G56   This is the formula:

$$=E56*F56$$

We multiply Cell E56 (relative PEG ratio) times Cell F56 (the weight assigned to the relative PEG ratio).

Rows 57 through 59   The other boldface cells in Column C hold other data relevant to stock valuation. The boldface cells in Column D hold other data relevant to S&P 500 valuation. The formulas in Column E are similar to the one in Cell E56; for each row, we divide the stock valuation ratio in Column C by the S&P 500 valuation ratio in Column D. The boldface cells in Column F hold the weights we assign to each of those other relative valuation ratios. The formulas in Column G are similar to the one in Cell G56; for each row, we multiply the relative valuation ratio in Column E by the weight in Column F.

Cell F61   This is the formula:

$$=SUM(F56:F59)$$

It's where we add all the weights that will be used to compute the weighted average.

Cell G61   This is the formula:

$$=SUM(G56:G59)$$

It's where we add all the weighted values that will be used to compute the weighted average.

Cell G62   This is the formula:

$$=G61/F61$$

We divide the sum of the weighted values (G61) by the sum of the weights (F61) and wind up with the weighted average. This is the number picked up in Cell D16 as the recommendation for predicted future relative P/E. We can accept it (and copy it into Cell D15) or modify it as we wish.

USING SALES PER SHARE TO CALCULATE THE EXPECTATION INDEX

Many of the concepts used in this portion of the template are the same as those just discussed and will, therefore, be summarized briefly. Our main focus will be on portions of the spreadsheet that are unique to the use of sales per share in lieu of EPS.

Our sales-per-share approach is done on the worksheet named "Exp. Index based on Sales." The sheet starts with Figure 8B.4.

	A	B	C	D	E	F	G	H	I
1	**AMZN**		**Expectation Index (based on sales)**						
2	10/26/02			**1.32**					
3									
4		**General Expectations**							
5	Time Horizon (years)			5		Quarterly Sales (in millions)			
6	Year-shift for base sales per share			-1		4 qtrs. Ago		**1115.171**	
7	Risk-free annual return			5.0%		3 qtrs. Ago		**847.422**	
8	Annual Risk Premium			4.5%		2 qtrs. Ago		**805.605**	
9	Beta			2.77		latest qtr,		**851.299**	
10	Required Return			17.5%					
11	Current Price			19.3		TTM Sales		**3619.497**	
12	Base level sales per share			9.513		# shares (in millions)		**380.47**	
13	Current market P/E			**24.58**					
14	Current market Price/Sales			2.95					
15						TTM Sales per share		9.513	
16	Growth capacity estimate								
17	recommendation			**24.51%**					
18	number to be used			**24.51%**					
19									
20		**Interim Calculations**							
21	Current market P/S-to-P/E			0.120					
22	Predicted future Market P/S-to-P/E			**0.120**					
23									
24	Predicted future market P/E			20					
25	Predicted future market P/S			2.4					
26	Predicted future relative Price/Sales (P/S)								
27	recommendation			0.681					
28	number to be used			**0.681**					
29									
30	Predicted future stock P/S			1.6344					
31	Predicted future share price			43.16					
32	Predicted future Sales per share			26.41					
33	Expected annual growth rate			18.55%	<======				

FIGURE 8B.4 The Header, General Expectations, and Interim Calculations Sections of the Expectation Index (Based on Sales) Spreadsheet

The Header

The header is similar to what we saw in the EPS version. But the data cells we need to calculate the expectation index itself are in different locations. In this sheet, the formula in Cell D2 is based on the following formula:

$$=(D16/D33)$$

General Expectations

Note the area in Columns F, G, and H where we calculate sales per share.

Cells H6, H7, H8, and H9   Input quarterly company sales data. The formulas used here assume these numbers will be in millions. In the AMZN example, sales for the most recent quarter were $851,299,000. Expressed in millions, the number was 851.299.

Cell H11   This is the formula:

$$=SUM(H6:H9)$$

It's the sum of four quarterly sales figures. Usually, this will be the last four quarters (the TTM period). But if you like, you can use an older period (if you think the last four quarters are not representative of the company's underlying capabilities) or an estimate of future sales (if you have access to such data).

Cell H12   Input the number of common shares. Again, the formulas assume this number will be expressed in millions.

Cell H13   This is the formula:

$$=H11/H12$$

It's sales per share.

The rest of this section is similar to what we saw in the EPS version.

Cell D5   Input the time period you wish to use for your analysis.

Cell D6   Input adjustments based on whether you use, for base sales per share, a figure based on a noncurrent period. For trailing 12 month sales per share, which is the figure likely to be most readily available, I use a year shift of "–1."

Cell D7   Input your assumption of the risk-free annual rate of return.

Cell D8   Input your assumption for annual risk premium.

Cell D9   Input the stock's beta.

Cell D10   This cell contains the following formula that calculates the return you require to make this stock worthwhile.

$$=D7+(D8*D9)$$

Be especially attentive to this number. When you use sales per share to generate an expectation index, you are usually dealing with higher-risk situations (companies losing money or trading at nonmeaningful P/E ratios). Make sure the required return is high enough to compensate for this risk. If this is not accomplished through an unusually high beta, set the risk premium (in Cell D8) higher than you would for a normally profitable company.

Cell D11   Input the current price of the stock.

Cell D12   This is the formula:

$$=H15$$

It picks up the base sales per share, the starting point for your growth calculation.

Cell D13   Input the current S&P 500 TTM P/E ratio (you can find this on the MultexInvestor.com Ratio Comparison report for any stock).

Cell D14   Input the current S&P 500 TTM price/sales (P/S) ratio (you can find this on the MultexInvestor.com Ratio Comparison report for any stock).

Cell D17   This is a recommended number you can use as a growth capacity estimate. It is picked up from one of the spreadsheet's work areas using the following formula:

$$=E56$$

Cell D18   Input your growth capacity estimate. Often, you will choose to simply copy the number that appears in Cell D15. But this is not mandatory.

Interim Calculations

As illustrated in Figure 8B.4, key components of this section are also contained in Column D. This entire area consists mainly of numbers calculated from data elsewhere on the spreadsheet. Here are the formulas.

Cell D21   Calculate the market's current P/S-to-P/E ratio using the following formula:

$$=D14/D13$$

Cell D22   Input your assessment of the market's current P/S-to-P/E ratio. Unless you believe the data you input into Cells D13 and D14 are impacted by unusual developments, you should simply copy the number that appears in Cell D21.

Cell D24   This is an estimate of the future (based on the number of years you specify in Cell D5) P/E for the overall market. It is the reciprocal of the risk-free rate. Here is the formula.

$$=1/D7$$

Needless to say, you are free to change this should you so desire.

Cell D25   This is your prediction of the future market P/S ratio based on the future P/E multiplied by the estimated future P/S-to-P/E ratio. It is calculated based on the following formula:

$$=D24*D22$$

Cell D27   This is a recommended number you can use as a predicted relative future P/S. It is picked up from one of the spreadsheet's work areas using the following formula:

$$=H68$$

Cell D28   Input your prediction for what the stock's relative (to the market) P/S will be in the future. Often, you will choose to simply copy the number that appears in Cell D27. But this is not mandatory.

Cell D30   This is the predicted future P/S for the stock, based on the predicted market P/S and the prediction you made of what the stock's relative P/S will be. Here is the formula.

$$=D28*D25$$

Cell D31 This is the predicted future price of the stock based on the following formula:

=((1+(D7+(D8*D9)))^(D5))*D11

Cell D32 This is the level of future sales per share that is required to justify the predicted future stock price. Here is the formula.

=D31/D30

Cell D33 This is the annual rate of growth from the base sales per share to predicted future sales per share. Here is the formula.

=((D32/D12)^(1/(D5–D6)))–1

Growth Capacity Estimate

This section of the spreadsheet is illustrated in Figure 8B.5.

Microsoft Excel - Expectation Analysis

File Edit View Insert Format Tools Data Window FactSet Alacra Help

	A	B	C	D	E
1	**AMZN**		**Expectation Index (based on sales)**		
2	**10/26/02**			**1.32**	
35		**Growth Capacity Estimate**			
36			Actual	Weight	Weighted Value
37	Company Sales Growth				
38		MRQ	**33.17%**	1	0.3317
39		TTM	**21.48%**	1	0.2148
40		5 Yr. Avg.	**188.05%**	0	0
41	Industry Sales Growth				
42		MRQ	**19.49%**	1	0.1949
43		TTM	**18.33%**	1	0.1833
44		5 Yr. Avg.	**30.06%**	1	0.3006
45	Sector Sales Growth				
46		MRQ	**9.85%**	0	0
47		TTM	**9.07%**	0	0
48		5 Yr. Avg.	**19.70%**	0	0
49					
50	S&P 500 Sales Growth				
51		MRQ	**6.93%**	0	0
52		TTM	**2.23%**	0	0
53		5 Yr. Avg.	**11.52%**	0	0
54					
55	Total			5	1.2253
56	Raw Result				24.51%

Exp. Index based on EPS | **Exp. Index based on Sales**

FIGURE 8B.5 The Growth Capacity Estimate Section of the Expectation Index (Based on Sales) Spreadsheet

Conceptually, this is similar to the growth capacity section of the EPS sheet. We take a weighted average of the relevant data items. MultexInvestor.com Ratio Comparison reports provide all the company, industry, sector, and S&P 500 data you'll need. Usually, you'll give the heaviest weightings—in many cases, all the weightings—to the company data. Use the other information for reference if you question the extent to which the company's data reflects potential future results. Remember, too, that Cell D18 gives you another opportunity to add your subjective judgment to this analysis.

Data inputs go into Column C. Input your chosen weightings into Column D. In Column E, calculate weighted values for use in a weighted average computation. The weighted value in Cell E38 uses the following formula.

$$=D38*C38$$

Similar formulas are used for the other rows in Column E.

Cell D55   This is the formula:

$$=SUM(D38:D53)$$

Cell E55   This is the formula:

$$=SUM(E38:E53)$$

Cell E56   This is the formula:

$$=E55/D55$$

This is the weighted average. The number is picked up in Cell D15 as the recommended growth capacity estimate. We can accept it (and copy it into Cell D16) or modify it as we wish.

Predicted Relative Price/Sales

This section of the spreadsheet is illustrated in Figure 8B.6.

This area is similar to the Predicted Relative P/E section of the EPS version. Column D holds company valuation metric data, and Column E holds S&P 500 valuation data.

Column F contains formulas for calculating relative (company to S&P 500) valuation metrics. The formula for Cell F61 is:

$$=D61/E61$$

	A	B	C	D	E	F	G	H	I
1	**AMZN**			**Expectation Index (based on sales)**					
2	10/26/02			**1.32**					
58									
59			**Predicted Relative Price/Sales**						
60				Company	S&P 500	Ratio	Weight	Weighted Value	
61	Price/Sales TTM			2.03	**2.98**	0.681	1	0.681	
62	Price/Book TTM				**4.45**	0.000	0	0.000	
63	Price/Tangible Book TTM				**7.4**	0.000	0	0.000	
64	Price/Cash Flow TTM				**18.48**	0.000	0	0.000	
65	Price/Free Cash Flow TTM			470.73	**26.12**	18.022	0	0.000	
66									
67					Totals		1	0.681	
68					Raw Result			0.681	

Exp. Index based on EPS \ **Exp. Index based on Sales**

FIGURE 8B.6 The Predicted Relative Price/Sales Section of the Expectation Index (Based on Sales) Spreadsheet

Use similar formulas for rows 62 through 65.

Column G is where you input the weight that is to be given to each relative metric. Notice that there is only one ratio that relates to sales. The others deal with different valuation approaches. Often, you will wind up giving a full weighting (1) to the relative price/sales and zero to the others. The alternatives serve as general guidelines for cases where you suspect the present relative price/sales may not be reflective of what can be expected over a longer term. And, of course, Cell D28 offers you another opportunity to use your judgment regarding relative price/sales.

Column H contains formulas to calculate the products that will be used to compute a weighted average. The formula for Cell H61 is:

$$=F61*G61$$

Use similar formulas for rows 62 through 65.

Cell G67 This is the formula:

$$=SUM(G61:G65)$$

Cell H67 This is the formula:

$$=SUM(H61:H65)$$

Cell H68   This is the formula:

$$=H67/G67$$

This is the weighted average relative price/sales ratio. It's the number that is picked up in Cell D27 as the recommendation for predicted future relative price/sales. We can accept it (and copy it into Cell D28) or modify it as we wish.

Buy . . . the Best Value Connected Opportunities

## CHAPTER 9

Weighing
and
Balancing

C hapter 8, which explained how to analyze an individual stock, kept us hopping. We performed two separate analytic tasks, one focusing on the stock (the valuation metrics) and one focusing on the company itself. And as if that weren't enough, we performed an expectation analysis that linked the good-company and good-stock concepts.

It would be wonderful if all three tasks produced answers that point in the same direction—all three indicating the stock is attractive, or all three suggesting we should pass it by. But that will rarely happen. Usually, investment opportunities are a mixture of pro and con. Step 3 (Buy) provides a systematic framework for weighing and balancing the good and the bad in such a way as to help us arrive at a final buy-or-avoid decision.

The process, introduced in *Screening the Market*, starts with three Analysis Keys. These are yes/no questions designed to reveal the strengths and weaknesses of a specific opportunity. The keys will produce one of eight possible combinations of yes-or-no answers. We assign each one to a Decision Path. The paths are ranked from best to worst. The stocks on the top path are our strongest buys. Conversely, stock on the lowest path are the ones we should eliminate first. The middle paths are structured in such a way as to help us prioritize among the stocks that have both pros and cons.

We will use the same Analysis Keys and Decision Paths here for the value connection. Below, we'll explain each key and path, and see how value connection considerations influence the way we respond to each key. In Chapter 10, we'll examine real-life case studies to see how they can be put into action in conjunction with Step 2 (Analyze).

THE ANALYSIS KEYS

Answering the Analysis Keys, a set of three yes/no questions, brings us face-to-face with all aspects of the value connection style and helps us organize our thoughts in a way that will make it easy to determine how attractive, or unattractive, a stock is. Here are the keys.

Analysis Key 1: Does the Situation Truly Fit the Theme You Originally Chose?

In *Screening the Market*, Analysis Key 1 was presented as a tool that, in effect, asks us if the stock complies with the spirit of the law as we established it when we chose our primary investment theme. We know the stock complies with the letter of the law merely by the fact that the stock makes the screen. But screening is an inexact process, and stocks that are really of no interest to us can pass muster based on data oddities.

An obvious example relating to the value connection would be a stock that has a low P/E ratio because earnings are inflated by an item that cannot be expected to recur in the future. A stock like this would fail to meet the spirit of the law. In such a case, we would say "no" in response to Analysis Key 1.

Another way Analysis Key 1 comes into play is the fact that no screen can include every possible test that might appeal to us, lest we drive our result set down to zero. Analysis Key 1 is where we take an opportunity to consider a gray zone for tests that did not find their way into our screen. For example, we may implement a middle-market strategy by using a screen that contains the core P/E tests (the growth comparison and the peer comparison). But, although we're somewhat interested in asset-oriented metrics such as price/book value or price/net working capital, we do not include these in our screen because we would rather add tests based on a well-articulated secondary or alternative theme. We'll look at the asset-oriented valuation metrics in Step 2 (Analyze). We won't necessarily apply the sort of rigid test we might create in a screen, such as a requirement that price/book value be less than the industry average. But we will take note of whether this ratio is at least close to the industry average. If the ratio exceeds the average by too much (a subjective judgment), we might answer "no" to Analysis Key 1.

The latter example raises an important wrinkle to the value connection version of Analysis Key 1: Answer "yes" or "no" based on the good-company or good-stock theme as a whole (whichever one was used as a primary theme). Chapter 8 assumed, for the sake of convenience, that the good-stock theme was primary, that we look at the price tag before we examine the merchandise. In such a case, the answer to Key 1 should be based on the entire good-stock analysis as described in Chapter 8. If we reverse the sequence by looking at the merchandise first (i.e., good-company concepts serve as our primary screening theme), the answer to Key 1 should depend on whether the company passes muster based on the good-company assessment described in Chapter 8.

Analysis Key 2: Are There Factors Different from Your Original Theme That You Consider Positive?

The classic function of Analysis Key 2 is to allow for the occurrence of the "happy accident." This happens when we find an investment idea that offers something we did not originally expect to get.

An example would be near-term earnings momentum. This theme is very popular on the Street today. But it's not a core aspect of the value connection. As we saw in Chapters 5 and 8, our method focuses much more heavily on fundamental indicators that aim for a longer-term, more sustainable view of company prospects. We'll certainly monitor current developments to see if there's reason to suspect historic trends may experience a sustained alteration for better or worse. But we will maintain perspective. We won't hastily buy and sell based on every news-related development.

But suppose Company A, which we uncover in our screens, just happens to have an attractive near-term earnings story, one that would appeal to many other investors. We weren't looking for it. But now that we found it, we ought not ignore it. Suppose in terms of basic value connection parameters, Company A is equivalent to Company B. If Company A also features the positive earnings story, but Company B does not, we'll favor A, since its shares will appeal to a wider pool of investors. As discussed in Chapter 7 in connection with alternative screening themes, that's an important consideration in a world where prices are established through supply and demand.

Analysis Key 2, as presented in *Screening the Market*, focuses our attention on any additional positives that may be present. It does not matter how alien to our style they may be. All we ask is whether they exist.

In the context of the value connection, we add an important wrinkle. We consistently spoke in terms of two themes, good-stock (check the price tag) and good-company (check the merchandise), and suggested that one be selected as the primary theme. Analysis Key 1 addressed the issue of whether that primary theme is deemed satisfied by the Step 2 analytic process. Now we shift gears. Analysis Key 2 includes attention to the theme that was deemed secondary.

In other words, if good-stock tests are our primary focal point, the answer to Analysis Key 1 will be based on whether the good-stock issues stood up to scrutiny in Step 2 (Analyze). And a satisfactory showing under good-company factors will determine whether we say "yes" or "no" to Analysis Key 2. Conversely, if our primary theme is based on good-company tests, we'll use those to drive our response to Analysis Key 1, and use good-stock tests to determine how we respond to Key 2.

Let's suppose Company A came to our attention through a good-company screen, and passed the check-the-merchandise phase of Step 2 (Analyze) with flying colors. And as per the example, our analysis uncovers an appealing near-term earnings momentum story. Suppose, however, that the stock has run up based on the earnings expectations and that it fails the check-the-price phase of the analysis. Should we say "yes" to Key 2 based on the presence of the earnings story? Or should we say "no" based on Company A's failure to meet good-stock tests?.

A purist would adopt the latter approach and refuse to answer "yes" to Key 2 if the second half of the good-company/good-stock story comes up short. I suggest an in-between approach. If the second half of the story (in this example, the good-stock angle) is satisfactory, that alone produces a "yes" for Key 2. But if the second half of the story falters, one might still say "yes" to Key 2 if an alternative investment theme is present.

Put another way, the secondary value-connection theme can help Key 2 if present, but need not automatically hurt it if absent. We can afford to relax this way because of Key 3, which is discussed next.

Analysis Key 3: Is This Investment Opportunity Free of Any Factors That You Consider Negative?

The first thing we notice here is the roundabout wording of the question. We're not asking if there are any negative factors present. We're asking if the situation is free from negative factors. The purpose of the grammatical juggling is to produce, for Key 3, a "yes" answer if the situation is such that we are inclined to invest, and a "no" answer if the situation points us away from buying. When actually working with the Decision Paths, it's a lot easier to quickly recognize that a set of answers reading "yes-yes-yes" is very bullish. If the most bullish response pattern was expressed as "yes-yes-no," we'd constantly wind up double-checking the strict phrasing of the keys, something we'd get tired of very quickly.

Whether or not a particular set of circumstances is negative within the meaning of Key 3 depends on one's individual investment style. An example that is recurring often as of this writing (late 2002) is the economy. Frequently, companies have issued earnings-related announcements to the effect that business conditions remain disappointing and many investors fear the economy will not recover much, if at all, in the months ahead.

Is this the sort of concern that should prompt us to answer "no" to Key 3 (i.e., saying the situation is not free of factors we deem negative)? An investor pursuing a theme based on growth or momentum would clearly be troubled by this and give a negative answer to Key 3. But the same would not necessarily hold true for others. If we decide, up front, that we are not going to attempt to time turns in the business cycle, we may well choose to accept cyclical risk and refuse to allow this issue to drive us away from a stock we otherwise like. In that case, we'd answer "yes" to Key 3 (i.e., say the situation is free of factors we deemed negative).

There is one special wrinkle to Key 3 that is geared toward the value connection method. That's based on the third part of the analysis we did in Chapter 8, the part where we used the expectation analysis to decide if we're getting our money's worth. In the context of the value connection, we should always answer "no" to Key 3 if the expectation analysis leaves us feeling uncomfortable.

Summary of the Analysis Keys

Here's a recap on how the analysis keys should be applied in the context of the value connection method.

Shoppers Who Check the Price First   Some implemented Step 1 (Find) by using one of three strategies that gave primacy to good-stock considerations. In Chapter 7, we referred to these as the S-C (Stock-Company), S-C-A (Stock-Company-Alternative), or S-A (Stock-Alternative) blueprints. Presumably, those who used one of these approaches implemented Step 2 (Analyze) by checking the price tag first, then checking the merchandise, and finishing up with a determination of whether we're getting our money's worth. This group should approach the analysis keys as follows.

- **Analysis Key 1: Does the Situation Truly Fit the Theme You Originally Chose?** Focus, here, on whether you come away satisfied from your review of valuation metrics. If so, answer this key "yes." If not, answer this key "no."
- **Analysis Key 2: Are There Factors Different from Your Original Theme That You Consider Positive?** Focus, here, on all themes other than valuation metrics. If your analysis of company fundamentals leaves you satisfied, answer "yes" to this key regardless of whether any additional positives are present. If you are unimpressed with the fundamentals, answer "yes" or "no" depending on whether any other positives are present.

- **Analysis Key 3: Is This Investment Opportunity Free of Any Factors That You Consider Negative?** If you are uncomfortable with what you saw in the expectation analysis, answer "no" to this key. If the expectation analysis proved satisfactory, answer "yes" or "no" depending on whether any other negatives are present.

Shoppers Who Check the Merchandise First Others implemented Step 1 (Find) by using one of three strategies that gave primacy to good-company considerations. In Chapter 7, we referred to these as the C-S (Company-Stock), C-S-A (Company-Stock-Alternative), or C-A (Company-Alternative) blueprints. Presumably, those who used one of these approaches implemented Step 2 (Analyze) by checking the merchandise first, then checking the price tag, and winding up with an assessment of whether we're getting our money's worth. This group should approach the analysis keys as follows.

- **Analysis Key 1: Does the Situation Truly Fit the Theme You Originally Chose?** Focus, here, on whether you come away satisfied from your review of company fundamentals. If so, answer this key "yes." If not, answer this key "no."
- **Analysis Key 2: Are There Factors Different from Your Original Theme That You Consider Positive?** Focus, here, on all themes other than company fundamentals. If your analysis of stock valuation metrics leaves you satisfied, answer "yes" to this key regardless of whether any additional positives are present. If you are unimpressed with the valuation, answer "yes" or "no" depending on whether any other positives are present.
- **Analysis Key 3: Is This Investment Opportunity Free of Any Factors That You Consider Negative?** If you are uncomfortable with what you saw in the expectation analysis, answer "no" to this key. If the expectation analysis proved satisfactory, answer "yes" or "no" depending on whether any other negatives are present.

THE DECISION PATHS

Whether our primary theme was company oriented or stock oriented, we've now reached the same place. We all have a three-way combination of yes-or-no answers for each stock under consideration.

The Decision Paths will take us to the finish line, a decision to buy a stock or pass on it. It's easy to recognize that a "yes-yes-yes" set of answers is the best combination and that these stocks are the most buyable. We can also recognize that a "no-no-no" set of answers is the worst combination and these stocks should be avoided. The paths provide the most help in dealing with the six combinations in between these two extremes.

Table 9.1 shows the eight possible Decision Paths, each corresponding to a particular three-way yes-or-no pattern. The paths are ranked from best (A) to worst (H).

Let's look now at each Decision Path. Then, in Chapter 10, we'll see how they apply in real-life situations.

Decision Path A: Yes-Yes-Yes

Here are the qualities a stock must exhibit to be on Decision Path A.

- **Analysis Key 1—Yes:** The situation meets our primary theme (good-company or good-stock).
- **Analysis Key 2—Yes:** The situation offers attractive investment features apart from the primary theme. These positives may or may not include the secondary theme (good-company or good-stock, the one we didn't make primary).
- **Analysis Key 3—Yes:** The expectation analysis was satisfactory, and the situation is free from any other factors that we regard as negative.

This is the best of all possible worlds. Our primary theme is satisfied. And we've got something extra. The "yes" answer to Key 2 tells us the stock has appeal based on at least one additional theme. That means the stock is also being identified and considered attractive by others whose areas of emphasis differ from ours. That increases the likelihood of strong

TABLE 9.1 The Decision Paths

Decision Path	Analysis Key 1 (Primary Theme)	Analysis Key 2 (Secondary and/or Alternative Themes)	Analysis Key 3 (Expectation Analysis and/or Other Themes)
A	Yes	Yes	Yes
B	Yes	No	Yes
C	No	Yes	Yes
D	Yes	Yes	No
	The Neutral Zone		
E	No	No	Yes
F	Yes	No	No
G	No	Yes	No
H	No	No	No

demand for the stock. And to top it off, the "yes" answer to Key 3 tells us the stock is free of things we might regard as negative baggage.

This does not guarantee we have a winner. The themes that appeal to us may be about to turn cold in the market. But we do know that this particular stock is a strong example of the sort investors who follow our style ought to be buying. If we have conviction about our chosen theme, it's appropriate to be patient with stocks like this.

Decision Path B: Yes-No-Yes

Here are the qualities a stock must exhibit to be on Decision Path B.

- **Analysis Key 1—Yes:** The situation meets our primary theme (good-company or good-stock).
- **Analysis Key 2—No:** The situation does not measure up under our secondary theme (good-company or good-stock, the one we didn't make primary), nor does it offer any other positives.
- **Analysis Key 3—Yes:** The expectation analysis was satisfactory, and the situation is free from any other factors that we regard as negative.

Many who don't follow the sort of analytic process set forth in Step 2 (Analyze) think this is the best of all possible worlds. The stocks meet their requirements and don't carry any negative baggage. Many aren't in the habit of checking for additional positive factors. Accordingly, we can feel comfortable buying Path B stocks. The only time we'd pass on them is if other stocks under consideration wind up on Path A.

Decision Path C: No-Yes-Yes

Here are the qualities a stock must exhibit to be on Decision Path C.

- **Analysis Key 1—No:** The situation does not really meet our primary theme (good-company or good-stock).
- **Analysis Key 2—Yes:** The situation offers attractive investment features apart from the primary theme. These positives may or may not include the secondary theme (good-company or good-stock, the one we didn't make primary).
- **Analysis Key 3—Yes:** The expectation analysis was satisfactory, and the situation is free from any other factors that we regard as negative.

Path C is represents the "happy accident." The bad news is that stock does not satisfy our original goals. The good news is that it is appealing on some other basis and carries no noteworthy negative baggage. Note that our "yes" answer to Key 3 tells us the stock did pass muster on the expectation analysis. In other words, valuation metrics may not have been quite good enough to satisfy our primary good-stock theme, but they may be good enough to get by given that the company fared very well under a secondary good-company theme, or perhaps an alternative theme like growth. Among Path C stocks, it is reasonable to give priority to companies that draw a "yes" for Key 2 because of a good-company or good-stock secondary theme.

Decision Path D: Yes-Yes-No

Here are the qualities a stock must exhibit to be on Decision Path D.

- **Analysis Key 1—Yes:** The situation meets our primary theme (good-company or good-stock).
- **Analysis Key 2—Yes:** The situation offers attractive investment features apart from the primary theme. These positives may or may not include the secondary theme (good-company or good-stock, the one we didn't make primary).
- **Analysis Key 3—No:** The situation is not free of negative factors; this may or may not include an unsatisfactory conclusion from the expectation analysis.

There is some baggage here. But we hesitate to eliminate the stock, because it satisfies our primary theme as well as at least one other style.

Realistically, we're going to encounter Path D stocks very frequently because in the real world we'll find many reasons to worry and say "no" to Key 3. So we could wind up with unrealistically slim pickings if we discard every situation on this path.

Considering that in the value connection we imposed certain method-specific requirements on Keys 2 and 3, we are able to prioritize among Path D stocks. I suggest doing so as follows:

Top Path D Priority (Path D1) The stock satisfies the expectation analysis (i.e., the baggage arises from a different issue). Also, the "yes" to Key 2 comes from the stock's having at least satisfied a secondary value connection theme (if there's also an unrelated alternative theme, so much the better).

Second Path D Priority (Path D2) The stock satisfies the expectation analysis (i.e., the baggage arises from a different issue). Also, the "yes" to Key 2 comes from the stock's having satisfied an alternative theme unrelated to the value connection.

Third Path D Priority (Path D3)　　The stock does not satisfy the expectation analysis. But it got a "yes" to Key 2 because it came up favorably when analyzed on the basis of a secondary value connection theme. This is a bit dicey. Why would we consider buying a stock that falters under the expectation analysis (i.e., for which we cannot comfortably say we're getting our money's worth)? Many may, justifiably, pass on any such stock. But others may elect to base a decision on the favorable outcomes of the here-and-now good-company and good-stock inquiries, and relax regarding the future-oriented expectation analysis. Our willingness to do this should depend on how easily we can come up with plausible new assumptions that will enable the stock to pass expectation analysis.

Lowest Path D Priority (Path D4)　　The stock does not satisfy the expectation analysis. Also, it falters under the secondary value connection theme. In such cases, the "yes" to Key 2 would be the result of an unrelated alternative theme. This is probably too far a stretch. Unless we have a gut feeling about the stock, we're better off crossing it off the list and moving on to something else.

The Neutral Zone

We saw that Paths A and B represent stocks that are clearly excellent investment opportunities. The stocks on Paths C and D are not quite as powerful, and we might even decide, as a matter of course, to avoid the low-priority Path D4 stocks. But for the most part, the stocks that are on Paths C and D are acceptable. Just going through Step 1 (Find) and Step 2 (Analyze), followed by the Step (3) process that enables us to place a stock on Path C or Path D positions us to know exactly why we're buying a particular stock at this time and at this price. That's a lot more than many investors can claim (even if it's a matter of openly acknowledging that the numbers for a Path D4 stock don't quite add up and that we're going forward on a hunch).

The remaining paths present a different story. The best we find here is Path E, consisting of stocks that offer nothing positive, but also carry no negatives. Many investors wind up doing a lot worse than that. But after all the systematic work we've done up till now, we have to hope we can find better ways to invest our money. And if we really can't do that, it may be preferable to stay out of the market until the right kinds of opportunities present themselves.

In fact, Paths E, F, G, and H are more relevant to Step 4 (Sell), a topic we'll tackle in Chapter 11. It will wind up using the same principles we will have discussed up to that point and culminating in eight Reconsideration

Paths that are analogous to the eight Decision Paths being discussed here. Table 9.2 summarizes the two path hierarchies.

Accordingly, we'll present only a general sense of Paths E through H, and defer closer consideration to Chapter 11.

Decision Path E: No-No-Yes

Here are the qualities a stock must exhibit to be on Decision Path E.

- **Analysis Key 1—No:** The situation does not really meet our primary theme (good-company or good-stock).
- **Analysis Key 2—No:** The situation does not measure up under our secondary theme (good-company or good-stock, the one we didn't make primary), nor does it offer any other positives.
- **Analysis Key 3—Yes:** The expectation analysis was satisfactory, and the situation is free from any other factors that we regard as negative.

As noted, the best we can say about these stocks is that although they offer nothing attractive, they feature no distinct negatives. That is hardly a glowing recommendation. We'll aim higher than that.

Decision Path F: Yes-No-No

Here are the qualities a stock must exhibit to be on Decision Path F.

- **Analysis Key 1—Yes:** The situation meets our primary theme (good-company or good-stock).

TABLE 9.2 The Decision Paths in Context

Decision Paths		Reconsideration Paths	
A			A
B	Buy Zone	Hold Zone	B
C			C
D			D
E			E
F	Avoid Zone	Sell Zone	F
G			G
H			H

- **Analysis Key 2—No:** The situation does not measure up under our secondary theme (good-company or good-stock, the one we didn't make primary), nor does it offer any other positives.
- **Analysis Key 3—No:** The situation is not free of negative factors; this may or may not include an unsatisfactory conclusion from the expectation analysis.

This path is a matter of perspective. On the plus side, the stock meets our primary theme. On the down side, there are negative factors to wrestle with. If stock screens didn't exist and we had a hard time finding interesting investment opportunities, it would be tempting to invest in some of these stocks. We might well say a satisfactory showing under the primary theme more than offsets the negatives. But screens do exist, and we can do better. If we're going to expose ourselves to stocks that garner a "no" to Key 3, we should demand extra compensation: stocks that go beyond our primary theme and also satisfy a secondary and/or alternative theme (as is required for Path D).

Decision Path G: No-Yes-No

Here are the qualities a stock must exhibit to be on Decision Path G.

- **Analysis Key 1—No:** The situation does not really meet our primary theme (good-company or good-stock).
- **Analysis Key 2—Yes:** The situation offers attractive investment features apart from the primary theme. These positives may or may not include the secondary theme (good-company or good-stock, the one we didn't make primary).
- **Analysis Key 3—No:** The situation is not free of negative factors; this may or may not include an unsatisfactory conclusion from the expectation analysis.

Now we're dropping far down on the food chain. As with Path F, we balance negative baggage against the fact that the stock satisfies at least one investment theme. The problem is that here, the themes that work don't match the one we really wanted.

Decision Path H: No-No-No

Here are the qualities a stock must exhibit to be on Decision Path H.

- **Analysis Key 1—No:** The situation does not really meet our primary theme (good-company or good-stock).

- **Analysis Key 2—No:** The situation does not measure up under our secondary theme (good-company or good-stock, the one we didn't make primary), nor does it offer any other positives.
- **Analysis Key 3—No:** The situation is not free of negative factors; this may or may not include an unsatisfactory conclusion from the expectation analysis.

This is as bad as it gets. The stock fails to satisfy any discernible investment theme and features some negative baggage. There is no rational reason to consider buying a stock like this.

## CHAPTER 10

Buying Value Connection Stocks: Case Studies

U p till this point, the process of finding, analyzing, and buying value connection stocks has been explained in depth. It's now time to shift our style from telling to showing. We'll see here how these principles apply in the real world.

To do this, we'll turn the clock back and look at three stocks that appeared on some of my value connection screens on April 20, 2000, four that appeared on April 20, 2001, and two that appeared on April 23, 2002. (All the screens referred to here are described in the appendix to Chapter 7.) We'll analyze the companies based on information you would have seen the date the company appeared in the screen. I mean that literally. The data won't even be adjusted for stock splits that occurred later on. Expectation indexes will be computed using the spreadsheet template described in Appendix B to Chapter 8. The one gray area will involve assumptions for the risk-free rate of return and the general equity risk premium. Regardless of what was actually happening at the time to interest rates, we'll assume in all cases the vantage point of an investor who was making a long-term assumption of a 5 percent risk-free rate and a 4 to 5 percent equity risk premium. We'll also answer the Analysis Keys and consider the Decision Paths as of that time. Then, Chapter 11 will explain Step 4 (Sell), and in Chapter 12 we'll revisit the stocks deemed buys and decide whether they should continue to be held or sold.

As you go through these buy-or-avoid case studies, note the following points.

- **Let the numbers carry the story.** The text presented for each case may strike you as sparse relative to analyses you've seen in other places. I deliberately refrain from overwhelming you with facts, which you can easily look up in the descriptive material presented on Multex-Investor.com and other financial web sites, or on company web pages (or SEC filings). The goal here is to spotlight the extent to which the data can drive you directly to the most critical portions of the analysis.

- **Recognize how the qualitative considerations can be combined with a quantitative story.** As data oriented as this style is, we most definitely do not reduce our analysis to mere number crunching. Note how easy it is to recognize when raw historic data cannot be relied on to predict what the future will hold.

- **See how "buzz" can be constructively used.** These case studies show you how ideas you pick up from analysts and the financial media can enhance your efforts. The key is to use this material in Step 2 (Analyze) rather than Step 1 (Find).

- **Notice the variety of conclusions that can be drawn.** I do not attempt to exhaustively recite every conclusion that can be drawn from the numbers. Instead, I include a very extensive collection of data tables so you can scan the numbers on your own and see what, if any, other ideas you get. Feel free to disagree with my conclusions. After all, every transaction has both a buyer and a seller. But note that if you do disagree, how easy it is to identify points of difference. (That's important. Such recognition helps you monitor your investments and make prompt changes if necessary.)

- **Observe how the art and science of analysis interact**, especially in the expectation analysis. Observe how easily I can examine the situations under modified assumptions and the way gut-level comfort factors (including margin of error) interact with hard numbers.

For stocks called to our attention through screens having a primary good-stock theme, Step 2 (Analyze) will be implemented first by checking the price and then moving on to an examination of the "merchandise" and the expectation analysis, consistent with the sequence presented in Chapter 8. For stocks that come to light via screens whose primary themes are based on good-company concepts, we'll start Step 2 (Analyze) by examining the merchandise. Then we'll address the price-related metrics and the expectation analysis.

The data tables presented in the "Checking the Merchandise" sections are generally consistent with the MultexInvestor.com format. In all cases, the following abbreviations are used.

TTM   Trailing 12 months
MRQ   Most recent quarter

NA   Data is not available
NM   Data is not meaningful
E   Estimated

AAON INCORPORATED (AAON)

On April 20, 2000, AAON, a micro-cap (market capitalization: $121.75 million) manufacturer of commercial rooftop air conditioners, appeared in my Growth at a Reasonable Price screen.

Checking the Price

Applying Chapter 8's shopping analogy, AAON seems to be a middle-market play. Table 10.1 assesses the price based on metrics relevant to that style.

Clearly, AAON shares are dirt cheap. The P/E and PEG ratios are well below benchmark averages. In fact, the PEG ratio is shockingly low; we'll make a point of looking more closely at that when we assess the credibility of growth projections. The asset-based valuation metrics seem neutral. Net cash is not meaningful (there's more debt than cash) and the stock is priced well above net working capital per share. Hence the market does not seem to be anticipating any quick windfall (e.g., buyout). AAON's price/book ratio is low, but that's characteristic of its industry (miscellaneous capital goods).

TABLE 10.1   AAON Incorporated, Valuation Metrics Data as of April 20, 2000

	Company	Industry	S&P 500
P/E based on estimate of next year's EPS	8.62	18.11	34.56
Projected long-term EPS growth rate	38.00	15.32	18.56
PEG ratio	0.23	1.18	1.86
P/E (TTM)	12.01	17.58	37.01
P/E—5-year high	26.79	31.56	48.78
P/E—5-year low	7.49	13.02	16.55
Yield	—	—	—
5-year dividend growth	—	—	—
Yield + growth	—	—	—
Payout ratio (TTM)	—	—	—
Price/book value (TTM)	3.82	3.25	9.75
MRQ price/net working capital	10.64	NM	NM
MRQ price/net cash (cash minus total debt)	NM	NM	19.97
Return on enterprise value (%)	12.8	9.9	4.1

Checking the Merchandise

Getting Acquainted   The news flow was generally uneventful, and the stock had scant analyst coverage. The few who covered AAON commented favorably on the company's fundamentals, but wondered about how future prospects would fare if the giant mass merchants like Wal-Mart, Target, and Home Depot slowed the pace of expansion. This was a major customer group for AAON, so a slowdown in new store openings could conceivably impact AAON's sales growth. The bullish side of the argument was that AAON was gaining market share among its major customer group and was branching out into new markets such as office buildings, schools, and factories.

Exploring the Fundamentals   We start this phase by examining estimates and considering their credibility. Right away, Table 10.2 tells us that the estimates we see for AAON are based on the work of only a single analyst. That reduces our willingness to read much into the long-term growth projection (which was 38 percent) and the resulting low PEG ratio, especially since it seems out of line when compared with historic sales growth rates, as shown in Table 10.2.

The TTM and three-year EPS growth rates are, indeed, impressive, but they are not matched by the gains in sales. Margin improvement, the engine for such EPS growth, cannot be expected to persist indefinitely. Hence those numbers cannot lend credence to the 38 percent long-term growth projection.

Meanwhile, the near-term projections, depicted in Table 10.3, seem more plausible in light of the company's recent performance. Indeed, they are arguably conservative; the projected year-to-year percentage EPS growth for the next two quarters assumes moderation due to fears that near-term interest rate hikes will hamper commercial construction.

We note, though, that the expectations are less moderate than they re-

TABLE 10.2   AAON Incorporated, Growth Rates Data as of April 20, 2000

Growth Rates: Historic and Long-Term Forecast				
	TTM	**3 Years**	**5 Years**	**10 Years**
Sales (%)	16.93	26.77	9.99	15.12
EPS (%)	88.20	65.86	13.13	44.06
	Consensus	**Low**	**High**	**# Analysts**
Long-term (%)	38.00	38.00	38.00	1

TABLE 10.3 AAON Incorporated, EPS Trends Data as of April 20, 2000

EPS Trends: Historic and Forecasted

	3 Years Ago	2 Years Ago	1 Year Ago	Current Year
1st quarter	0.110	0.170	0.270	0.490
2nd quarter	0.120	0.200	0.380	.41E
3rd quarter	0.080	0.220	0.430	.47E
4th quarter	0.170	0.230	0.410	.57E
Total	0.480	0.820	1.490	1.94E
	Consensus	**Low**	**High**	**# Analysts**
Estimate current quarter	0.41	0.41	0.41	1
Estimate next quarter	0.47	0.47	0.47	1
Estimate current year	1.94	1.94	1.94	1
Estimate next year	2.35	2.35	2.35	1

cently were. Table 10.4 shows that all numbers were revised upward within the past month.

Moving on to examine general sentiment, we note that even though AAON is tiny and covered by just one analyst, the stock has been a very strong performer relative to the market and its industry peers, as shown in Table 10.5. This is an example of a hot stock within a lackluster industry.

Moving on to examine fundamental footprints of success, we start with growth comparisons, shown in Table 10.6. The EPS growth comparisons seem to favor AAON, but we noted earlier that this is probably not sustainable. Comparing growth in sales and capital spending, we see that AAON has certainly not been scrimping in the latter. The capital spending growth rate is more than double the rate of sales growth.

Tables 10.7, 10.8, 10.9, and 10.10 show the margin, efficiency, return, and financial strength comparisons. Table 10.7 starts in a manner some

TABLE 10.4 AAON Incorporated, EPS Estimates Data as of April 20, 2000

EPS Estimates: Recent Revisions

	Current	4 Weeks Ago	8 Weeks Ago	13 Weeks Ago
Estimate current quarter	0.41	0.32	0.32	0.32
Estimate next quarter	0.47	0.44	0.44	0.44
Estimate current year	1.94	1.70	1.70	1.70
Estimate next year	2.35	—	—	—

TABLE 10.5 AAON Incorporated, Price Data as of April 20, 2000

Price Performance

Period	Actual (%)	Vs. S&P 500 (%)	Company Rank in Industry*	Industry Rank*
4 weeks	18.5	24.6	93	37
13 weeks	45.2	48.1	86	28
26 weeks	51.8	37.2	76	32
52 weeks	81.9	70.2	82	47
YTD	43.9	48.1	77	35

*Ranks are percentiles: 0 is worst, 99 is best.

TABLE 10.6 AAON Incorporated, Growth Data as of April 20, 2000

Growth Comparisons (%)

	Company	Industry
Sales MRQ vs. quarter 1 year ago	14.86	22.86
Sales TTM vs. TTM 1 year ago	16.93	26.71
Sales—5-year growth rate	9.99	16.57
EPS MRQ vs. quarter 1 year ago	81.48	9.51
EPS TTM vs. TTM 1 year ago	88.20	9.69
EPS—5-year growth rate	13.13	11.85
Capital spending—5-year growth	23.00	16.24

TABLE 10.7 AAON Incorporated, Margin Data as of April 20, 2000

Margin Comparisons (%)

	Company	Industry
Gross margin—TTM	23.99	32.32
Gross margin—5-year average	18.44	31.75
EBITD margin—TTM	14.87	12.83
EBITD margin—5-year average	11.46	12.76
Operating margin—TTM	12.48	10.23
Operating margin—5-year average	8.44	9.81
Pretax margin—TTM	12.22	10.30
Pretax margin—5-year average	7.08	9.16
Net margin—TTM	8.25	5.32
Net margin—5-year average	4.51	5.41
Tax rate—TTM	38.00	38.50
Tax rate—5-year average	35.48	37.50

TABLE 10.8 AAON Incorporated, Efficiency Data as of April 20, 2000

Efficiency Comparisons

	Company	Industry
Revenue/employee—TTM	144,808	201,548
Net income/employee—TTM	11,949	13,160
Receivable turnover—TTM	6.35	7.01
Inventory turnover—TTM	8.67	6.16
Asset turnover—TTM	2.41	1.30

TABLE 10.9 AAON Incorporated, Return Data as of April 20, 2000

Return Comparisons (%)

	Company	Industry
Return on assets—TTM	19.85	7.60
Return on assets—5-year average	9.84	7.97
Return on investment—TTM	28.81	10.21
Return on investment—5-year average	13.76	10.78
Return on equity—TTM	36.42	16.82
Return on equity—5-year average	21.17	16.95

TABLE 10.10 AAON Incorporated, Financial Strength Data as of April 20, 2000

Financial Strength

	Company	Industry
Quick ratio MRQ	1.24	1.08
Current ratio MRQ	2.12	2.00
Long-term debt/equity MRQ	0.20	0.54
Total debt/equity MRQ	0.21	0.67
Interest coverage TTM	27.83	12.09

might interpret as disappointing. It shows that AAON's gross margins are below average. But recall from Chapter 5 that this calculation depends on company decisions regarding classification of expenses as direct and indirect. We can bypass such considerations if we focus on operating margins, which incorporate all basic business expenses, however they are classified. Here, we see that AAON is above average for both time periods. We note, too, that AAON's time-series margin comparisons (TTM versus

five-year averages) are impressive, in contrast to the more modest showing for the industry as a whole.

Table 10.8 shows that AAON's revenue per employee is below average,
as is income per employee. But the latter is very close to the industry average, a nice feat considering AAON's small size and, presumably, disec-
onomies of scale. The company's receivables turnover is below par;
presumably, tiny AAON can't pound the table and demand that Home Depot pay up today, as opposed to next week. But AAON's data suggests that
its customers pay quickly enough to enable it to function properly. Meanwhile, AAON's inventory and asset turnover are above average.

Table 10.9 shows the inevitable combination of good margins and
good asset turnover: strong returns on capital. AAON looks good in all
company-industry comparisons, and over time has been improving while
the industry has been cool.

Finally, Table 10.10 shows the financial strength comparisons. The
company and industry are about equal in terms of liquidity (current and
quick) ratios, but AAON's debt burden is lighter.

Finishing Touches Examination of the financial statements in a search
for anything that may have fallen through the cracks raises no red flags.

Getting Our Money's Worth

Table 10.11 summarizes the results of our expectation analysis. To arrive at
a predicted relative P/E for the growth expectation, I averaged the relative

TABLE 10.11 AAON Incorporated, Analysis as of
April 20, 2000

Expectation Analysis	
Time horizon (years)	5.0
Assumed risk-free return (annual %)	5.0
Assumed equity risk premium (annual %)	4.5
Beta	1.07
Current share price	20.69
Base-level EPS	2.35
Predicted future relative stock P/E	0.442
Predicted future market P/E	20.0
Predicted future stock P/E	8.84
Predicted future share price	33.04
Predicted future EPS	3.74
Expected annual EPS growth rate (%)	12.30
Estimated growth capacity (%)	15.90
Expectation index	1.29

(company-to-S&P 500) P/Es for the TTM period, the five-year high, and the five-year low. I believe the relative PEG ratio (a mere 0.124) is excessively low. Indeed, the prospect of a better relative valuation is at the heart of our interest in the stock. On the whole, we see that AAON's present stock price is reasonable if the company can earn $2.35 a share one year hence (or assumed base-level EPS) and post annual EPS gains of 12.30 percent or better in years two through five. In estimating growth capacity we used all the sales growth figures shown in Table 10.7 and only the five-year EPS growth figure; the TTM and MRQ numbers are obviously not representative of a sustainable growth rate for AAON. As to the return on capital in Table 10.10, we eliminated the return on equity data from the calculation.

The Analysis Keys

1. **Does the situation truly fit the theme you originally chose?** We found AAON on a good-stock screen (Growth at a Reasonable Price). We take this stock's PEG ratio with a grain of salt because of the very high growth projection supplied by only one analyst. But that's not enough to defeat our overall sense that the stock is reasonably priced. I'll answer this key "yes."

2. **Are there factors different from your original theme that you consider positive?** The core company fundamentals are impressive. I'll answer this key "yes."

3. **Is this investment opportunity free of any factors that you consider negative?** The expectation analysis gets us off to a good start with an index of 1.29, well above the 1.00 threshold of neutrality. A modest change in the relative P/E assumption, raising it from 0.442 to 0.50, cuts the growth target to 8.89 percent and boosts the expectation index to 1.78. Hence we have lots of margin for error if we are inclined to wonder about the sustainability of the historic growth rates we used to calculate growth capacity. But as good as this and the other numbers are, I can't quite shake loose my concern that skeptics are correct when they point to AAON's dependence on one market segment (large retailers) and near-term cyclical risk (back in early 2000, the investment community was wondering if or when rising interest rates would stifle the general economy). If a company is to depend on a single market segment, mass merchants aren't a bad group. Even if they run out of opportunities for their large store formats, they might enter smaller markets with smaller "footprints." That, too, could mean orders for air-conditioning equipment from AAON. And there is the company's effort to increase sales to other kinds of customers. But these aren't sure things. I'm going to answer this key "no."

The Decision Path

The yes-yes-no answer pattern we get for the AAON Analysis Keys corresponds to Decision Path D, the lowest round of the buying zone.

Chapter 9 reminded us that we're going to find ourselves on this path very often, since investors tend to worry a lot and often answer "no" to Analysis Key 3. Among the many Path D stocks we'll find, Chapter 9 tells us that situations such as AAON are the highest priority (Path D1). That's because our "yes" answer to Key 2 is based on solid value connection (in this case, good-company) principles, and because the "no" response to Key 3 is based on something other than a failure to pass the expectation analysis.

So on the whole, although AAON is not the best stock we'll find, it would have been a reasonable buy on April 20, 2000.

ORACLE CORPORATION (ORCL)

On April 20, 2000, new-economy superstar ORCL appeared on my Strong Return on Investment screen, which in retrospect turned out to be one of my best good-company screens. At the time, we didn't even have to look at data to know that ORCL was a very high-priced stock. All we needed to do to know that was be aware of what was going on in the market. But if William Miller could purchase Amazon.com for his value fund, who knows? Maybe ORCL, too, is worth the money. Let's see.

Checking the Merchandise

Getting Acquainted   Back in early 2000, this vendor of database software and information management services was widely regarded as a potential winner in the emergence of new-economy technology. Earnings were soaring. So was the stock. People talked much about future visions. The main point of skepticism related to competition with Microsoft.

One detail worth noting is that in the latest quarter, ORCL's EPS included a nonrecurring $0.08-a-share gain. So had the TTM P/E been calculated based on normalized EPS, it would have been even higher than the astronomical level (110.64) we'll see later in Table 10.18.

Exploring the Fundamentals   New-economy stocks like ORCL were investments in the future, or so the Street assumed. Skipping the visionary rhetoric, that boils down to growth, and lots of it. Tables 10.12 and 10.13 get us right to the heart of the matter. The top of Table 10.12 is generally supportive of the consensus projection of a 25.56 percent future long-term

TABLE 10.12 Oracle Corporation, Growth Rates Data as of April 20, 2000

Growth Rates: Historic and Long-Term Forecast

	TTM	3 Years	5 Years	10 Years
Sales (%)	16.91	27.86	34.56	31.51
EPS (%)	63.26	29.57	37.57	32.04
	Consensus	**Low**	**High**	**# Analysts**
Long-term (%)	25.56	15.00	35.00	18

TABLE 10.13 Oracle Corporation, Growth Data as of April 20, 2000

Growth Comparisons (%)

	Company	Industry
Sales MRQ vs. quarter 1 year ago	17.82	36.99
Sales TTM vs. TTM 1 year ago	16.91	41.67
Sales—5-year growth rate	34.56	42.85
EPS MRQ vs. quarter 1 year ago	160.20	61.04
EPS TTM vs. TTM 1 year ago	63.27	45.31
EPS—5-year growth rate	35.57	43.40
Capital spending—5-year growth	5.62	33.11

EPS growth rate for ORCL. We recognize that MRQ and TTM EPS growth rates are boosted by a nonrecurring gain. But the 25.56 percent target seems in line with longer-term numbers.

But it's not a slam dunk. Life cycle considerations force us to wonder how long any company can maintain such an above-normal pace. In the TTM period, the pace of sales growth already dipped below 20 percent. And we see in Table 10.13 that company-to-industry comparisons do not favor ORCL.

There's another thing that's especially troubling. The bottom part of Table 10.12 shows that the range on the 25.56 percent consensus growth projection is especially wide, ranging from a low of 15 percent to a high of 35 percent. We note that there are 18 analysts in the picture here. That, in and of itself, is neutral. But it becomes disturbing when we consider it in relation to Table 10.14.

Here are some "takeaways" from Tables 10.12, 10.13, and 10.14 that trouble me.

- The high-low range on the upcoming quarterly estimates is wide, but tolerable. But the ranges on the annual estimates are disconcerting.

TABLE 10.14   Oracle Corporation, EPS Trends Data as of April 20, 2000

EPS Trends: Historic and Forecasted

	3 Years Ago	2 Years Ago	1 Year Ago	Current Year
1st quarter	.037	.003	.065	.087
2nd quarter	.060	.063	.095	.130
3rd quarter	.057	.073	.100	.250*
4th quarter	.120	.137	.180	.25E
Total	.274	.276	.440	.62E
	Consensus	**Low**	**High**	**# Analysts**
Estimate current quarter	.25	.22	.28	25
Estimate next quarter	.11	.09	.12	14
Estimate current year	.62	.70	.55	32
Estimate next year	.79	.69	.90	30

*Includes 0.08 in nonrecurring gains.

- The number of analysts issuing quarterly estimates is significantly lower than the number issuing full-year estimates. This is very odd, because one would think an analyst publishing an annual estimate would have also forecasted the quarters (indeed, the annual is usually the sum of the four quarterly estimates).
- The number of analysts publishing long-term forecasts is significantly lower than the number who publish annual estimates.

My confidence in the 25.56 percent projection is now dashed. Erratic trends in range and number of analysts issuing forecasts leads me to wonder how many analysts are simply pulling numbers out of thin air. I suppose I could read individual analyst reports and make judgments regarding which analysts are better at defending their projections. But that may not be relevant. A high-priced stock like this could prove vulnerable if investors lose confidence in earnings estimates. If things later go wrong, investors will not take the trouble to think back about whether the earlier estimates were thoughtfully conceived.

Another red flag is raised by Tables 10.15 and 10.16, which contain sentiment-oriented data presentations. Table 10.15 shows that analysts have been getting more bullish in recent weeks. Frankly, I'm worried about an increasingly bullish analyst rating profile occurring at a time when projections seem to be all over the landscape. (Those who looked at data like this back in early 2000 were way ahead of journalists and politicians in wondering about why analysts were rating stocks as they were!) Meanwhile, Table 10.16 shows that ORCL stock had already started to

TABLE 10.15 Oracle Corporation, Analyst Data as of April 20, 2000

Analyst Ratings

	Current	4 Weeks Ago	8 Weeks Ago	13 Weeks Ago
1—Buy	17	16	15	14
2—Outperform	9	11	14	14
3—Hold	3	3	2	3
4—Underperform	0	0	0	0
5—Sell	0	0	0	0
Average rating	1.52	1.57	1.58	1.65

TABLE 10.16 Oracle Corporation, Price Data as of April 20, 2000

Price Performance

Period	Actual (%)	Vs. S&P 500 (%)	Company Rank in Industry*	Industry Rank*
4 weeks	−15.8	−11.4	87	1
13 weeks	24.0	26.5	81	20
26 weeks	216.5	185.9	86	92
52 weeks	487.0	449.4	93	76
YTD	26.4	30.1	75	23

*Ranks are percentiles: 0 is worst, 99 is best.

cool, not so much because anyone was looking closely at the company (its stature within the software and programming industry remained quite high) but because the industry itself went from very hot to very cold.

Switching gears, Table 10.17 shows that ORCL does have fundamental footprints worthy of respect. We recall that there was a nonrecurring gain in the most recent quarter. That impacts the TTM numbers, but not enough to override our general conclusion that ORCL's capital utilization is quite strong. We might be further impressed if we examine more fundamental data. But I'm not going to bother. In the stock market, where our fortunes are tied to the interaction of supply and demand, it doesn't help for ORCL to be a legitimately good company if those who bid for and offer shares are confused, as appears to be the case here.

Finishing Touches Review of the financial statements shows that ORCL has been buying back shares. That's probably contributing to the company's high returns on capital. On the one hand, that's disappointing; we wish the high returns were entirely the result of a superprofitable

TABLE 10.17   Oracle Corporation, Return Data as of April 20, 2000

Return Comparisons (%)

	Company	Industry
Return on assets—TTM	28.39	11.40
Return on assets—5-year average	19.75	14.06
Return on investment—TTM	46.60	18.16
Return on investment—5-year average	34.48	23.78
Return on equity—TTM	53.34	21.46
Return on equity—5-year average	38.49	28.28

business. But on the other hand, it's good to see an executive team choosing to shrink its capital base, rather than put the resources to bad use in ventures that don't produce suitable returns.

Checking the Price

The screen is not specifically targeted toward upscale candidates. But considering the way ORCL shares had been behaving (trading at $70.81 within an $11.28 to $90.00 52-week high-low range and fetching a superhigh P/E), we can recognize right away that we need to assess this high-priced merchandise on that basis. Table 10.18 shows the upscale valuation metrics that were visible on April 20, 2000.

The whole industry is richly valued, but the metrics for ORCL shares were above the sky-high industry norms; the premium is especially noticeable in ORCL's very high PEG ratio. Interestingly, though, ORCL's projected growth rate is below the industry average. This most certainly does not alleviate our aforementioned worries.

TABLE 10.18   Oracle Corporation, Valuation Metrics Data as of April 20, 2000

	Company	Industry	S&P 500
P/E based on estimate of next year's EPS	93.91	83.54	34.56
Projected long-term EPS growth rate	25.56	32.19	18.56
PEG ratio	3.67	2.59	1.86
P/E (TTM)	110.64	46.20	37.01
P/E—5-year high	161.62	84.16	48.78
P/E—5-year low	24.43	28.54	16.55
Price/sales (TTM)	21.82	24.15	7.70
Price/free cash flow (TTM)	98.08	63.80	49.25
Price/cash flow (TTM)	91.61	53.64	27.42

Getting Our Money's Worth

Table 10.19 summarizes the results of our expectation analysis. The predicted relative P/E is based on an average of all the P/E components on the expectation analysis template. For the growth capacity estimate, we eliminated only the TTM and MRQ EPS growth rates, the ones most heavily influenced by the nonrecurring gain.

The 0.77 expectation index is very low. If we raise the predicted relative P/E to 3.00, the index is 0.97, still below the 1.00 neutrality threshold. If we also raise the growth capacity number to 26.5, a bit ahead of the consensus prediction, we can just get to 1.00.

The Analysis Keys

1. **Does the situation truly fit the theme you originally chose?** We found ORCL on a good-company screen (Strong Return on Investment). ROI is, indeed, strong. But our discomfort with the expectations, coupled with the presence of a nonrecurring gain and the fact that growth is not special compared to industry peers, removes a lot of the luster I expect from a true good-company investment. I'll answer this key "no."

2. **Are there factors different from your original theme that you consider positive?** I am not satisfied with the share price valuation metrics. The stock is valued richly relative to growth prospects and

TABLE 10.19 Oracle Corporation, Analysis as of April 20, 2000

Expectation Analysis	
Time horizon (years)	5
Assumed risk-free return (annual %)	5.0
Assumed equity risk premium (annual %)	4.5
Beta	1.40
Current share price	70.81
Base-level EPS	0.79
Predicted future relative stock P/E	2.438
Predicted future market P/E	20.0
Predicted future stock P/E	48.8
Predicted future share price	120.94
Predicted future EPS	2.48
Expected annual EPS growth rate (%)	33.11
Estimated growth capacity (%)	25.50
Expectation index	0.77

the peer group. And I see no alternative theme that gives me comfort. So my response to this key is "no."

3. **Is this investment opportunity free of any factors that you consider negative?** ORCL fails the expectation analysis. My initial assumptions produced an unacceptable index of 0.77. I was able to get the index up to a neutral position. But frankly, the assumptions I had to make to do that are imprudently generous. So I'll answer this key "no."

The Decision Path

The no-no-no answer pattern we get for the ORCL Analysis Keys corresponds to Decision Path H, which is at the bottom of the selling zone.

Today, we can look back and say, in retrospect, that stocks like ORCL should have been avoided in early 2000. This bearishness is not based on 20/20 hindsight. We just saw how any investor who turned away from the bubble-era gossip and hoopla and looked at readily available data in a disciplined manner could have concluded that ORCL, priced at about $70, should have been avoided.

BEBE STORES (BEBE)

Shares of BEBE, a retail chain featuring stylish apparel for (mainly younger) women, got pounded in early 2000, after the company hit a rough patch in terms of same-store sales growth. On April 20, 2000, it was priced at $9.69, toward the bottom of a 52-week $8.75 to $42.13 range. At that time, it showed up on my Contrarian Opportunities screen, which has a strong good-company primary theme.

Checking the Merchandise

Getting Acquainted   The chain had garnered a nice measure of respect in the marketplace for the appeal of its apparel and the efficiency of its operation. But investors reacted badly to the announcement that the vice president in charge of merchandising left the company. Things got worse for the stock when subsequent sales data seemed to confirm the bears' fears. In February 2000, year-to-year comparable store sales barely rose at all (up 0.2 percent) and in March they fell 10.1 percent. April was likewise looking bad; comps were expected to be down almost as much as in March. This compared poorly to year-ago growth above 20 percent. The problem was described as inadequate inventory, resulting from the transition in merchandising management.

It's hard to say what, if anything, the market thought of the fact that this micro-cap company (capitalization: $236.98 million) was 90 percent owned by insiders. The float, at 2.4 million shares, was small and probably added to price volatility.

Exploring the Fundamentals One thing is obvious from Tables 10.20, 10.21, and 10.22. Up until the departure of the merchandising executive, BEBE could lay claim to being a legitimate growth story. Table 10.20 shows that its sales and EPS gains beat the daylights out of a generally strong retail apparel industry, and the deceleration we see is reasonable in light of life cycle considerations.

TABLE 10.20 Bebe Stores, Growth Data as of April 20, 2000

Growth Comparisons (%)		
	Company	Industry
Sales MRQ vs. quarter 1 year ago	31.54	18.88
Sales TTM vs. TTM 1 year ago	35.86	18.74
Sales—5-year growth rate	43.93	18.60
EPS MRQ vs. quarter 1 year ago	30.69	25.58
EPS TTM vs. TTM 1 year ago	41.13	18.65
EPS—5-year growth rate	79.71	28.35
Capital spending—5-year growth	16.88	21.51

TABLE 10.21 Bebe Stores, EPS Trends Data as of April 20, 2000

EPS Trends: Historic and Forecasted				
	3 Years Ago	2 Years Ago	1 Year Ago	Current Year
1st quarter	−0.010	0.160	0.210	0.300
2nd quarter	0.110	0.230	0.380	0.490
3rd quarter	0.050	0.140	0.210	0.21E
4th quarter	0.080	0.200	0.300	0.32E
Total	0.230	0.730	1.100	1.32E
	Consensus	Low	High	# Analysts
Estimate current quarter	.21	.19	.22	5
Estimate next quarter	.32	.31	.34	5
Estimate current year	1.32	1.30	1.35	6
Estimate next year	1.59	1.55	1.62	6

TABLE 10.22   Bebe Stores, Growth Rates Data as of April 20, 2000

Growth Rates: Historic and Long-Term Forecast

	TTM	3 Years	5 Years	10 Years
Sales (%)	35.86	41.17	43.92	NA
EPS (%)	41.13	469.12	79.71	NA
	Consensus	**Low**	**High**	**# Analysts**
Long-term (%)	19.50	18.00	20.00	4

Table 10.21 is especially intriguing. Considering how negative the recent rhetoric surrounding BEBE had become and how badly the stock got hit, we might have legitimately expected to see estimates all over the place, as we did for ORCL. But that's not the case. The range is quite reasonable. And note the EPS estimate for the upcoming third fiscal quarter. BEBE isn't expected to fall over a cliff. The predicted year-to-year trend is flat.

Realistically, life cycle considerations suggest we ought not expect the company to continue to deliver the sort of growth rates we see for various historic periods in the top portion on Table 10.22. But look at the expectations at the bottom of the table. The analysts have already factored lifecycle issues into their projections. And the high-to-low range is not wide.

Tables 10.23 and 10.24 make for an interesting juxtaposition. Table 10.23 shows the extreme degree to which analyst sentiment deteriorated. But Table 10.24 shows that the deterioration of estimates has been quite mild by comparison.

Is the market overreacting? Short sellers may be thinking along consistent lines. Table 10.25 shows that relative to the small float, the number of shares sold short has been extremely high. But the latest month's data

TABLE 10.23   Bebe Stores, Analyst Data as of April 20, 2000

Analyst Ratings

	Current	4 Weeks Ago	8 Weeks Ago	13 Weeks Ago
1—Buy	1	2	2	4
2—Outperform	1	1	3	3
3—Hold	5	4	1	0
4—Underperform	0	0	0	0
5—Sell	0	0	0	0
Average rating	2.57	2.29	1.83	1.43

TABLE 10.24 Bebe Stores, EPS Estimates Data as of April 20, 2000

EPS Estimates: Recent Revisions				
	Current	**4 Weeks Ago**	**8 Weeks Ago**	**13 Weeks Ago**
Estimate current quarter	0.210	0.210	0.240	0.250
Estimate next quarter	0.320	0.330	0.340	0.340
Estimate current year	1.320	1.340	1.370	1.340
Estimate next year	1.590	1.620	1.660	1.600

TABLE 10.25 Bebe Stores, Short Interest Data as of April 20, 2000

Short Interest				
	Shares (Millions)	**% Outstanding**	**% Float**	**Days**
Latest month	1.392	5.691	58.000	5.233
1 month ago	2.025	8.278	84.375	6.289
2 months ago	1.782	7.285	74.250	4.842
3 months ago	1.597	6.529	66.542	12.098

suggests the hard-core bears are cashing out, thinking, perhaps, that the bottom has been reached.

To this point, the scenario can be characterized as investors overreacting to a snag encountered by a formerly hot growth company. But before locking in on such a picture, let's see if the growth is supported by solid fundamental footprints of success, or was accomplished with smoke and mirrors. Tables 10.26, 10.27, 10.28, and 10.29 help us do that.

The margin comparisons depicted in Table 10.26 are nothing short of stupendous. This applies to cross-section and time-series matchups. Table 10.27 shows that BEBE's asset turnover is modestly below the industry average. Interestingly, though, inventory turnover is above the norm. Usually in retail, high margins are associated with slower turnover. BEBE's data stands as evidence supporting the company's reputation, that is, that young women really do like its merchandise.

Table 10.28 shows that BEBE's hefty margins more than offset the mundane asset turnover, and generate powerful returns on capital. Especially impressive is the fact that BEBE, with no debt and lots of liquidity (see Table 10.29) has returns on equity that are still a shade above its industry peers, even though the others use leverage to boost their returns.

TABLE 10.26 Bebe Stores, Margin Data as of April 20, 2000

Margin Comparisons (%)		
	Company	Industry
Gross margin—TTM	52.23	37.89
Gross margin—5-year average	46.92	34.92
EBITD margin—TTM	23.96	15.63
EBITD margin—5-year average	14.92	14.77
Operating margin—TTM	22.18	12.43
Operating margin—5-year average	13.23	11.28
Pretax margin—TTM	23.28	12.25
Pretax margin—5-year average	13.46	11.25
Net margin—TTM	14.05	7.60
Net margin—5-year average	8.00	7.11
Tax rate—TTM	39.68	38.77
Tax rate—5-year average	40.36	37.83

TABLE 10.27 Bebe Stores, Efficiency Data as of April 20, 2000

Efficiency Comparisons		
	Company	Industry
Revenue/employee—TTM	159,372	187,071
Net income/employee—TTM	22,385	14,130
Receivable turnover—TTM	26.574	54.57
Inventory turnover—TTM	5.93	4.57
Asset turnover—TTM	2.20	2.56

TABLE 10.28 Bebe Stores, Return Data as of April 20, 2000

Return Comparisons (%)		
	Company	Industry
Return on assets—TTM	30.84	20.15
Return on assets—5-year average	22.90	16.66
Return on investment—TTM	39.65	33.65
Return on investment—5-year average	32.40	24.25
Return on equity—TTM	41.24	40.47
Return on equity—5-year average	36.54	32.47

TABLE 10.29 Bebe Stores, Financial Strength Data as of April 20, 2000

Financial Strength		
	Company	**Industry**
Quick ratio MRQ	2.99	0.37
Current ratio MRQ	3.75	1.54
Long-term debt/equity MRQ	0.00	0.35
Total debt/equity MRQ	0.00	0.43
Interest coverage TTM	NM	14.61

Finishing Touches Examination of the financial statements in a search for anything that may have fallen through the cracks raises no red flags.

Checking the Price

Considering the extent to which BEBE's shares plunged and the way analysts jumped ship, Table 10.30, which examines BEBE's stock on the basis of downscale criteria, shows what the bargain counter looks like. The earnings-related metrics are way below industry averages. The general asset metrics are likewise lower. The shares are not selling at a discount to the per-share value of liquid assets, but they are within hailing distance.

TABLE 10.30 Bebe Stores, Valuation Metrics Data as of April 20, 2000

	Company	**Industry**	**S&P 500**
P/E based on estimate of next year's EPS	6.36	16.20	34.56
Projected long-term EPS growth rate	19.50	19.06	18.56
PEG ratio	0.326	.855	1.86
P/E (TTM)	7.43	24.00	37.01
P/E—5-year high	NA	47.36	48.78
P/E—5-year low	NA	12.21	16.55
Price/sales (TTM)	1.04	1.89	7.70
MRQ price/book value	2.33	11.60	9.75
MRQ price/tangible book value	2.33	2.825	13.42
MRQ price/net cash (cash minus total debt)	2.825	NM	19.969
MRQ price/cash	2.818	NM	NM
MRQ price/net working capital	3.141	NM	NM
MRQ price/working capital	2.995	NM	14.45
Return on enterprise value (%)	34.1	8.3	4.1

And BEBE's return on enterprise value is in the stratosphere. Now, the 90 percent insider ownership takes on an interesting flavor. If the market doesn't upgrade BEBE's valuation, insiders probably have an opportunity to take matters into their own hands through a buyout.

Getting Our Money's Worth

Table 10.31 shows the results of the expectation analysis we conducted for BEBE. The stock did not have sufficient data to compute a beta, so on my own I plugged in a number that assumes BEBE shares will be 50 percent more volatile than the market. I also had to wing it with the predicted relative P/E. Currently available data produced an average of .188. But it would be ridiculous to use that. The whole point of an investment in BEBE would be an assumption that the market overreacted to the company's slipup and that the relative P/E will improve. I think my 0.50 assumption is reasonably conservative. Meanwhile, averaging all the relevant historic data relating to growth capacity would produce a 38.87 percent result, which is obviously way too high. So I plugged in the 19.50 percent assumption the analysts maintain.

Note the resulting 12.85 expectation index. Recall that the point of neutrality is 1.00. Obviously, we have an enormous margin for error in the extent to which we can modify assumptions and still come up with a bullish answer.

TABLE 10.31	Bebe Stores, Analysis as of April 20, 2000
Expectation Analysis	
Time horizon (years)	5
Assumed risk-free return (annual %)	5.0
Assumed equity risk premium (annual %)	4.5
Beta	1.50
Current share price	9.69
Base-level EPS	1.59
Predicted future relative stock P/E	0.50
Predicted future market P/E	20
Predicted future stock P/E	10
Predicted future share price	16.89
Predicted future EPS	1.69
Expected annual EPS growth rate (%)	1.52
Estimated growth capacity (%)	19.50
Expectation index	12.85

The Analysis Keys

1. **Does the situation truly fit the theme you originally chose?** The company did slip recently, but let's not kid ourselves: There's no such thing as a company that never falters. All in all BEBE passed our good-company tests with flying colors. I'll answer "yes" to this key.

2. **Are there factors different from your original theme that you consider positive?** The powerful good-stock story alone merits a "yes" answer to this key. Even without that, we could arguably also say "yes" based on the presence of a growth story, subject to the possible hitch we'll discuss next.

3. **Is this investment opportunity free of any factors that you consider negative?** The market may be hyper. It exaggerates. But it's rarely stupid. We have to respect the possibility that the impact of the merchandising snags may be prolonged. So I'll answer "no" to this key.

The Decision Path

The yes-yes-no answer pattern we get for the BEBE Analysis Keys corresponds to Decision Path D. This is the lowest path in the buying zone. But as we did with AAON, we'll recall that many stocks fall on this path because investors almost always seem to worry about something. We'll drill down and prioritize within Path D based on why we said "no" to Key 3. BEBE falls on Path D1, the highest subgroup, by virtue of its having passed the expectation analysis and the fact that it satisfies the secondary good-stock theme.

All in all, despite low valuation and great fundamentals, BEBE isn't a perfect stock. But it is definitely buyable.

PATTERSON DENTAL COMPANY (PDCO)

Have you ever heard of this company? I didn't until I noticed it appearing in various screens. While the firm is hardly a giant, it's not exactly tiny. On April 20, 2001, when it appeared in my Fastest Turnover screen, it had a market capitalization of about $2 billion. And the stock had enough fans to enable it to trade at $30, close to the top of its $18.75 to $34.50 52-week range. Its anonymity probably stems from the nature of its business, distribution of dental supplies, and to a lesser extent, equipment used in dentists' offices. (I won't discuss a branching out into veterinary supplies, since that hadn't been a factor back in April 2001.)

Checking the Merchandise

Getting Acquainted This particular situation was easy to grasp, given that the business is readily understandable. The buzz among those in the investment community who knew of it was that the shares were expensive, but worth it considering the company's consistent performance, driven by market share gains made possible by enlargement of the sales force.

Exploring the Fundamentals Tables 10.32, 10.33, and 10.34 get us off to a nice start by confirming PDCO's reputation. Its growth trends won't make anyone jump up and shout. But the numbers do look both good and consistent. The impact of the life cycle is visible, if we squint.

TABLE 10.32 Patterson Dental Company, Growth Data as of April 20, 2001

Growth Comparisons (%)		
	Company	Industry
Sales MRQ vs. quarter 1 year ago	11.04	9.66
Sales TTM vs. TTM 1 year ago	12.50	10.86
Sales—5-year growth rate	13.24	18.54
EPS MRQ vs. quarter 1 year ago	18.11	8.32
EPS TTM vs. TTM 1 year ago	21.09	31.72
EPS—5-year growth rate	20.62	19.48
Capital spending—5-year growth	20.01	20.36

TABLE 10.33 Patterson Dental Company, EPS Trends Data as of April 20, 2001

EPS Trends: Historic and Forecasted				
	3 Years Ago	2 Years Ago	1 Year Ago	Current Year
1st quarter	0.125	0.150	0.210	0.240
2nd quarter	0.150	0.180	0.220	0.280
3rd quarter	0.165	0.210	0.250	0.300
4th quarter	0.175	0.210	0.270	0.31E
Total	0.615	0.750	0.950	1.13E
	Consensus	Low	High	# Analysts
Estimate current quarter	.31	.31	.32	8
Estimate next quarter	.29	.29	.29	3
Estimate current year	1.13	1.12	1.15	9
Estimate next year	1.33	1.31	1.35	8

TABLE 10.34 Patterson Dental Company, Growth Rates Data as of April 20, 2001

Growth Rates: Historic and Long-Term Forecast				
	TTM	**3 Years**	**5 Years**	**10 Years**
Sales (%)	12.50	14.78	13.24	16.78
EPS (%)	21.09	24.16	20.62	25.44
	Consensus	**Low**	**High**	**# Analysts**
Long-term (%)	20.00	20.00	20.00	7

The deceleration we see is occurring at a very gentle pace. I wonder about the dearth of analysts publishing estimates for the next quarter, but in the context of the rest of the data, I would not go so far as to describe this situation as an ORCL-style red flag. The fact that all seven analysts who publish long-term projections are using the exact same 20 percent number (Table 10.34) suggests they may be following company guidance.

The only chill we feel is the fact that sales are not growing as quickly as earnings. That sort of thing cannot be sustained forever. But as a distributor gets bigger and gains market share, economies of scale do kick in. Offhand, I see no reason to dismiss the possible management guidance to the effect that a 20 percent growth rate can be maintained throughout the forecast horizon, at least not now (I'll revisit this in the expectation analysis).

Tables 10.35 and 10.36 confirm the other aspect of the grapevine, that some on the Street consider the stock expensive. After a solid showing, it has taken a breather, underperforming the S&P 500 over the past four weeks. We also see that institutions, although owning a healthy percentage of the common shares, have pulled back a bit in the latest reporting period. My guess is that much of the selling was done by the more value-oriented accounts.

TABLE 10.35 Patterson Dental Company, Price Data as of April 20, 2001

	Price Performance			
Period	**Actual (%)**	**Vs. S&P 500 (%)**	**Company Rank in Industry***	**Industry Rank***
4 weeks	0.4	−7.9	42	31
13 weeks	1.7	9.8	64	41
26 weeks	11.9	25.7	75	34
52 weeks	26.3	45.8	80	62
YTD	−11.4	−5.9	32	18

*Ranks are percentiles: 0 is worst, 99 is best.

TABLE 10.36 Patterson Dental Company,
Institutional Data as of April 20, 2001

Institutional Activity	
# of institutions	366
% shares owned	60.92
Industry average	35.79
Net shares purchased last 3 months	−0.286

Tables 10.37 and 10.38 bear imprints of PDCO's distribution business—low margins and high turnover. But at least PDCO's margins, such as they are, demonstrate positive time-series comparisons.

Table 10.39 shows the impact of the margin-turnover combination. PDCO's returns on capital are impressive. We see some minor time-series softening, consistent with life cycle issues. But cross-sectional comparisons are attractive. And I'm especially impressed by PDCO's ability to post above-average return on equity considering that, unlike others in the medical and equipment supplies industry, this company is not using debt to boost returns (Table 10.40).

Finishing Touches Looking at the financial statements, particularly the Statement of Cash Flows, I notice that PDCO has a propensity to make small acquisitions. Acquirers always face integration-related risks, but PDCO's returns on capital show that up to this point, it has handled such issues skillfully.

TABLE 10.37 Patterson Dental Company, Margin Data as of
April 20, 2001

Margin Comparisons (%)		
	Company	Industry
Gross margin—TTM	36.84	61.23
Gross margin—5-year average	36.51	59.94
EBITD margin—TTM	10.76	25.57
EBITD margin—5-year average	9.04	21.97
Operating margin—TTM	9.85	20.92
Operating margin—5-year average	8.23	16.75
Pretax margin—TTM	10.44	20.83
Pretax margin—5-year average	8.51	15.76
Net margin—TTM	6.54	13.31
Net margin—5-year average	5.32	9.69
Tax rate—TTM	37.41	31.51
Tax rate—5-year average	37.53	36.54

TABLE 10.38 Patterson Dental Company, Efficiency Data as of April 20, 2001

Efficiency Comparisons		
	Company	Industry
Revenue/employee—TTM	296,437	237,897
Net income/employee—TTM	19,380	37,371
Receivable turnover—TTM	8.66	5.27
Inventory turnover—TTM	6.82	2.78
Asset turnover—TTM	2.39	0.91

TABLE 10.39 Patterson Dental Company, Return Data as of April 20, 2001

Return Comparisons (%)		
	Company	Industry
Return on assets—TTM	15.59	10.98
Return on assets—5-year average	14.79	9.42
Return on investment—TTM	20.61	14.75
Return on investment—5-year average	20.97	12.70
Return on equity—TTM	21.10	20.59
Return on equity—5-year average	23.95	17.44

TABLE 10.40 Patterson Dental Company, Financial Strength Data as of April 20, 2001

Financial Strength		
	Company	Industry
Quick ratio MRQ	2.40	1.90
Current ratio MRQ	3.39	2.88
Long-term debt/equity MRQ	0.00	0.35
Total debt/equity MRQ	0.00	0.45
Interest coverage TTM	NM	8.76

Checking the Price

Table 10.41 analyzes the stock's valuation metrics on a midscale basis. My impression here is generally favorable, albeit not nearly as spectacularly so as with the downscale BEBE situation. All cross-sectional comparisons except return on enterprise value favor PDCO. But ROEV is not really significant. PDCO's number is close to the industry average. And

TABLE 10.41 Patterson Dental Company, Valuation Metrics Data as of April 20, 2001

	Company	Industry	S&P 500
P/E based on estimate of next year's EPS	22.87	27.41	23.99
Projected long-term EPS growth rate	20.00	17.71	15.67
PEG ratio	1.144	1.589	1.606
P/E (TTM)	27.65	37.67	28.38
P/E—5-year high	32.61	79.20	50.41
P/E—5-year low	18.35	22.54	17.31
Yield	—	—	—
5-year dividend growth	—	—	—
Yield + growth	—	—	—
Payout ratio (TTM)	—	—	—
Price/book value (TTM)	5.24	8.34	6.17
MRQ price/net working capital	7.164	1.411	NM
MRQ price/net cash (cash minus total debt)	12.848	30.393	7.924
Return on enterprise value (%)	5.9	6.2	5.0

frankly, neither PDCO's ROEV nor those of the comparative benchmarks raise the prospect of a serious buyout opportunity.

Getting Our Money's Worth

Table 10.42 contains my expectation analysis of PDCO. I played it pretty straight with the growth expectation and capacity assumptions. In both cases, I started by averaging all numbers in the respective data sets. Originally this resulted in a bullish expectation index of 1.17. But the stock's actual beta, 0.19, left me uncomfortable from a common sense standpoint. I did some trial and error to find a beta that would bring the index down to the 1.00 point of neutrality. I got that result when I used a beta of 0.60.

Notice, though, that my growth capacity calculation trails the consensus 20 percent target. If I use the 20 percent number, I can raise the beta to 0.95 and still wind up with an index of 1.00.

The Analysis Keys

1. **Does the situation truly fit the theme you originally chose?** I searched for a good turnover-oriented company, and that's exactly what I got. And that's a theme worth pursuing. As discussed in Chapter 5, companies that take the turnover route to good returns and growth are not always as well appreciated as those that rely on mar-

TABLE 10.42	Patterson Dental Company, Analysis as of April 20, 2001
Expectation Analysis	
Time horizon (years)	5
Assumed risk-free return (annual %)	5.0
Assumed equity risk premium (annual %)	4.5
Beta	0.60
Current share price	30.00
Base-level EPS	1.33
Predicted future relative stock P/E	0.85
Predicted future market P/E	20
Predicted future stock P/E	17
Predicted future share price	43.47
Predicted future EPS	2.56
Expected annual EPS growth rate (%)	17.75
Estimated growth capacity (%)	17.80
Expectation index	1.00

gins. So there will often be a valuation opportunity. I'll answer "yes" to this key.

2. **Are there factors different from your original theme that you consider positive?** Indeed, the valuation opportunity here is real. The good-stock angle is solid if unspectacular. So, too, is the growth story. I'll answer "yes" to this key.

3. **Is this investment opportunity free of any factors that you consider negative?** At first glance, a 1.00 expectation index seems unexciting. But we saw that this number results from conservative beta and growth capacity assumptions. It's easy to come up with assumptions that push the index above 1.00. So on the whole PDCO passes this test. I see no other noteworthy negatives. So I'll answer "yes" to this key.

The Decision Path

The yes-yes-yes answer pattern we get for the PDCO Analysis Keys corresponds to Decision Path A, which is top dog. This stock is about as buyable as any we'll see. This may be surprising to the uninitiated. After all, it has a PEG ratio above 1.00, and the Street is complaining that the stock is richly valued. Herein lies the essence of the value connection method. We'll pay a good price for PDCO because the company is sufficiently good to make it worth our while.

GRACO INCORPORATED (GGG)

On April 20, 2001, GGG appeared on my Relative Value screen. Until then, I had never heard of this small (market capitalization: $848.65 million) manufacturer of a variety of industrial products. The shares, priced at $27.60, were closer to the upper end of a 52-week $20.13 to $40.00 trading range.

Checking the Price

Table 10.43 examines middle-market valuation metrics and shows GGG to be an attractively priced stock. The projected long-term EPS growth rate was modestly below the average for the miscellaneous capital goods group, but the P/E ratios were considerably lower, more than seemed warranted by the slower projected growth rate.

    The traditional asset-based valuation metrics gave no cause for excitement, but the return on enterprise value was high. We'll note, in the back of our minds, that insiders controlled 32 percent of the common shares, with one person owning 29 percent. That does not necessarily dampen trading activity; there are 20.9 million shares' worth of float. But if the stock unjustifiably languishes for too long, we might consider the possibility this major shareholder would be motivated to effect some sort of deal or buyout.

    Meanwhile, the dividend yield, on its own, was nothing to write home about, but if the company would maintain the historic pace of dividend growth, the income angle would be quite viable.

TABLE 10.43   Graco Incorporated, Valuation Metrics Data as of April 20, 2001

	Company	Industry	S&P 500
P/E based on estimate of next year's EPS	10.68	21.48	23.99
Projected long-term EPS growth rate	14.00	17.04	15.67
PEG ratio	0.763	1.262	1.606
P/E (TTM)	12.16	21.88	28.38
P/E—5-year high	20.18	31.64	50.41
P/E—5-year low	10.21	12.44	17.31
Yield	1.45	1.79	1.59
5-year dividend growth	13.70	3.79	8.86
Yield + growth	15.15	5.58	10.45
Payout ratio (TTM)	16.47	17.20	29.12
Price/book value (TTM)	7.57	3.10	6.17
MRQ price/net working capital	51.059	7.228	NM
MRQ price/net cash (cash minus total debt)	NM	6.743	7.924
Return on enterprise value (%)	12.7	7.1	5.0

Checking the Merchandise

Getting Acquainted The core of GGG's business consisted of fluid handling equipment for industrial and commercial applications. The automotive industry was an important customer group. Key products included vehicle lubrication products, valves, filters, and spray guns. Internet data presentations as of April 20, 2001, covered results through the end of calendar year 2000. But the news links showed that earnings for the first quarter of 2001 were released on April 18th. It would be a few days before the data would appear in web site financial tables, but we won't wait that long to factor it into our analysis, especially since, as we'll see, it might be a difference maker.

Exploring the Fundamentals Table 10.44 shows the EPS up through the first-quarter results reported by the company on April 18. We see that in the latest period, the year-to-year comparison was unfavorable, breaking what had been a nice string of positive-growth quarters. The problem was as basic as it gets: the economy. GGG's customers had experienced some cyclical softness in the period, and naturally that impacted the extent to which they bought from GGG.

The earnings announcement contained two bits of good news. One was the extent to which GGG's margins were able to hold up despite lackluster business conditions. The other was the fact that management, although still generally cautious, was a bit more optimistic for the upcoming quarter than was the case in the recent past.

Table 10.45 shows that analysts balanced the bad (the results of the

TABLE 10.44 Graco Incorporated, EPS Trends Data as of April 20, 2001

EPS Trends: Historic and Forecasted				
	3 Years Ago	2 Years Ago	1 Year Ago	Current Year
1st quarter	0.227	0.360	0.480	0.420
2nd quarter	0.320	0.570	0.590	.59E
3rd quarter	0.353	0.480	0.590	.61E
4th quarter	0.467	0.480	0.610	.65E
Total	1.367	1.890	2.270	2.27E
	Consensus	Low	High	# Analysts
Estimate current quarter	.59	.53	.60	2
Estimate next quarter	.61	.58	.63	2
Estimate current year	2.27	2.15	2.38	2
Estimate next year	2.58	2.50	2.65	2

TABLE 10.45 Graco Incorporated, EPS Estimates Data as of April 20, 2001

EPS Estimates: Recent Revisions

	Current	4 Weeks Ago	8 Weeks Ago	13 Weeks Ago
Estimate current quarter	.59	.61	.61	.65
Estimate next quarter	.61	.63	.63	.62
Estimate current year	2.27	2.38	2.38	2.47
Estimate next year	2.58	2.67	2.67	NA

latest period) and the good (guidance for the next quarter) by trimming estimates for the second time in 13 weeks.

But this isn't the end of the world. Tables 10.46 and 10.47 show that GGG hadn't been much of a growth story up till now.

EPS gains have been fine, but sales growth has been modest for most time periods, the TTM interval being a positive exception. But despite the

TABLE 10.46 Graco Incorporated, Growth Rates Data as of April 20, 2001

Growth Rates: Historic and Long-Term Forecast

	TTM	3 Years	5 Years	10 Years
Sales (%)	11.73	6.10	5.06	4.41
EPS (%)	19.80	25.83	26.19	16.76
	Consensus	**Low**	**High**	**# Analysts**
Long-term (%)	14.00	14.00	14.00	1

TABLE 10.47 Graco Incorporated, Growth Data as of April 20, 2001

Growth Comparisons (%)

	Company	Industry
Sales MRQ vs. quarter 1 year ago	7.62	7.96
Sales TTM vs. TTM 1 year ago	11.73	9.72
Sales—5-year growth rate	5.06	14.28
EPS MRQ vs. quarter 1 year ago	26.20	−2.73
EPS TTM vs. TTM 1 year ago	19.80	10.24
EPS—5-year growth rate	26.19	8.55
Capital spending—5-year growth	−6.06	12.56

modest sales growth, the Street has had a generally favorable view of GGG. For most time periods, its share price performance has been strong relative to industry peers and the S&P 500 (Table 10.48). And its level of institutional ownership has been quite respectable considering the small market capitalization (Table 10.49). Meanwhile, I make a mental note of the declining rate of capital spending.

Table 10.50 adds some interesting color. Cross-sectional margin comparisons are outstanding. Time-series comparisons are also quite good, but probably not so good as to constitute the main reason why EPS have been growing so much more quickly than sales.

Moving on, Tables 10.51, 10.52, and 10.53 paint a picture of GGG as an enormously efficient, profitable, and conservatively financed company.

Finishing Touches This is where we find the key that unlocks the mystery as to why GGG is as well regarded, among those in the know, as it is. The financial statements show modest acquisition activity ($18.4 million worth in December 1999). But more importantly, we also see a propensity on the part of GGG to buy back its own shares, with an especially large purchase taking place in 1998.

TABLE 10.48 Graco Incorporated, Price Data as of April 20, 2001

	Price Performance			
Period	Actual (%)	Vs. S&P 500 (%)	Company Rank in Industry*	Industry Rank*
4 weeks	9.0	0.0	73	35
13 weeks	0.8	8.9	63	38
26 weeks	28.1	44.0	83	63
52 weeks	29.6	49.6	83	52
YTD	0.1	6.3	46	59

*Ranks are percentiles: 0 is worst, 99 is best.

TABLE 10.49 Graco Incorporated, Institutional Data as of April 20, 2001

Institutional Activity	
# of institutions	245
% shares owned	70.28
Industry average	41.52
Net shares purchased last 3 months	.237

TABLE 10.50 Graco Incorporated, Margin Data as of April 20, 2001

Margin Comparisons (%)

	Company	Industry
Gross margin—TTM	50.74	29.71
Gross margin—5-year average	50.18	20.00
EBITD margin—TTM	25.63	13.00
EBITD margin—5-year average	21.20	12.62
Operating margin—TTM	22.50	10.27
Operating margin—5-year average	18.00	10.24
Pretax margin—TTM	21.42	9.46
Pretax margin—5-year average	17.23	9.69
Net margin—TTM	14.18	5.99
Net margin—5-year average	11.62	6.08
Tax rate—TTM	33.80	36.60
Tax rate—5-year average	32.37	39.18

TABLE 10.51 Graco Incorporated, Efficiency Data as of April 20, 2001

Efficiency Comparisons

	Company	Industry
Revenue/employee—TTM	257,486	203,385
Net income/employee—TTM	36,515	13,141
Receivable turnover—TTM	5.86	5.90
Inventory turnover—TTM	6.66	5.21
Asset turnover—TTM	2.09	1.18

TABLE 10.52 Graco Incorporated, Return Data as of April 20, 2001

Return Comparisons (%)

	Company	Industry
Return on assets—TTM	29.68	6.28
Return on assets—5-year average	21.36	8.21
Return on investment—TTM	44.46	8.59
Return on investment—5-year average	31.63	11.06
Return on equity—TTM	85.62	14.74
Return on equity—5-year average	72.93	17.74

TABLE 10.53 Graco Incorporated, Financial Strength Data as of April 20, 2001

Financial Strength		
	Company	Industry
Quick ratio MRQ	1.18	1.58
Current ratio MRQ	1.76	2.54
Long-term debt/equity MRQ	0.16	0.54
Total debt/equity MRQ	0.32	0.68
Interest coverage TTM	26.96	9.25

The share buybacks combined with the strong dividend growth rate and the powerful returns on investment communicate to us that GGG is an extremely profitable operation. Management is not unwilling to use capital to make acquisitions. But the combination of dividend growth and share buybacks shows that management is quite willing to return surplus capital to shareholders one way or another. That's a welcome relief from a business culture that encourages too many firms to delude themselves about how much growth prospects they really have and wind up wasting capital on ill-conceived ventures. In this context, the capital spending shrinkage is acceptable. And we now understand why earnings per share have been growing so briskly. It's the impact of a shrinking share base.

Getting Our Money's Worth

Table 10.54 shows the expectation analysis for GGG. I computed predicted relative P/E by the book: by averaging all the P/E-related data on the template. To compute growth capacity, I eliminated the staggeringly high returns on capital and averaged all the sales and EPS growth data. I don't usually average sales and EPS growth rates when one line item is so high relative to the other. But I'll make an exception here and give GGG full credit for the high EPS growth rates because it's coming from a source (use of surplus capital to buy back stock) that's more sustainable than would be the case if it were relying only on cost-cutting projects. That produces a bullish index of 1.23. Arguably, I could rely solely on EPS growth rates to push the capacity number up to 24.06 and the index to 1.83. But the 1.23 index tells me all I really need to know—to wit, that the price of the shares is reasonable relative to the merchandise we get.

TABLE 10.54   Graco Incorporated, Analysis as of April 20, 2001

Expectation Analysis	
Time horizon (years)	5
Assumed risk-free return (annual %)	5.0
Assumed equity risk premium (annual %)	4.5
Beta	0.60
Current share price	27.60
Base-level EPS	2.58
Predicted future relative stock P/E	0.473
Predicted future market P/E	20.00
Predicted future stock P/E	9.46
Predicted future share price	39.99
Predicted future EPS	4.23
Expected annual EPS growth rate (%)	13.14
Estimated growth capacity (%)	16.10
Expectation index	1.23

The Analysis Keys

1. **Does the situation truly fit the theme you originally chose?** GGG passes the good-stock test with flying colors, and merits a "yes" answer to this key.

2. **Are there factors different from your original theme that you consider positive?** This situation includes a strong good-company angle. I'll answer "yes" to this key.

3. **Is this investment opportunity free of any factors that you consider negative?** GGG passes the expectation index test with room to spare. It's tempting to cite cyclical risk as a negative, but I'm not going to do that here. The stock did not get hammered in response to the lackluster first quarter. Nobody was under illusions about GGG being a hot business growth story that stood to be derailed by an economic slump. I'm going to take a realistic view of what GGG is, and on that basis answer "yes" to this key.

The Decision Path

The yes-yes-yes answer pattern we get for the GGG Analysis Keys corresponds to Decision Path A, which makes the stock as strong a buy as we're likely to see.

ENGINEERED SUPPORT SYSTEM (EASI)

EASI is another company in the miscellaneous capital goods group that appeared in my Relative Value screen on April 20, 2001. But there's a potentially interesting story angle. Unlike GGG, much of EASI's business is done with the military. EASI is a very small firm (market capitalization: $213.5 million), but the float, 6.2 million shares, is enough to make the issue reasonably tradable. At the time, the stock was priced at $23.50, just above the middle of the 52-week $8.50 to $31.70 trading range.

Checking the Price

Table 10.55 shows EASI's valuation metrics, which are reviewed under middle-market standards. The asset-oriented metrics are reasonable, and the P/E-related measures are better than reasonable. Strictly speaking, there is a dividend; but the yield is low and I would not want to draw conclusions based on the probably unsustainably high historic dividend growth rate.

Checking the Merchandise

Getting Acquainted   EASI makes military support products and electronic equipment. It's a play on the prospect that military procurement,

TABLE 10.55   Engineered Support System, Valuation Metrics Data as of April 20, 2001

	Company	Industry	S&P 500
P/E based on estimate of next year's EPS	12.81	21.48	23.99
Projected long-term EPS growth rate	18.89	17.04	15.67
PEG ratio	0.678	1.262	1.606
P/E (TTM)	15.27	21.88	28.38
P/E—5-year high	21.20	31.64	50.41
P/E—5-year low	8.41	12.44	17.31
Yield	0.12	1.79	1.59
5-year dividend growth	51.57	3.79	8.86
Yield + growth	NM	5.58	10.45
Payout ratio (TTM)	2.69	17.20	29.12
Price/book value (TTM)	2.59	3.10	6.17
MRQ price/net working capital	NM	7.228	NM
MRQ price/net cash (cash minus total debt)	NM	6.743	7.924
Return on enterprise value (%)	10.5	7.1	5.0

after having been stagnant for a while, is poised for improved growth. Even before September 11, 2001, this possibility was being discussed. The company's offerings include chemical and biological defense products, air-conditioning and heat transfer systems, aircraft cargo loaders, and tactical bridging, radar, and fire control systems. Insofar as they are sold for defense use, they are relevant to an important military agenda: rapid-deployment limited-scale warfare. Earnings trends have been healthy. The backlog in April 2001 was good, and the company was actively pursuing more defense contracts.

Exploring the Fundamentals   Tables 10.56 and 10.57 show that historic growth numbers are huge. How is that? Bullish defense prospects were a future consideration. The recent past had not exactly resembled a 1980s-style military buildup. And why wasn't the stock fetching higher P/E ratios, especially since, as noted, the backlog was good? And why was the projection of future growth so far below the historic record?

TABLE 10.56   Engineered Support System, Growth Data as of April 20, 2001

Growth Comparisons (%)		
	Company	**Industry**
Sales MRQ vs. quarter 1 year ago	5.29	7.96
Sales TTM vs. TTM 1 year ago	63.75	9.72
Sales—5-year growth rate	40.71	14.28
EPS MRQ vs. Qtr. 1 year ago	37.46	–2.73
EPS TTM vs. TTM 1 year ago	47.98	10.24
EPS—5-year growth rate	29.19	8.55
Capital spending—5-year growth	33.49	12.56

TABLE 10.57   Engineered Support System, Growth Rates Data as of April 20, 2001

Growth Rates: Historic and Long-Term Forecast				
	TTM	**3 Years**	**5 Years**	**10 Years**
Sales (%)	63.75	59.81	40.71	19.64
EPS (%)	47.98	24.23	29.19	40.47
	Consensus	**Low**	**High**	**# Analysts**
Long-term (%)	18.89	15.00	25.56	4

These are pressing questions, and it's pointless to continue with our company analysis at this time while they remain unanswered. So we're going to step out of sequence and "look between the cracks" now, instead of after we've reviewed the fundamentals.

Looking Ahead at What Usually Are Finishing Touches We did well by digging into the details now, since the answer we seek is quickly visible. EASI has made some sizable acquisitions, one in fiscal 1998 (financed by debt and equity) and another in fiscal 1999 (financed by debt). But the company isn't anxious to keep too much capital out in the marketplace. In fiscal 2000, the company repaid some debt and bought back some shares.

Back to the Fundamentals Now we understand the growth data. The numbers were boosted by acquisitions and are not necessarily representative of what we could expect EASI to accomplish in the future (unless there are more acquisitions).

Table 10.58 shows that future growth is expected to moderate. Table 10.59 shows a pattern of generally favorable sentiment toward EASI, as the stock has been consistently strong relative to the S&P 500 and the industry. But Table 10.60 shows that institutions are not really on board. Considering EASI's status as a micro-cap, there's just so much institutional presence we can expect. But the percentage of ownership is below the industry average at present, and recent activity shows net selling, rather than buying.

TABLE 10.58 Engineered Support System, EPS Trends Data as of April 20, 2001

EPS Trends: Historic and Forecasted

	3 Years Ago	2 Years Ago	1 Year Ago	Current Year
1st quarter	0.152	0.224	0.288	0.400
2nd quarter	0.216	0.272	0.288	.41E
3rd quarter	0.232	0.216	0.416	.43E
4th quarter	0.336	0.264	0.440	.44E
Total	0.936	0.976	1.432	1.68E
	Consensus	**Low**	**High**	**# Analysts**
Estimate current quarter	.41	.40	.42	3
Estimate next quarter	.43	.42	.43	3
Estimate current year	1.68	1.68	1.69	4
Estimate next year	2.01	2.00	2.02	2

TABLE 10.59 Engineered Support System, EPS Trends Data as of April 20, 2001

| | Price Performance | | | |
| | Actual | Vs. S&P | Company Rank in | Industry |
Period	(%)	500 (%)	Industry*	Rank*
4 weeks	13.3	3.9	81	35
13 weeks	21.8	31.5	87	38
26 weeks	54.6	73.8	95	63
52 weeks	152.7	191.7	98	52
YTD	35.1	43.5	84	59

*Ranks are percentiles: 0 is worst, 99 is best.

TABLE 10.60 Engineered Support System, Institutional Data as of April 20, 2001

Institutional Activity	
# of institutions	54
% shares owned	35.69
Industry average	41.52
Net shares purchased last 3 months	−0.344

Tables 10.61, 10.62, and 10.63 show that EASI's core fundamentals are solid but unspectacular.

Margins are generally a bit below industry averages. The business-oriented gross, operating, and EBITD margins are trending upward on a time-series basis, but the overall pretax and net margins are not following suit. The latter reflects increased interest expense for acquisition-related debt. The efficiency data is mixed; EASI is not especially labor efficient, but turnover numbers are satisfactory. Returns on assets and investment look modestly favorable compared to industry averages. Return on equity is noticeably above average, reflecting EASI's greater use of debt, as demonstrated in Table 10.64.

Getting Our Money's Worth

Table 10.65 shows the expectation analysis for EASI. The predicted relative P/E is based on an average of all P/E-related data items in the table. I took a conservative approach to estimating growth capacity given the inherent uncertainties that are present anytime acquisitions figure prominently in the picture. I eliminated all growth data as well as the

TABLE 10.61 Engineered Support System, Margin Data as of April 20, 2001

Margin Comparisons (%)		
	Company	Industry
Gross margin—TTM	19.50	29.71
Gross margin—5-year average	18.75	20.00
EBITD margin—TTM	11.69	13.00
EBITD margin—5-year average	11.34	12.62
Operating margin—TTM	8.84	10.27
Operating margin—5-year average	8.77	10.24
Pretax margin—TTM	6.51	9.46
Pretax margin—5-year average	7.77	9.69
Net margin—TTM	3.91	5.99
Net margin—5-year average	4.66	6.08
Tax rate—TTM	40.00	36.60
Tax rate—5-year average	40.00	39.18

TABLE 10.62 Engineered Support System, Efficiency Data as of April 20, 2001

Efficiency Comparisons		
	Company	Industry
Revenue/employee—TTM	158,538	203,385
Net income/employee—TTM	6,197	13,141
Receivable turnover—TTM	12.28	5.90
Inventory turnover—TTM	5.20	5.21
Asset turnover—TTM	1.57	1.18

TABLE 10.63 Engineered Support System, Return Data as of April 20, 2001

Return Comparisons (%)		
	Company	Industry
Return on assets—TTM	6.13	6.28
Return on assets—5-year average	8.32	8.21
Return on investment—TTM	9.43	8.59
Return on investment—5-year average	11.66	11.06
Return on equity—TTM	19.22	14.74
Return on equity—5-year average	19.26	17.74

TABLE 10.64 Engineered Support System, Financial Strength Data as of April 20, 2001

Financial Strength		
	Company	**Industry**
Quick ratio MRQ	0.41	1.58
Current ratio MRQ	1.21	2.54
Long-term debt/equity MRQ	0.70	0.54
Total debt/equity MRQ	1.20	0.68
Interest coverage TTM	3.71	9.25

TABLE 10.65 Engineered Support System, Analysis as of April 20, 2001

Expectation Analysis	
Time horizon (years)	5
Assumed risk-free return (annual %)	5.0
Assumed equity risk premium (annual %)	4.5
Beta	0.43
Current share price	23.50
Base-level EPS	2.01
Predicted future relative stock P/E	0.622
Predicted future market P/E	20.00
Predicted future stock P/E	12.44
Predicted future share price	32.86
Predicted future EPS	2.64
Expected annual EPS growth rate (%)	7.07
Estimated growth capacity (%)	8.89
Expectation index	1.26

leverage-boosted returns on equity. I derived my estimate by averaging the data for the returns on assets and investment.

My assumptions produced a bullish expectation index of 1.26. Interestingly, my growth capacity estimate is less than half the 18.89 percent consensus long-term EPS growth projection. The range of estimates among the four analysts is very wide (15.00 percent to 25.56 percent). As discussed in connection with ORCL, ranges like that detract from credibility. But my growth capacity estimate, a mere 8.89 percent, is much lower than the bottom of the range of analyst forecasts. So the bullish expectation index has a large margin for error. (If I use the low end of the analyst range, 15.00 percent, the expectation index jumps to 2.12.)

The Analysis Keys

1. **Does the situation truly fit the theme you originally chose?** EASI is a solid good-stock story. I can easily give a "yes" answer to this key.

2. **Are there factors different from your original theme that you consider positive?** Perhaps a legitimate growth story will emerge as the company, enhanced by acquired units, obtains more defense contracts. But I'm not inclined to go out on a limb and say a growth story exists at present. And the good-company data, while not necessarily bad, doesn't inspire me to cite EASI as a here-and-now good-company story. So I'll answer "no" to this key.

3. **Is this investment opportunity free of any factors that you consider negative?** I'm quite satisfied with the expectation analysis. As to other potential red flags, I do notice the leveraged balance sheet. But the continued earnings progress and the high returns on equity indicate that the debt is manageable. There's a risk that no new defense contracts will emerge, but that's always the case in this business. I see no reason to single EASI out as possessing more such risk than other firms. On the whole, I'll say "yes" to this key; that is, the situation is free of factors I deem negative.

The Decision Path

The yes-no-yes answer pattern we get for the EASI Analysis Keys corresponds to Decision Path B. It's not the best possible scenario. But it's quite good and positions EASI as a solid buy.

SONIC CORPORATION (SONC)

So far we've seen dental supplies, fluid handling equipment, military supplies, and rooftop air-conditioning units. What do we have to do to find a fun company? Need we gamble with new economy hype (ORCL) or wait for stocks to get pounded (BEBE)? On April 20, 2001, our Industry Leaders screen showed all we need do is keep looking. Among the stocks it featured on that date was SONC, proprietor of 1950s-style drive-in restaurants (including carhops). The company was small (market capitalization: $731.31 million). But the stock was not beaten up or neglected. It was priced at $27.70, near the top of the $16.25 to $29.10 52-week range.

Checking the Merchandise

Getting Acquainted   The chain consisted of 2,219 units at the time, approximately 1,900 of which were franchised. (Many restaurant chains rely heavily on franchisees.) But depending on where you live, you may never have seen a Sonic drive-in. Given the nature of the concept, the company confines itself to warm-weather states.

The chain was still in a growth mode. Plans in early 2001 called for about 200 units over the next two years, mainly in existing territories, where they could benefit from brand recognition and get off to good starts. Indeed, emphasis on good starts for new units was an important growth driver. Restaurants opened during fiscal 1999 experienced volumes 20 percent better than the new establishments opened the prior year, and the debut performances were improving in 2000 and 2001 (evidence of the success of management's revised site selection strategies). An escalating franchise royalty structure (higher royalty rates than in the past for new franchisees and for existing franchisees whose agreements came up for renewal) contributed to growth. Operational performance was being enhanced by a new point-of-sale information system, a promotion strategy that eschewed price cutting in favor of interesting menu promotions (such as hickory bacon dogs and watermelon slushies), as well as stepped-up advertising efforts. Further plans called for the testing of a breakfast menu to penetrate a new day part. As it was, SONC's day-part profile was favorable. A large portion of revenues came from off-peak (nonlunch, nondinner) hours.

The only fly in the ointment was lackluster EPS growth in the latest quarter. But that was attributable to unusually bad weather in SONC's normally meteorologically friendly territories.

Exploring the Fundamentals   Tables 10.66 and 10.67 show that SONC has been growing more quickly than others in the restaurant indus-

---

TABLE 10.66   Sonic Corporation, Growth Data as of April 20, 2001

Growth Comparisons (%)		
	Company	Industry
Sales MRQ vs. quarter 1 year ago	8.24	7.83
Sales TTM vs. TTM 1 year ago	8.19	7.83
Sales—5-year growth rate	17.74	9.06
EPS MRQ vs. quarter 1 year ago	8.70	0.85
EPS TTM vs. TTM 1 year ago	19.79	6.37
EPS—5-year growth rate	20.00	15.77
Capital spending—5-year growth	0.55	1.85

TABLE 10.67 Sonic Corporation, Growth Rates Data as of April 20, 2001

Growth Rates: Historic and Long-Term Forecast

	TTM	3 Years	5 Years	10 Years
Sales (%)	8.19	15.03	17.74	19.83
EPS (%)	19.79	22.75	20.00	35.48
	Consensus	**Low**	**High**	**# Analysts**
Long-term (%)	19.25	18.00	20.00	8

try. But the time-series comparisons leave something to be desired. We know about the bad weather in the latest quarter, but that does not explain the extent of the drop-off in the TTM period. This suggests a true need for stepped-up advertising and efforts to get new units off the ground more quickly, not to mention the breakfast launch.

Table 10.68 indicates that analysts are comfortable with future growth prospects. And the articulated strategies seem plausible, so we won't necessarily dismiss such assumptions. After all, when it comes to room to grow, Sonic is hardly like McDonald's, which seems to already be on every corner.

Meanwhile, the analysts aren't the only ones comfortable with SONC's prospects. Table 10.69 shows that the stock has been very much in favor compared with the S&P 500 and the restaurant industry as a whole. And Table 10.70 shows more institutional presence than we might expect with a company this size.

TABLE 10.68 Sonic Corporation, EPS Trends Data as of April 20, 2001

EPS Trends: Historic and Forecasted

	3 Years Ago	2 Years Ago	1 Year Ago	Current Year
1st quarter	.173	.207	.260	.310
2nd quarter	.120	.147	.187	.200
3rd quarter	.153	.267	.333	.40E
4th quarter	.253	.320	.393	.48E
Total	.699	.941	1.173	1.39E
	Consensus	**Low**	**High**	**# Analysts**
Estimate current quarter	.40	.39	.41	6
Estimate next quarter	.48	.47	.48	6
Estimate current year	1.39	1.38	1.41	10
Estimate next year	1.65	1.63	1.68	7

TABLE 10.69 Sonic Corporation, Price Data as of April 20, 2001

	Price Performance			
Period	**Actual (%)**	**Vs. S&P 500 (%)**	**Company Rank in Industry***	**Industry Rank***
4 weeks	16.9	7.2	78	58
13 weeks	15.4	24.7	75	30
26 weeks	20.2	35.1	73	49
52 weeks	46.4	69.0	86	46
YTD	18.8	26.2	62	25

*Ranks are percentiles: 0 is worst, 99 is best.

TABLE 10.70 Sonic Corporation, Institutional Data as of April 20, 2001

Institutional Activity	
# of institutions	260
% shares owned	85.96
Industry average	51.86
Net shares purchased last 3 months	0.255

But the view from the Street is not unanimous. Table 10.71 shows that short interest, while hardly huge, has inched up modestly (although the latest month represented a respite from the earlier uptrend).

Meanwhile, Table 10.72 shows that company fundamentals are quite solid. Margin comparisons look good based on both cross-sectional and time-series comparisons. Table 10.73 shows that SONC is enormously efficient. Receivables and inventory turnover are not crucial in the restaurant industry. We do note that SONC's asset turnover is below average. But that's well balanced by the solid margins. Table 10.74 shows strong cross-sectional

TABLE 10.71 Sonic Corporation, Short Interest Data as of April 20, 2001

	Short Interest			
	Shares (Millions)	**% Outstanding**	**% Float**	**Days**
Latest month	0.508	1.924	4.097	3.820
1 month ago	0.549	2.079	4.427	3.636
2 months ago	0.376	1.424	3.032	1.194
3 months ago	0.143	0.542	1.153	0.386

TABLE 10.72 Sonic Corporation, Margin Data as of April 20, 2001

Margin Comparisons (%)

	Company	Industry
Gross margin—TTM	63.35	37.82
Gross margin—5-year average	56.98	47.72
EBITD margin—TTM	27.93	22.35
EBITD margin—5-year average	23.71	21.70
Operating margin—TTM	20.64	16.55
Operating margin—5-year average	16.96	15.76
Pretax margin—TTM	18.79	14.58
Pretax margin—5-year average	15.78	13.59
Net margin—TTM	11.71	9.35
Net margin—5-year average	9.89	9.09
Tax rate—TTM	37.25	33.95
Tax rate—5-year average	37.35	36.91

TABLE 10.73 Sonic Corporation, Efficiency Data as of April 20, 2001

Efficiency Comparisons

	Company	Industry
Revenue/employee—TTM	1,124,012	70,200
Net income/employee—TTM	131,663	6,423
Receivable turnover—TTM	29.42	25.52
Inventory turnover—TTM	307.27	33.40
Asset turnover—TTM	1.05	1.22

TABLE 10.74 Sonic Corporation, Return Data as of April 20, 2001

Return Comparisons (%)

	Company	Industry
Return on assets—TTM	12.35	9.16
Return on assets—5-year average	10.71	7.66
Return on investment—TTM	13.39	11.37
Return on investment—5-year average	11.72	9.60
Return on equity—TTM	22.33	18.99
Return on equity—5-year average	17.39	16.44

and time-series return on capital comparisons. And Table 10.75 shows that SONC's financial strength measures are reasonable.

Finishing Touches   Review of the financial statements showed no additional factors having a material impact on our analysis.

Checking the Price

Table 10.76 shows SONC's valuation metrics, viewed under midscale criteria. On the whole, SONC is not cheap. Its projected and TTM P/Es are above industry averages. But so, too, is the projected growth rate. The asset-oriented valuation metrics show SONC to be slightly expensive relative to the industry.

TABLE 10.75   Sonic Corporation, Financial Strength Data as of April 20, 2001

Financial Strength		
	Company	Industry
Quick ratio MRQ	0.54	0.52
Current ratio MRQ	0.69	0.76
Long-term debt/equity MRQ	0.52	0.62
Total debt/equity MRQ	0.52	0.67
Interest coverage TTM	9.24	9.76

TABLE 10.76   Sonic Corporation, Valuation Metrics Data as of April 20, 2001

	Company	Industry	S&P 500
P/E based on estimate of next year's EPS	17.58	15.77	23.99
Projected long-term EPS growth rate	19.25	13.91	15.67
PEG ratio	0.913	1.17	1.606
P/E (TTM)	22.43	20.69	28.38
P/E—5-year high	30.30	39.88	50.41
P/E—5-year low	14.51	15.71	17.31
Yield	—	—	—
5-year dividend growth	—	—	—
Yield + growth	—	—	—
Payout ratio (TTM)	—	—	—
Price/book value (TTM)	4.45	3.55	6.17
MRQ price/net working capital	NM	NM	NM
MRQ price/net cash (cash minus total debt)	NM	NM	7.924
Return on enterprise value (%)	7.3	7.8	5.0

Getting Our Money's Worth

Table 10.77 shows the expectation analysis for SONC. The growth capacity estimate is based on an average of all the return on capital data items used in the spreadsheet template. The result is well below the consensus analyst projection, which may indicate some margin for error. The predicted relative P/E estimate is based on an average of all P/E data on the template.

The initial result looks unfavorable. The expectation index is a bearish 0.85. But let's look at margin for error.

- If we use the low end of the projected growth rate (18 percent) for growth capacity, the index jumps to a moderately bullish 1.04.
- We could keep our conservative growth capacity estimate and plug in 0.79 for predicted relative P/E. This would work if we accept the TTM company-to-industry ratio. That would bring the index up to 1.06.
- If we make the adjustments to both the predicted relative P/E and growth capacity, the index jumps to 1.31.

The Analysis Keys

1. **Does the situation truly fit the theme you originally chose?** The good-company story here is not the most powerful we've seen. But it is sufficiently solid to merit a "yes" answer for this key.

TABLE 10.77 Sonic Corporation, Analysis as of April 20, 2001

Expectation Analysis	
Time horizon (years)	5
Assumed risk-free return (annual %)	5.0
Assumed equity risk premium (annual %)	4.5
Beta	1.01
Current share price	27.7
Base-level EPS	1.65
Predicted future relative stock P/E	0.70
Predicted future market P/E	20.00
Predicted future stock P/E	14.00
Predicted future share price	43.70
Predicted future EPS	3.12
Expected annual EPS growth rate (%)	17.28
Estimated growth capacity (%)	14.63
Expectation index	0.85

2. **Are there factors different from your original theme that you consider positive?** The good-stock story is not necessarily bad. The growth story seems credible, but it's not a lock, at least not enough to drive me to accept the story for purposes of this key. I'd rather consider margin for error in the context of the third key. For this key, I'll simply answer "no."

3. **Is this investment opportunity free of any factors that you consider negative?** This key is going to make or break the stock based on the expectation analysis, since I see no other red flags. As to that analysis, the initial pass turned up a bearish 0.85 result. But I did leave considerable cushions, on both growth capacity and predicted relative P/E. One who is sufficiently strict to dismiss all growth except that which is present could still drive the index above 1.00 simply by assuming today's relative TTM company-to-market P/E ratio will persist. It gets easier to make the expectation analysis work by factoring in some of the prospective growth. The ease with which we can generate a bullish expectation index leads me to give a "yes" answer to this key.

The Decision Path

The yes-no-yes answer pattern we get for the SONC analysis keys corresponds to Decision Path B, the second highest path and a very solid buy. My gut is fine with the buy conclusion, but feels a bit queasy with the vigor of Path B.

I'm not prepared to dismiss the growth story, because it does sound believable. What I will do, though, is revisit the paths, say the growth story is sufficient to justify a "yes" answer to the second key, and keep my original expectation analysis that produced a "no" answer to the third key. That changes the pattern to yes-yes-no and drops SONC down to Path D, the lowest in the buying zone. More specifically, we're on Path D4, the absolute bottom of the buy zone. That's because SONC is now deemed to have failed the expectation analysis and because the "yes" to the second key is based on a theme (growth) that is outside the value connection.

This is an example of how we can factor the art of stock analysis and selection into our rational process. But our actions aren't necessarily a breach of our methodological discipline. However much we wavered, we never lost sight of the key make-or-break issue for this stock, the extent to which the growth strategies (in-market expansion, increased advertising, testing of a breakfast menu, etc.) were credible. There can never be a hard-and-fast answer to such questions. But at least we articulated them carefully, and stayed aware of how our answers matched up with share price valuation considerations.

UNIVERSITY OF PHOENIX ONLINE (UOPX)

In Chapter 7, we saw the MultexInvestor.com High P/E Ratios screen, a good-stock screen that turns conventional value notions upside down and uses high metrics as a signal that company quality might be high. To get an idea of the kinds of situations we might find this way, consider UOPX, which appeared on the screen on April 23, 2002.

Checking the Price

Table 10.78 shows the valuation metrics for UOPX, which are assessed from an upscale perspective. We should not be surprised that the ratios are all high. That was the key to the screen's primary theme.

The stock's price volatility (it traded at $30.74, near the middle of a $19.07 to $43.78 52-week range) raised an eyebrow. First, as high as the P/Es already are, we note that at one time in the recent past, the stock still traded more than 40 percent higher. And we see, from the experience of those who bought near the high, that large losses had been sustained. Considering the P/Es are still sky-high, is the stock heading for more trouble ahead?

We saw high metrics before with ORCL. But Table 10.78 shows something important that was conspicuously absent from that situation: an above-average projected EPS growth rate resulting in a below-average PEG ratio. Obviously, we have to consider the credibility of the projection.

Admittedly, a 39.40 percent projected growth rate is high enough to raise eyebrows. But I'll keep an open mind since high expectations are typical of UOPX's industry. It's possible that expectations are too high for the other firms as well. But this isn't a group of fancy high-tech outfits; it's the schools industry, which is not a darling of bubble-era speculators. So at

TABLE 10.78 University of Phoenix Online, Valuation Metrics Data as of April 26, 2002

	Company	Industry	S&P 500
P/E based on estimate of next year's EPS	52.93	35.62	22.40
Projected long-term EPS growth rate	39.40	24.87	13.54
PEG ratio	1.343	1.421	1.654
P/E (TTM)	86.59	49.83	29.33
P/E—5-year high	NA	70.51	50.02
P/E—5-year low	NA	23.12	17.60
Price/sales (TTM)	13.63	5.92	3.40
Price/free cash flow (TTM)	57.35	45.16	35.42
Price/cash flow (TTM)	74.07	38.07	22.10

this point in the analysis, I have at least some reason to hope I'm not wasting my time.

Checking the Merchandise

Getting Acquainted   UOPX isn't a garden-variety stock. It's a tracking issue. The key is a publicly traded company known as Apollo Group (APOL), which provides higher education for adults. Programs focus on such practical skills areas as business, education, information technology, and nursing. One of the schools owned by APOL is the University of Phoenix. The Internet branch of that school, University of Phoenix Online, was performing especially well, so APOL decided to take advantage of that during the new economy boom. In late 2000, it sold a special kind of common stock that would be pegged solely to the results of this online education unit. That is the UOPX issue we're considering now. UOPX is 88 percent owned by APOL. But market capitalization ($2.6 billion) was respectable, and the float (13.10 million shares) and volume (daily average: 210,000 shares) were tolerable.

It could well have been a disaster, as were so many financing vehicles based on Internet and late-1990s communication technology. But it just so happened that at least through the spring of 2002, this particular new economy business was looking very much for real. Enrollments were soaring and so were earnings. The Street understood that the 80 percent enrollment growth rates that were being experienced would not be sustainable. But consensus opinion was that growth would remain strong enough to justify the stock's admittedly rich valuation.

Exploring the Fundamentals   Tables 10.79 and 10.80 show that analysts still expected great things from the bottom line. And this was after some fine-tuning had already occurred. Note Table 10.80, which shows that estimates had been modestly trimmed in the past four weeks.

The top of Table 10.81 shows historic growth rates that are, clearly, way above what UOPX is likely to do in the future. Remember life cycle considerations; there's a presumption that growth rates will decelerate from supernormal levels as companies age.

The bottom of Table 10.81 seems a bit disconcerting. While analysts understand deceleration will occur, they, as a group, seem to have no idea how much slowing is likely to occur in the next few years. The high-to-low range is ridiculously wide. And three of the analysts who published current-year estimates didn't even bother to come up with a long-term assumption.

This, obviously, brings to mind the ORCL situation, where it looked

TABLE 10.79 University of Phoenix Online, Growth Trends Data as of April 26, 2002

EPS Trends: Historic and Forecasted				
	3 Years Ago	**2 Years Ago**	**1 Year Ago**	**Current Ago**
1st quarter	0.015	0.035	0.030	0.090
2nd quarter	0.020	0.035	0.053	0.105
3rd quarter	0.030	0.050	0.083	.17E
4th quarter	0.015	0.065	0.075	.16E
Total	0.080	0.185	0.241	.57E
	Consensus	**Low**	**High**	**# Analysts**
Estimate current quarter	.17	.13	.18	8
Estimate next quarter	.16	.14	.17	9
Estimate current year	.57	.45	.61	8
Estimate next year	.82	.66	.90	7

TABLE 10.80 University of Phoenix Online, EPS Estimates Data as of April 26, 2002

EPS Estimates: Recent Revisions				
	Current	**4 Weeks Ago**	**8 Weeks Ago**	**13 Weeks Ago**
Estimate current quarter	.17	.17	.16	.16
Estimate next quarter	.16	.16	.15	.15
Estimate current year	.57	.59	.52	.52
Estimate next year	.82	.86	.82	.82

TABLE 10.81 University of Phoenix Online, Growth Rates Data as of April 26, 2002

Growth Rates: Historic and Long-Term Forecast				
	TTM	**3 Years**	**5 Years**	**10 Years**
Sales (%)	89.51	58.80	58.98	NA
EPS (%)	83.94	69.83	96.80	NA
	Consensus	**Low**	**High**	**# Analysts**
Long-term (%)	39.40	25.00	60.00	5

like numbers were being picked out of a hat. We also saw wide ranges here
for the nearer-term estimates in Table 10.79. But there's an important difference here. For UOPX, we see pretty much the same number of analysts
issuing estimates for annual and quarterly figures. For ORCL, many analysts who issued annual forecasts were not issuing estimates for the quarters. That's what gave a sense of carelessness there. But let's face it. For a
new business like that of UOPX, there is no reliable way to generate pre-
dictions. So difference of opinion alone won't put us off. All we can seek is
a legitimate effort to try, and that does seem to be happening with the
UOPX numbers, as opposed to the sloppiness of the ORCL situation.

Table 10.82 presents another point of differentiation from ORCL. With
the latter, analysts had a preponderance of recommendations in the top
category and, as a group, were getting more bullish even though they had
no handle at all on the earnings estimates. For UOPX, the preponderance
of ratings is in the second category (outperform) and has been more stable
over time than the ORCL profile. And the most recent change in average
rating for UOPX represented a pulling back of the throttle.

Table 10.83 shows that analysts aren't the only ones who hit the brakes
recently. Over the past four weeks, the stock turned in a negative performance, albeit not enough to cause it to underperform the weak S&P 500.

Table 10.84 is quite interesting. It shows short interest to be much
more modest than one might expect for a highflier like UOPX. Perhaps
brokers are reluctant to lend the stock for short selling. But in the past,
they did loan enough for short interest to reach 8.26 percent of the float.
And the short interest has declined from that point. Perhaps the fall from
the 52-week high is being read by the bears as a signal that it's time to
cover short positions.

Given UOPX's brief history as a firm that files its own financial statements, it's hard to draw conclusions from the return on capital data in
Table 10.85.

TABLE 10.82 University of Phoenix Online, Analyst Data as of
April 23, 2002

Analyst Ratings				
	Current	4 Weeks Ago	8 Weeks Ago	13 Weeks Ago
1—Buy	3	4	3	2
2—Outperform	7	7	7	7
3—Hold	0	0	0	0
4—Underperform	0	0	0	0
5—Sell	0	0	0	0
Average rating	1.70	1.64	1.70	1.78

TABLE 10.83 University of Phoenix Online, Price Data as of April 23, 2002

	Price Performance			
Period	Actual (%)	Vs. S&P 500 (%)	Company Rank in Industry*	Industry Rank*
4 weeks	−2.1	4.4	34	73
13 weeks	21.1	27.5	75	88
26 weeks	52.4	56.4	75	76
52 weeks	110.9	145.6	84	96
YTD	25.7	34.1	64	85

*Ranks are percentiles: 0 is worst, 99 is best.

TABLE 10.84 University of Phoenix Online, Short Interest Data as of April 23, 2002

	Short Interest			
	Shares (Millions)	% Outstanding	% Float	Days
Latest month	0.738	0.874	5.634	1.736
1 month ago	0.769	0.911	5.870	5.870
2 months ago	0.950	1.126	7.252	4.077
3 months ago	1.082	1.282	8.260	6.479

TABLE 10.85 University of Phoenix Online, Return Data as of April 23, 2002

Return Comparisons (%)		
	Company	Industry
Return on assets—TTM	29.28	15.58
Return on assets—5-year average	63.62	18.61
Return on investment—TTM	39.61	22.22
Return on investment—5-year average	201.79	17.99
Return on equity—TTM	40.47	23.01
Return on equity—5-year average	NA	20.70

But Table 10.86 is encouraging because it shows margins to be healthy under both cross-sectional and time-series comparisons. Table 10.87 is especially appealing. Many corporations that establish subsidiaries as separate publicly traded entities saddle the offspring with weak balance sheets. APOL did not do that. It sent its child into the world with a strong balance sheet.

TABLE 10.86 University of Phoenix Online, Margin Data as of April 23, 2002

Margin Comparisons (%)		
	Company	Industry
Gross margin—TTM	58.63	47.40
Gross margin—5-year average	47.08	43.87
EBITD margin—TTM	28.40	20.54
EBITD margin—5-year average	21.33	18.45
Operating margin—TTM	27.76	16.84
Operating margin—5-year average	20.16	13.36
Pretax margin—TTM	29.18	17.21
Pretax margin—5-year average	20.56	13.88
Net margin—TTM	17.75	10.38
Net margin—5-year average	12.30	8.05
Tax rate—TTM	39.17	39.16
Tax rate—5-year average	40.38	39.40

TABLE 10.87 University of Phoenix Online, Financial Strength Data as of April 23, 2002

Financial Strength		
	Company	Industry
Quick ratio MRQ	2.66	1.72
Current ratio MRQ	2.72	2.01
Long-term debt/equity MRQ	0.00	0.10
Total debt/equity MRQ	0.00	0.10
Interest coverage TTM	NM	NM

Finishing Touches   Review of the financial statements produced no information that materially alters the impression we formed of UOPX to this point.

Getting Our Money's Worth

Table 10.88 contains our UOPX expectation analysis. Here is where we'll really tackle the credibility of growth projections.

The growth credibility issue turns out to be quite straightforward. There was no way I could utilize the historic growth and return data in a way that would produce a growth capacity estimate that comports with common sense. So I simply used 25 percent, the low end of the range of

TABLE 10.88 University of Phoenix Online, Analysis as of April 23, 2002

Expectation Analysis	
Time horizon (years)	5
Assumed risk-free return (annual %)	5.0
Assumed equity risk premium (annual %)	4.5
Beta	2.0
Current share price	30.74
Base-level EPS	.82
Predicted future relative stock P/E	1.50
Predicted future market P/E	20.00
Predicted future stock P/E	30.00
Predicted future share price	59.19
Predicted future EPS	1.97
Expected annual EPS growth rate (%)	24.54
Estimated growth capacity (%)	25.00
Expectation index	1.02

analyst growth projections. It's also in line with the average 24.82 percent growth projection for the other publicly traded firms in the industry. Using the historic data to predict a relative P/E proved likewise challenging. Averaging the available data produced a ratio of 1.882. I eyeballed it down to 1.50. That produced an acceptable index value of 1.02. Also, there wasn't enough historic data to compute beta, so I plugged in a conservative 2.00 assumption.

The Analysis Keys

1. **Does the situation truly fit the theme you originally chose?** Considering the high valuation metrics here, I'm going to answer "no" to this key. That's not a surprise. I knew when I used the High P/E Ratios screen that this is what I was in for. I was using high valuation as behavioral evidence of other virtues, and this investment opportunity will make or break on those.

2. **Are there factors different from your original theme that you consider positive?** The good-company story is okay, although the short history and resulting unconvincing return on capital data make me reluctant to use this as a basis for an affirmative answer to this key. But the alternative theme, growth, does work. I'm not comfortable with the official consensus, but I can accept the merits of the story even if growth comes in at the low end of the forecast range, which

matches the industry average expectation. So the alternative theme allows me to answer "yes" to this key.

3. **Is this investment opportunity free of any factors that you consider negative?** I'm going to accept the 1.02 expectation index as a passing score in that analysis. As explained earlier, I'm already comfortable with the growth capacity number I plugged into the model. The predicted relative P/E is a source of uncertainty. But my 1.50 assumption allows me to assume the existing relative TTM P/E (2.952) will be cut approximately in half. The conservatism of my beta assumption also provides a margin for error. Since I see no other red flags, I'll answer "yes" to this key.

The Decision Path

The no-yes-yes answer pattern we get for the UOPX Analysis Keys corresponds to Decision Path C, which equates to a respectable, if not compelling, buy. And I understand going in that the sensitive point in the decision is my use of a 1.50 predicted relative P/E based on a switch from the science to the art part of the process.

GROUP 1 AUTOMOTIVE INC. (GPI)

As of April 23, 2002, GPI, the sixth largest chain of auto dealerships in the United States, was well regarded. Shares of this small-sized issue (market capitalization: $991.80 million) were priced at $43.50, near the top of a 52-week $17.50 to $45.69 range. At that time, GPI appeared in my Fastest Turnover screen.

Checking the Merchandise

Getting Acquainted   This specialty retail outfit is a new-style automobile dealer. Instead of pushing one brand, as traditional mom-and-pop dealerships do, GPI, like other publicly traded dealerships, sells many brands (30 different ones in GPI's case), both foreign and domestic. These outfits have active used car businesses with lucrative servicing units, and they get more involved in the customer finance process than traditional dealerships have done. And as was the case with others like it, GPI was continuing to grow by acquiring smaller operators. As of early 2002, GPI's skills at integrating acquired units and generating economies of scale were quite solid.

But cyclical risk was definitely present when the stock appeared in the screen. Bulls maintained that the impact of a weaker economy would be mitigated by manufacturer price incentives, by shorter and more innovative product cycles, and by the wealth (buying power) consumers obtained through a wave of home mortgage refinancings. In any case, as of April 23, 2002, reports of softening in new car sales and used car pricing were already incorporated into analyst estimates.

Insiders owned 34 percent of GPI, and two other shareholders accounted for another 15 percent. But float was a respectable 11.6 million shares and daily trading volume averaged a solid 270,000 shares.

Exploring the Fundamentals Tables 10.89 and 10.90 paint an erratic growth picture. Acquisitions (and economies of scale) are noticeable on the bottom line, but recent sales growth has not shown much zip, suggesting cyclical issues are already making themselves felt.

Tables 10.91 and 10.92 open my eyes a bit. Rhetoric at the time had it

TABLE 10.89 Group 1 Automotive Inc., Growth Data as of April 23, 2002

Growth Comparisons (%)		
	Company	Industry
Sales MRQ vs. quarter 1 year ago	1.85	8.74
Sales TTM vs. TTM 1 year ago	9.81	9.59
Sales—5-year growth rate	70.00	28.20
EPS MRQ vs. quarter 1 year ago	37.77	29.00
EPS TTM vs. TTM 1 year ago	41.32	13.28
EPS—5-year growth rate	61.59	24.06
Capital spending—5-year growth	60.20	3.24

TABLE 10.90 Group 1 Automotive Inc., Growth Rates Data as of April 23, 2002

Growth Rates: Historic and Long-Term Forecast				
	TTM	3 Years	5 Years	10 Years
Sales (%)	9.81	34.84	70.00	46.58
EPS (%)	41.32	30.80	61.59	36.16
	Consensus	Low	High	# Analysts
Long-term (%)	16.98	12.90	25.00	6

TABLE 10.91 Group 1 Automotive Inc., EPS Trends Data as of April 23, 2002

EPS Trends: Historic and Forecasted

	3 Years Ago	2 Years Ago	1 Year Ago	Current Year
1st quarter	0.310	0.400	0.470	0.640
2nd quarter	0.420	0.540	0.680	.77E
3rd quarter	0.480	0.540	0.750	.79E
4th quarter	0.350	0.410	0.680	.67E
Total	1.560	1.890	2.580	2.87E
	Consensus	**Low**	**High**	**# Analysts**
Estimate current quarter	.77	.79	.74	5
Estimate next quarter	.79	.83	.77	4
Estimate current year	2.87	2.70	3.10	6
Estimate next year	3.33	3.12	2.58	4

TABLE 10.92 Group 1 Automotive Inc., EPS Estimates Data as of April 23, 2002

EPS Estimates: Recent Revisions

	Current	4 Weeks Ago	8 Weeks Ago	13 Weeks Ago
Estimate current quarter	.77	.72	.72	.71
Estimate next quarter	.79	.77	.77	.76
Estimate current year	2.87	2.75	2.75	2.61
Estimate next year	3.33	3.20	3.20	NA

that estimates had accounted for potential softening of car sales. But I don't see it in the data. While the near-term projected year-to-year comparisons incorporate some time-series deceleration, culminating in a marginally unfavorable fourth-quarter comparison, yet I also notice that the estimates had been raised in the past four weeks. Are we getting into a pipe dream here? Often, when cyclical weakness appears to be on the way, companies and analysts create convincing stories of why it won't seriously hurt the company at hand. But often, by the time the dust settles, those stories falter. I could live with estimates being held steady, but raising them at a time when softening business conditions are under discussion seems odd. And I recall, from Table 10.90, a very wide range of expectations for the projected long-term growth rate. All in all, I'm not convinced that analysts have much of a grip on the situation.

Table 10.93 leaves me similarly discontented. It shows that the rating profile has been getting more bullish as we approach a possible auto slump. Then, on closer reflection, I feel I need to modify my first impression. The reason why the average rating is rising is because analysts with lower ratings have been dropping coverage. One wonders what the rating profile might look like had they continued to rate the stock. My sense of discomfort persists.

Even so the stock has kept pace with the strong specialty retail group and well ahead of the S&P 500 (Table 10.94). Table 10.95 shows that there has been some insider selling. But that sort of thing is present in many stocks. What's less prevalent, however, is insider buying. That has been happening at GPI. Institutions have also been buying (Table 10.96). Admittedly, data reporting lags are a factor. But if institutions had been selling recently, we should have seen that reflected in softening relative share price performance on Table 10.94. But that's not the case.

TABLE 10.93 Group 1 Automotive Inc., Analyst Data as of April 23, 2002

Analyst Ratings				
	Current	4 Weeks Ago	8 Weeks Ago	13 Weeks Ago
1—Buy	3	3	3	3
2—Outperform	2	2	2	3
3—Hold	0	1	1	1
4—Underperform	0	0	0	0
5—Sell	0	0	0	0
Average rating	1.40	1.67	1.67	1.71

TABLE 10.94 Group 1 Automotive Inc., Price Data as of April 23, 2002

Price Performance				
Period	Actual (%)	Vs. S&P 500 (%)	Company Rank in Industry*	Industry Rank*
4 weeks	11.4	18.8	70	89
13 weeks	59.0	67.5	88	70
26 weeks	53.7	57.7	64	88
52 weeks	139.0	178.3	83	90
YTD	52.6	62.8	75	72

*Ranks are percentiles: 0 is worst, 99 is best.

TABLE 10.95　Group 1 Automotive Inc., Insider Data as of April 23, 2002

Insider Activity	
Number of insider buy transactions	3
Number of insider sell transactions	8

TABLE 10.96　Group 1 Automotive Inc., Institutional Data as of April 23, 2002

Institutional Activity	
# of institutions	289
% shares owned	55.71
Industry average	57.55
Net shares purchased last 3 months	3.411

Someone's watching the future. Short interest is inching upward (Table 10.97).

Are you confused about the sentiment data? I am. It's hard to discern a coherent theme, especially one consistent with where the economy was assumed to be heading.

Meanwhile, as to core fundamentals, Table 10.98 shows that GPI is a low-margin business. But at least the time-series comparisons are favorable. We won't get upset about this because of how we found the stock: on a screen geared toward turnover. Table 10.99 soothes us by showing that turnover is, indeed, strong, as is labor efficiency. Table 10.100 makes us feel even better. Margin and turnover combine to produce returns on capital that look good under both cross-sectional and time-series comparisons.

Table 10.101 leaves us feeling less sanguine. The liquidity ratios are below average. So, too, is the long-term debt-to-equity ratio. But the

TABLE 10.97　Group 1 Automotive Inc., Short Interest Data as of April 23, 2002

	Shares (Millions)	% Outstanding	% Float	Days
Short Interest				
Latest month	1.910	5.224	10.267	4.428
1 month ago	1.188	5.211	10.241	3.070
2 months ago	1.023	4.487	8.819	4.043
3 months ago	0.826	3.623	7.121	2.961

TABLE 10.98 Group 1 Automotive Inc., Margin Data as of April 23, 2002

Margin Comparisons (%)		
	Company	**Industry**
Gross margin—TTM	15.37	30.86
Gross margin—5-year average	14.59	30.10
EBITD margin—TTM	3.75	7.38
EBITD margin—5-year average	3.53	6.80
Operating margin—TTM	3.36	5.56
Operating margin—5-year average	3.14	4.72
Pretax margin—TTM	2.47	4.87
Pretax margin—5-year average	2.01	4.17
Net margin—TTM	1.54	2.69
Net margin—5-year average	1.24	1.95
Tax rate—TTM	37.75	37.56
Tax rate—5-year average	37.78	38.50

TABLE 10.99 Group 1 Automotive Inc., Efficiency Data as of April 23, 2002

Efficiency Comparisons		
	Company	**Industry**
Revenue/employee—TTM	668,391	298,857
Net income/employee—TTM	10,269	10,108
Receivable turnover—TTM	165.37	38.54
Inventory turnover—TTM	7.11	5.67
Asset turnover—TTM	3.76	2.34

TABLE 10.100 Group 1 Automotive Inc., Return Data as of April 23, 2002

Return Comparisons (%)		
	Company	**Industry**
Return on assets—TTM	5.77	5.40
Return on assets—5-year average	4.69	5.40
Return on investment—TTM	12.58	7.44
Return on investment—5-year average	10.81	7.89
Return on equity—TTM	19.27	14.15
Return on equity—5-year average	15.90	14.97

TABLE 10.101 Group 1 Automotive Inc., Financial Strength Data as of April 23, 2002

Financial Strength		
	Company	Industry
Quick ratio MRQ	0.29	0.56
Current ratio MRQ	1.32	1.81
Long-term debt/equity MRQ	0.23	0.49
Total debt/equity MRQ	1.18	0.60
Interest coverage TTM	5.85	15.71

total debt-to-equity ratio is high, indicating heavy reliance on short-term debt. How long will the company stay oriented toward this kind of financing?

Finishing Touches   Review of the financial statements suggests the company is not looking to retire debt. In late 2001, it issued new equity to fund an acquisition war chest.

Checking the Price

Table 10.102 shows the valuation metrics for GPI, viewed under mid-scale standards. For the most part, GPI's numbers look good. I recall the

TABLE 10.102 Group 1 Automotive Inc., Valuation Metrics Data as of April 23, 2002

	Company	Industry	S&P 500
P/E based on estimate of next year's EPS	13.21	26.13	22.40
Projected long-term EPS growth rate	16.98	17.27	13.54
PEG ratio	0.778	1.515	1.654
P/E (TTM)	15.80	33.60	29.33
P/E—5-year high	53.76	49.97	50.02
P/E—5-year low	4.96	17.53	17.60
Yield	—	—	—
5-year dividend growth	—	—	—
Yield + growth	—	—	—
Payout ratio (TTM)	—	—	—
Price/book value (TTM)	2.41	4.72	5.13
MRQ price/net working capital	NM	10.331	NM
MRQ price/net cash (cash minus total debt)	NM	1.595	NM
Return on enterprise value (%)	10.2	4.4	4.2

wide range of long-term growth expectations and note that the PEG ratio would rise if I used the low end of the range of expectations. But doing so would keep the PEG at a still reasonable and below industry average 1.02 level.

Getting Our Money's Worth

Table 10.103 shows the expectation analysis for GPI. I calculate the predicted relative P/E by averaging all the available P/E-related data items. The growth capacity estimate presents a challenge because there are so many varying data items. I create my estimate by averaging the return on investment and equity items. This produces a modestly bearish index of 0.96.

Frankly, I don't feel overly confident in any of my assumptions. Reviewing the P/E data, I notice that the relative five-year high and low P/Es vary a lot from the current readings. If I stick to the current relative PEG and TTM ratios, the predicted relative P/E falls to .505 and the expectation index plunges to a very bearish 0.74.

And historic data gives me no comfort in my 14.64 percent growth capacity estimate. It's below the analyst consensus growth forecast, but above the low end of the range of expectations. And considering how wide that range is, analysts are obviously having similar trouble getting a handle on long-term prospects.

TABLE 10.103 Group 1 Automotive Inc., Analysis as of April 23, 2002

Expectation Analysis	
Time horizon (years)	5
Assumed risk-free return (annual %)	5.0
Assumed equity risk premium (annual %)	4.5
Beta	1.06
Current share price	43.50
Base-level EPS	3.33
Predicted future relative stock P/E	0.591
Predicted future market P/E	20.00
Predicted future stock P/E	11.82
Predicted future share price	69.33
Predicted future EPS	5.87
Expected annual EPS growth rate (%)	15.27
Estimated growth capacity (%)	14.64
Expectation index	0.96

The Analysis Keys

1. **Does the situation truly fit the theme you originally chose?** The basic footprints of success (margin, turnover, and return) are adequate. But I'm bothered by balance sheet issues: the low liquidity and the company's heavy use of short-term debt. And given that GPI is gearing up for more acquisitions, I have to wonder if the favorable footprints I see this far will persist. I'll be conservative and answer "no" to this key.

2. **Are there factors different from your original theme that you consider positive?** I'm satisfied with the good-stock angle and answer "yes" to this key.

3. **Is this investment opportunity free of any factors that you consider negative?** This key is a definite "no." The expectation analysis is modestly bearish, and reasonable changes in assumptions could push it lower. I'm worried about impending cyclical softness in the auto sector, and more worried about what appears to be a failure on the part of key investment community constituencies to fully address this.

The Decision Path

The no-yes-no answer pattern we get for the GPI analysis keys corresponds to Decision Path G, which is far down in the avoid zone.

Sell . . . Stocks for Which the Value Connection Has Weakened

## CHAPTER 11

Finding
the Exit

To many, the process of deciding whether to hold or sell is mysterious and difficult. That should come as no surprise considering the often contradictory rhetoric on the topic. Some advise investors to hold winning positions (ride profits) and dump losers. Others suggest selling winners to take money off the table and buying more of the losers to get a lower average purchase price. Both camps can't be right. Interestingly, though, both camps can be, and in fact are, wrong.

The problem with those strategies, and many others like them, is that they focus on whether the position is a winner or loser. And to describe a holding in such language, we have to be aware of the prices we paid when we purchased the stocks. That's where the difficulties arise. Our purchase prices are irrelevant. They reflect transactions that happened in the past. Nothing can change them. And most important, the market does not care. Our stocks will do whatever they do in the future (for better or worse) based on many factors, none of which include the prices we paid. If the companies have bright prospects, the stocks will probably perform well in the future, whether or not we paid higher prices for our shares in the past. If the companies have poor prospects, chances are the stocks will perform badly, whether or not we paid lower prices in the past. (Many who tried to ride paper profits on new economy stocks accumulated through 2000 learned the hard way that riding a winner doesn't work if the company is about to fall over a cliff.)

There is, of course, one exception to the notion that our purchase prices are irrelevant: taxes. Clearly, judicious selling can moderate our tax liabilities, especially when the market is experiencing extreme conditions, as was the case in late 2002, when investors had many (too many) opportunities to generate taxable losses. But it's important that you analyze your tax situation and your investment portfolio separately. If tax planning is going to motivate a hold-versus-sell decision, that's fine as long as you are consciously aware that this is what you are doing. Problems arise when one's opinion on a stock's merits gets clouded by tax considerations. If this happens, you may wind up forfeiting more because of poor investment decisions than you gain in tax benefits.

Tax considerations aside, the hold-versus-sell decision should be based on an assessment of future prospects. If company prospects seem bright and the stock seems reasonably valued, we should hold. If not, we should sell. In fact, a decision to hold or sell (the investment aspects of the decision, as distinct from tax considerations) is identical to a decision to buy or avoid. This becomes evident if you imagine yourself in the shoes of another investor with goals similar to yours who is considering whether to buy the same stock; perhaps this other individual may wind up buying the very shares you might sell. How do you think the other person will assess the shares? If you believe the other investor has reason to be bullish, that suggests you should hold on to your shares. Conversely, if the stock should seem unappealing to other investors with similar goals, that's probably a hint that you ought to be a seller.

Given this perspective, it should come as no surprise to learn that Step 4 (Sell) is, in a sense, a reprisal of the process we used to determine whether we should buy. We break this step down into three phases that are similar to the first three steps. Step 1 (Find) is adapted to what we refer to as Sell Phase A (Alert). Step 2 (Analyze) is adapted to Sell Phase B (Update). And Step 3 (Buy) translates to Sell Phase C (Reconsider). The latter uses three Update Keys (similar to the Analysis Keys) and eight Reconsideration Paths (similar to the Decision Paths).

We'll now look more closely at each of the sell phases. Then, in Chapter 12, we'll see how these concepts apply in real-life case studies.

SELL PHASE A: ALERT . . . CALLING ATTENTION TO THE NEED FOR REVIEW

Ideally, we will all check all our stocks every day. Realistically, this is not going to happen.

That's not the end of the world. Not every stock needs to be reviewed every day. In fact, some argue it's a good idea to refrain from looking too closely at our portfolios, lest we lose perspective and wind up acting as if certain events are more important than is really the case.

What we really need is a means for calling our attention to stocks that need to be reviewed at a particular point in time. Sell Phase A (Alert) is designed to do just that. There are three different circumstances that prompt us to review an individual stock holding: events, a review routine keyed to the passage of time, and sell-oriented screens.

Events

It's easy to recognize that events alert us to the need to review a position. We bought our stocks for particular reasons. Any event has the potential to alter the situation in such a way as to render our good-stock, good-company conclusions obsolete.

The key to the prior sentence is the word "potential." Most events will not alter the underlying company-stock stories. We examine events to the extent necessary to determine if this concern is serious.

Although all kinds of events are potentially important, there are three categories to which we should be especially attentive.

1. **Earnings Releases:** (This includes earnings guidance given in "pre-announcements" issued before earnings are formally reported.) News like this may be directly relevant to the extent the company's current latest results reflect considerations that are likely to prove sustainable for a prolonged period. In other words, examine earnings-related news for indications the company is likely to become more or less good than it has been in the past. Earnings releases are indirectly relevant in that the market tends to react vigorously to them. Whether we consider that right or wrong, we need to check to see if what might once have been a nice good-stock story has been materially altered.

2. **Significant Share Price Movements:** Extending the notion that the market's reaction to earnings news may alter a good-stock story, we should be attentive to any noteworthy share price movements, especially those that vary from overall market trends. Obviously, share price movements impact that valuation metrics that form the basis for our good-stock stories. And often, these movements can cue us to refresh our good-company stories. Stocks sometimes appear to move for no reason. But my experience has been that reasons for the movements, even if not discoverable right away, are always present. So whether or not we immediately recognize why a stock has moved sharply, we ought to consider ourselves alerted to the need for a review.

3. **Mergers/Acquisitions/Divestitures/Restructurings:** Events such as these change the very nature and character of the corporation

itself. So any good-company stories we may have articulated in the past must be refreshed.

Routine

No matter how quiet a company or stock seems on the surface, it's never prudent to let too much time pass before updating ourselves. Therefore, I suggest adopting a catchall policy of reviewing any company that has not been examined after the passage of a certain amount of time.

We can be flexible regarding how much time we're willing to let pass before we review a position. I suggest setting three months as the absolute outer limit. That's because companies are required to report results every three months (except for situations wherein non-U.S. companies have longer reporting intervals). Hence all the data we examined when we bought the stock is subject to a finite shelf life lasting no longer than three months.

Even those who consider themselves long-term investors should not let more than three months go by without a review. Under this perspective, a five-year investor is the same as a three-month investor who came up with the same answer at least 20 times in a row.

This addresses an important objection made by many to a so-called buy-and-hold style of investing. To me, the phrase "buy-and-hold" raises the specter of an investor who buys a stock and puts it away without looking at it for five years. That's reckless. A lot can happen during the holding period. So even if I hold a stock for five years, I would not accept the buy-and-hold label, as conventionally used. I'd refer to my approach as buy-and-review (with reviews being spaced no more than three months apart).

Sell-Oriented Screens

It's tempting to assume we should sell any stock that no longer makes the grade on the screen that brought it to light. That's not the case. Screens did initially call stocks to our attention, but our purchase decisions were based on much more comprehensive sets of facts. So, too, should our selling decisions. Still, we can use screening to help us recognize when we ought to go through the process of updating our analysis and making systematic hold-versus-sell decisions.

If we uncover a stock through a screen implemented pursuant to Sell Phase A (Alert), we do not necessarily sell. All we do is implement Sell Phase B (Update) and Sell Phase C (Reconsider). The latter is where the actual hold-versus-sell decision is made.

One way to create sell-oriented screens is to establish tests that directly define whether a company or stock fails to qualify as being good. In other words, we might screen for high valuation metrics, or poor company showings in such areas as margin, return, financial strength, and so forth. But this approach is subject to the same reservations expressed in Chapter 7 in connection with downscale value screening. There are countless reasons why a company or stock may no longer qualify as being good. If we attempt to prejudge a particular set of factors, we are likely to miss out on others we would want to know about.

Hence it is preferable to create sell-oriented screens using behavioral tests that seek evidence that others who look at the stock are concerned about its future. These screens are very simple, and often they'll include only one or two tests. We'll discuss them shortly.

Afterward, we'll address some logistics issues. Unlike what we did in Step 1 (Find), we're now screening against a much narrower "universe," the small number of stocks we own, as opposed to a full database. Not all applications are equally adaptable to that task. Also, our quest is more open-ended; we seek evidence that others may be wondering about the stock's merits. We're less attached to one sort of evidence as opposed to another. Hence it's a lot harder to choose from the available tests. That, too, is a logistical issue we'll address.

The Screening Tests Here are suggested testing approaches that can be used to alert us to the need for an updated analysis that might lead to a sale of the stock.

Relative Share Price Performance Since stock price trends reflect the aggregate of all opinions formed by all who examine a stock, these can be used as a cue that the Street's collective opinion has turned negative. And if we can zero in on lackluster relative performance, we're more likely to encounter situations where the negative opinion is based on company-specific, rather than general market, factors. Here are some suggested tests based on this approach.

Relative Strength Latest 4 Weeks < (Industry Average Relative Strength Last 4 Weeks) * .65

Relative Strength Latest 4 Weeks < (Relative Strength Last 13 Weeks) * .65

Price Change Last 4 Weeks < (Industry Average Price Change Last 4 Weeks) * .65

The multiplication factors help us avoid clutter. By definition, approximately half of all stocks are below average. And over time, stocks gain and lose relative stature even without significant changes in fundamentals. Hence, where possible, an alert screen should seek performances that are not just weak, but very weak.

If your screener allows for complex tests, as does the Multex premium application and Stock Investor Pro (in the latter, you'd need to create the separate components as custom fields), you can try something like this.

(Price Change Last 4 Weeks – Industry Average Price Change Last 4 Weeks) < (Price Change Last 13 Weeks – Industry Average Price Change Last 13 Weeks) * .65

This test searches for instances where the four-week stock-to-industry relationship is less favorable than the 13-week relationship. We use multiplication factors to identify situations where the relationship has deteriorated to a significant degree. Table 11.1 provides an example of the kinds of situations such a test can identify.

The alert is triggered, not by underperformance, but by a stock's narrower margin of victory. The strength of this test is that it can alert us early to stocks that may still be outperforming their respective industries. Its weakness lies in the fact that relative performance ebbs and flows all the time. Hence this test is probably best used in conjunction with others.

Practitioners of the value connection method may wish to reverse the price tests and seek exceptionally strong performance. Presumably, in such cases, the good-company aspects of the situation will be intact and may even have improved. But the valuation metrics may have changed in such a way as to diminish the good-stock story to the point where we no longer wish to hold.

Here are examples of how some of the earlier mentioned tests may be reversed to seek unusual share price strength.

Relative Strength Last 4 Weeks > (Industry Average Relative Strength Last 4 Weeks) * 1.35

TABLE 11.1 Deteriorating Relative Share Price Strength

	Share Price Performance	
	Last 4 Weeks	Last 13 Weeks
Stock	+2%	+5%
Industry average	+1%	−2%
Stock's "margin of victory"	+1%	+7%

(Price Change Last 4 Weeks – Industry Average Price Change Last 4 Weeks) > (Price Change Last 13 Weeks – Industry Average Price Change Last 13 Weeks) * 1.35

Analyst Actions   We use recommendations and/or changes in earnings estimates to identify situations toward which analysts have turned cool. Here are some examples.

Average Rating > (Average Rating 4 Weeks Ago) * 1.25

(Recall from Chapter 6 the definition of average rating: higher numbers are more bearish than lower numbers.) With a test like this, it can be useful to include multiplication factors (if permitted by your screener) to identify situations where the deterioration in analyst sentiment has been noteworthy.

The following tests aim directly at individual rating categories. Recall that normally, most analysts issue ratings within the top three (Strong Buy, Buy, or Hold) groups. Hence tests like these could alert us to the need for review.

Underperform Ratings > 0

Sell Ratings > 0

Underperform Ratings > 0 OR # Sell Ratings > 0

Underperform Ratings > # Underperform Ratings 4 Weeks Ago

Sell Ratings > # Sell Ratings 4 Weeks Ago

Buy Ratings 4 Weeks Ago – # Buy Ratings Now >= 3

In today's investment community culture, tests based on estimate revision need not go the extra mile to distinguish between large and modest alterations. Stocks react to almost any change, even those that amount to little more than fine-tuning. Hence the following tests could serve as useful alerts.

Latest Quarter Earnings Surprises < 0

Downward Estimate Revisions Last 4 Weeks > 0

Consensus Estimate Now < Consensus Estimate 4 Weeks Ago

But things change. Stay alert to the possibility that as time passes, share price reactions may distinguish between trivial and substantial estimate revisions. If that occurs, we should adjust our screening tests accordingly.

General Sentiment Criteria   The tests are not quite as powerful as the ones already discussed due to data-reporting lags. Still, tests like these can be helpful, especially if used in conjunction with tests based on price performance or analyst actions.

Institutional Shareholders < (# Institutional Shareholders 4 Weeks Ago) * .85

Institutional Net Shares Purchased < 0

Short Interest Now < Short Interest 4 Weeks Ago

Short Interest Now/Short Interest 4 Weeks Ago > 1.5

Note that I have not included a test based on insider selling. As discussed in Chapter 6, this occurrence is not as reliable an indicator of bearishness as we wish it could be.

Logistical Matters   Well-conceived sell-oriented screens, even those that use only one test, will often produce very large lists. It can be cumbersome to review them to see if they contain any of the stocks we own. The problem is magnified if we're not partial to any single alert category test and wish to use several screens. Moreover, some programs limit kinds of tests that can be created or the number of companies that can be listed. Here, we'll discuss ways to address these logistical issues.

Screeners That Are Unable to Handle the Tests   Not all screeners can handle sophisticated tests. If we use a simple screener, we may find ourselves especially frustrated if we try to create sophisticated relative share-price performance tests.

My first-choice recommendation to those who wish to get screen-generated alerts is to gain access to a screener capable of creating the best tests. For those unable to do so, *Screening the Market* presented a shadow screening technique that, although far from optimal, allows users of simple applications to get at least some screen-based assistance in generating alerts. The technique is described in Appendix A to this chapter.

Screeners That Limit the Result Set   Some screening applications limit the number of results that can be displayed. That means we can't take comfort in a stock's absence from a sell-oriented screen. For example, 1,500 stocks may meet an earnings revision test but the screener lists only the worst 300. If our stock met the test and was the 301st worst stock, it would not appear in the list. But we'd want to know about it.

There is no way around the fact that we will have to accept an imperfect solution. One, obviously, is to accept the results the screener gives including the fact that we will miss out on names we wish we could have seen, and wait for them to come to our attention through the other alerting mechanisms (event or routine).

Another option is to split the "universe" into several top-down categories and repeat the screen for each. In other words, we might couple an estimates revision screen with a requirement that stocks have market capitalizations above $5 billion. We might then repeat the estimates revision screen paired the next time with a test seeking market capitalizations between $1 billion and $5 billion. We could repeat for smaller market cap categories. By splitting the overall database into subgroups, we increase our workload, but we also increase the probability that the screener will be able to list all the stocks that meet the estimates revision test.

In fact, we can make sure all results can be displayed if we carefully design the top-down tests based on our portfolio composition. For example, if we own 15 stocks, 10 of which have market capitalizations between $125 million and $1.5 billion, while the rest are above $3 billion, we could use the following set of screens.

Consensus Estimate Now < Consensus Estimate 4 Weeks Ago
Market Capitalization >= $125 Million AND Market Capitalization < $300 Million

Consensus Estimate Now < Consensus Estimate 4 Weeks Ago
Market Capitalization >= $300 Million AND Market Capitalization < $500 Million

Consensus Estimate Now < Consensus Estimate 4 Weeks Ago
Market Capitalization >= $500 Million AND Market Capitalization < $750 Million

Consensus Estimate Now < Consensus Estimate 4 Weeks Ago
Market Capitalization >= $750 Million AND Market Capitalization < $1 Billion

Consensus Estimate Now < Consensus Estimate 4 Weeks Ago
Market Capitalization >= $1 Billion AND Market Capitalization <= $1.5 Billion

We may not need this exact number of groupings. We can use trial and error to determine how many we need based on the number of results we see in each list. If all the lists contain fewer names than the maximum the screener can display, then we can take comfort in knowing we'll see any of our stocks that pass the sell-oriented estimate revision test.

The applications that limit list sizes, SmartMoneySelect.com and MSN Money, also allow us to export our results to spreadsheets. We should use that option and in Excel combine all result sets into a single, comprehensive spreadsheet. (We'll see in Appendix B to this chapter how we can paste the ticker list into another spreadsheet template that quickly extracts the stocks we own.)

Very Large Result Sets   Obviously, one way to deal with very large result sets is to simply tough it out and search by eye (or via the spreadsheet Search feature if we downloaded our results into that format) to see whether each of the stocks we own is present. But there are better ways. One is to use an application like the Multex premium screener or Stock Investor Pro that allows us to create user portfolios. We should have one such portfolio listing the stocks we own. We then run the sell-oriented screens against that much smaller group, rather than against the entire database. If we use an application that cannot accommodate user portfolios but can download results to spreadsheet files (Smart MoneySelect.com and MSN Money), there is another solution. Appendix B to this chapter shows you how to create a simple spreadsheet template that searches through very large ticker lists (the screen results) to identify the ones that are also included on a much smaller list (the stocks you own).

Desire to Use a Variety of Alert Tests   Even those who use the best screeners can find sell-oriented screening to be a daunting process. That's because those who look at the sample tests presented earlier are highly tempted to want to use all of them. Obviously, we can force ourselves to narrow our choices to a reasonable number. But considering the nature of our task—identifying evidence of investment community concern—a case can be made for casting as wide a net as possible. But if we do that, just about every stock we own will always turn up with an alert.

Appendix C to this chapter offers a solution. It shows you how to create a spreadsheet template that will list the stocks that appear on each screen you create, contains a scoring mechanism that allows you to assign different levels of importance to each screen, and focuses on stocks generating the most urgent combination of alerts.

SELL PHASE B: UPDATE . . . THE SITUATION IN LIGHT OF NEW INFORMATION

Now we move to very familiar territory. In Sell Phase B (Update), we do the same things we discussed in Chapter 8 in connection with Step 2 (Analyze). We check the price tag of the merchandise we own by reviewing the valuation metrics relevant to our chosen (upscale, middle-market, or downscale) shopping style. We check the quality of the merchandise. And we use the expectation analysis to determine if we're getting our money's worth. The only difference between what we do now and what we did before is the information we see, which has changed as time passed.

The absence of an elaborate new evaluation procedure might strike some as a letdown. But in fact, this is a situation where the simple answer is the most powerful. As noted earlier, we're trying to see the situation through the eyes of a hypothetical investor who might be trying to decide whether to buy any shares we choose to sell. So it makes sense that our activities in Sell Phase B (Update) should mimic what he or she is doing in Step 2 (Analyze).

SELL PHASE C: RECONSIDER . . . WHETHER YOU SHOULD STILL HOLD THE STOCK

As was the case at the conclusion of Step 2 (Analyze), we find ourselves with a lot of information about our holdings and a lot of opinions about what we've learned. If everything strikes us as being negative, we'll sell. If everything strikes us as being positive, we'll hold. Unfortunately, life is rarely that simple. As with the buy decision, we're most likely to face both pros and cons. We'll weigh and balance these the way we did before by using a set of Update Keys and Reconsideration Paths that are similar to the Analysis Keys and Decision Paths described in Chapter 9.

Update Keys

Update Key 1: Is Your Original Reason for Buying the Stock Still Valid? In *Screening the Market*, I encouraged readers to apply this key based not on the original screening themes, but rather on the actual investment case that emerged from Step 3 (Buy). As we saw in Chapter 9, it is quite possible for the Analysis Keys to point us toward stocks that are quite different from what we had in mind when we started searching. But the situation here is different. We are dealing, here, with a specific style, the value connection. Even Decision Path C, which opens the way for happy accidents (stocks that shine for unanticipated reasons) keeps us fairly close to home: That path required a "yes" answer to Analysis Key 3, something that could not have occurred unless the situation came up as satisfactory in the expectation analysis. Hence, for the value connection method, we will interpret all the Update Keys the same way we interpreted the Analysis Keys, in light of the primary, secondary, and alternative themes we started with.

Accordingly, if we started with a primary theme based on good-company concepts, we will answer "yes" to Update Key 1 if our update shows the company to still be satisfactory in that regard. We will do this even if, in Step 3 (Buy), we wound up buying mainly because of a secondary good-stock theme and/or an unrelated alternative theme.

This promotes clarity given that we are focused here on one particular investment philosophy, the value connection. (This is different from the *Screening the Market* scenario. There we were neutral as to which investment philosophy one pursued.) Note, though, that by the time we complete all three keys, we will have had an opportunity to recreate any still viable alternative investment rationale that motivated us back on day one.

Update Key 2: Are There Any Other Factors You Regard as Positive?   Consistent with the value connection slant, we modified the phrasing of this key to prompt an affirmative answer if any "other" positive factors are present. (They need not qualify as "new" factors as in *Screening the Market*.) As was the case in Step 2 (Analyze), the second key focuses our attention on alternative or secondary themes. (Recall that if our primary theme was couched in good-company terms, good-stock concepts would constitute a secondary theme. Alternative themes are those that are unrelated to value connection principles.) Answer "yes" to Update Key 2 if you feel comfortable holding on the basis of the secondary theme. If the secondary theme is not satisfied, answer "yes" or "no" depending on whether any alternative themes could justify holding the stock.

Update Key 3: Is the Situation Free of Other Factors You Regard as Negative?   Regardless of how the situation fared under the expectation analysis originally performed as part of Step 2 (Analyze), we perform a new one based on updated information as part of Sell Phase B (Update). If the revised expectation analysis produces an unfavorable conclusion, answer "no" to this key. If the revised expectation analysis produces a satisfactory result, answer "yes" or "no" to this key depending on whether any other negatives appear at the time of the update.

Reconsideration Paths

As was the case in Step 3 (Buy), we now have a three-way combination of yes-or-no answers to the questions posed by the Update Keys. Each combination is assigned to a Reconsideration Path that helps us prioritize the stocks we review in terms of hold versus sell. Table 11.2 ranks the possible Update Key combinations from best to worst.

The stocks on Reconsideration Path A are the ones that can be most comfortably held. Any stock on Reconsideration Path H should be sold immediately. The other paths represent in-between scenarios.

Reconsideration Path A (Yes-Yes-Yes) Here are the qualities a stock must exhibit to be on Reconsideration Path A.

- **Update Key 1—Yes:** The situation remains consistent with our original primary (good-company or good-stock) theme.
- **Update Key 2—Yes:** Based on the updated information, we see attractive investment features apart from the primary theme. These positives may or may not include the secondary theme (good-company or good-stock, the one we didn't make primary).
- **Update Key 3—Yes:** The updated expectation analysis was satisfactory, and the situation is free from any other factors that we regard as negative.

These are our favorite stocks. They comply with our primary theme and at least one additional theme. And the updated expectation analysis shows a good match between what we pay and what we get for our

TABLE 11.2 The Reconsideration Paths

Reconsideration Path	Update Key 1 (Primary Theme)	Update Key 2 (Secondary and/or Alternative Themes)	Update Key 3 (Expectation Analysis and/or Other Themes)
A	Yes	Yes	Yes
B	Yes	No	Yes
C	No	Yes	Yes
D	Yes	Yes	No
The Neutral Zone			
E	No	No	Yes
F	Yes	No	No
G	No	Yes	No
H	No	No	No

money. If we didn't already own the stock, we'd probably buy it. Accordingly, we won't sell unless we want to reduce our exposure to equities in general or need to raise cash, and have no stocks on lower paths that can be sold instead.

Reconsideration Path B (Yes-No-Yes)   Here are the qualities a stock must exhibit to be on Reconsideration Path B.

- **Update Key 1—Yes:** The situation remains consistent with our original primary (good-company or good-stock) theme.
- **Update Key 2—No:** The updated information does not indicate the presence of an investment case based on our secondary theme (good-company or good-stock, the one we didn't make primary), nor does it reveal any other attractive investment features.
- **Update Key 3—Yes:** The updated expectation analysis was satisfactory, and the situation is free from any other factors that we regard as negative.

This situation is not perfect, but it's pretty darn good. The situation meets our primary theme and satisfies the expectation analysis. Even though it doesn't satisfy any additional themes, we'd probably still consider buying if we didn't already own the shares. Accordingly, given that we already have the stock, we'll consider it a solid hold (unless we have to sell something and the only alternatives are all on Path A).

Reconsideration Path C (No-Yes-Yes)   Here are the qualities a stock must exhibit to be on Reconsideration Path C.

- **Update Key 1—No:** The situation is no longer consistent with our original primary (good-company or good-stock) theme.
- **Update Key 2—Yes:** Based on the updated information, we see attractive investment features apart from the primary theme. These positives may or may not include the secondary theme (good-company or good-stock, the one we didn't make primary).
- **Update Key 3—Yes:** The updated expectation analysis was satisfactory, and the situation is free from any other factors that we regard as negative.

Now we're starting to drop down in terms of how comfortable we are continuing to hold. Basically, the situation is fine. The stock satisfies at least one rational investment case, and the situation passes muster under our expectation analysis.

The only fly in the ointment is that the theme that constitutes a basis for holding differs from our original primary theme. If we started out this way (i.e., we bought as a result of its having originally been on Decision Path C), we ought to feel comfortable holding. On the other hand, if we started by buying this stock due to its position on Decision Path A or B, its presence on Reconsideration Path C represents a decline, which might sway a borderline decision. Note, though, that we would still give greater sell priority to stocks on the lower paths.

Reconsideration Path D (Yes-Yes-No)   Here are the qualities a stock must exhibit to be on Reconsideration Path D.

- **Update Key 1—Yes:** The situation remains consistent with our original primary (good-company or good-stock) theme.
- **Update Key 2—Yes:** Based on the updated information, we see attractive investment features apart from the primary theme. These positives may or may not include the secondary theme (good-company or good-stock, the one we didn't make primary).
- **Update Key 3—No:** The present situation is not free of negative factors; this may or may not include an unsatisfactory conclusion from the updated expectation analysis.
  We worry about these stocks, but we continue to like them because, objectively speaking, they satisfy our primary goals as well as at least one other theme (secondary or alternative). The problem is that we now face some unpleasant baggage.

In theory, we should sell any such stock. But if we do that, we may wind up having few or no stocks. As noted in Chapter 9, investors love to worry, and we'll find ourselves saying "no" to Key 3 very often. Hence it's worth our while to dig more closely into these stocks. Within Path D, our hold priorities should match the buy priorities established for this path in Chapter 9.

- **Path D1:** The stock passes the expectation analysis; the baggage arises from a different issue. Also, the "yes" to Key 2 comes from the fact that at the very least the stock satisfies a secondary value connection theme (if there's also an unrelated alternative theme, so much the better).
- **Path D2:** The stock passes the expectation analysis; the baggage arises from a different issue. But the "yes" to Key 2 comes from the stock's having satisfied an alternative theme unrelated to the value connection.

- **Path D3:** The stock does not satisfy the expectation analysis. But we answered "yes" to Key 2 because it did satisfy a secondary value connection theme.
- **Path D4:** The stock does not satisfy the expectation analysis, and it does not satisfy a secondary value connection theme. (The "yes" to Key 2 relates to an unrelated alternative theme.) We're stretching here. Absent a gut feeling, we are probably better off selling.

The Neutral Zone   Reconsideration Path D already dips its toes into the sell zone (Path D4). But for the most part, these are stocks we can justify holding. The lower paths consist of stocks we should sell. Table 11.3 depicts the relationship between the paths as used in Step 3 (Buy) and as used here in Step 4 (Sell).

Paths E through H are ranked on a bad-to-worst hierarchy. However, it's hard to justify holding any of these stocks. The main purpose of the lower hierarchy is to spotlight how urgent it is to resist an often-recurring emotional attachment to stocks that ought not remain in our portfolios.

Reconsideration Path E (No-No-Yes)   Here are the qualities a stock must exhibit to be on Reconsideration Path E.

- **Update Key 1—No:** The situation is no longer consistent with our original primary (good-company or good-stock) theme.
- **Update Key 2—No:** The updated information does not indicate the presence of an investment case based on our secondary theme (good-company or good-stock, the one we didn't make primary), nor does it reveal any other attractive investment features.
- **Update Key 3—Yes:** The updated expectation analysis was satisfactory, and the situation is free from any other factors that we regard as negative.

TABLE 11.3 The Decision Paths in Context

Reconsideration Paths		Decision Paths	
A			A
B	Hold Zone	Buy Zone	B
C			C
D			D
E			E
F	Sell Zone	Avoid Zone	F
G			G
H			H

It's tempting to continue to hold these stocks based on inertia. Nothing really bad has surfaced. But there's nothing good happening, either. Try to resist inertia and to bring yourself to sell these stocks. If the value connection method cannot produce better opportunities, take that as a hint that the overall market may be facing tough times.

Reconsideration Path F (Yes-No-No)   Here are the qualities a stock must exhibit to be on Reconsideration Path F.

- **Update Key 1—Yes:** The situation remains consistent with our original primary (good-company or good-stock) theme.
- **Update Key 2—No:** The updated information does not indicate the presence of an investment case based on our secondary theme (good-company or good-stock, the one we didn't make primary), nor does it reveal any other attractive investment features.
- **Update Key 3—No:** The present situation is not free of negative factors; this may or may not include an unsatisfactory conclusion from the updated expectation analysis.

These stocks continue to satisfy our primary theme, so a decision to hold could not be attributed to inertia. But it might be attributed to a lack of diligence. That's because negative baggage has surfaced. Indeed, as value investors, there's one example of Path F we hope to be confronted with frequently: a stock that has moved high enough to create a condition of overvaluation. We'd love nothing more than to encounter baggage such as this, sell, and reinvest elsewhere.

Reconsideration Path G (No-Yes-No)   Here are the qualities a stock must exhibit to be on Reconsideration Path G.

- **Update Key 1—No:** The situation is no longer consistent with our original primary (good-company or good-stock) theme.
- **Update Key 2—Yes:** Based on the updated information, we see attractive investment features apart from the primary theme. These positives may or may not include the secondary theme (good-company or good-stock, the one we didn't make primary).
- **Update Key 3—No:** The present situation is not free of negative factors; this may or may not include an unsatisfactory conclusion from the updated expectation analysis.

As with Path F, there is negative baggage. But these stocks are a step lower since the goal they satisfy is not the one to which we give primary emphasis.

Reconsideration Path H (No-No-No)   Here are the qualities a stock must exhibit to be on Reconsideration Path H.

- **Update Key 1—No:** The situation is no longer consistent with our original primary (good-company or good-stock) theme.
- **Update Key 2—No:** The updated information does not indicate the presence of an investment case based on our secondary theme (good-company or good-stock, the one we didn't make primary), nor does it reveal any other attractive investment features.
- **Update Key 3—No:** The present situation is not free of negative factors; this may or may not include an unsatisfactory conclusion from the updated expectation analysis.

There is no reason to hold stocks like this. They carry negative baggage, and do not appear to satisfy any legitimate investment theme.

APPENDIX A TO CHAPTER 11

Shadow Screening Techniques

Shadow screening is a technique we can use to get sell alerts with a screener that is not sufficiently sophisticated to handle the kinds of tests described earlier in Chapter 11. I'm going to acknowledge up front that I do not use this admittedly cumbersome procedure. I use the Multex premium application, which can execute the screening suggestions made in the chapter. Those who seek a lower-priced application can create good sell screens with the Stock Investor Pro and SmartMoneySelect.com programs. Shadow screening is best suited for less sophisticated applications.

Generally, shadow screens are similar to the ones we created in Step 1 (Find), but the tests are less stringent. The procedure can be summed up as follows.

- Check the screen used to initially call attention to the stock. If the stock is still listed, no alert is generated.
- If the stock is no longer listed on the original screen, check to see whether it makes the less stringent shadow screen. If the stock is on the shadow screen, no alert is generated.
- If the stock fails to make the initial screen and also is absent from the less stringent shadow screen, treat this pair of omissions as an alert and proceed to Sell Phase B (Update). If a stock reviewed pursuant to this procedure emerges through the process as a hold, it is not necessary to repeat the procedure each and every time the

stock fails to appear on the initial screen. From this point on, wait until an alert is next prompted by an event or routine (i.e., the passage of time).

Here's an example of how we can use shadow screens.

Assume I select a stock based on the Relative Value screen, which is created using the Multex premium application and whose results are published on the MultexInvestor.com web site. As we saw in the appendix to Chapter 7, the tests are:

1. TTM P/E <= (Industry Average TTM P/E) * 1.1
2. TTM Price/Sales <= (Industry Average TTM Price/Sales) * 1.1
3. TTM Price/Free Cash Flow <= (Industry Average TTM Price/Free Cash Flow) * 1.1
4. Projected P/E Next Year <= (Long-Term Growth) * 2
5. TTM % EPS Growth >= (Industry Average TTM % EPS Growth) * 1.25
6. 3 Year % EPS Growth >= (Industry Average 3 Year % EPS Growth) * 1.25
7. Share Price % Change Last 4 Weeks > Industry Average Share Price % Change Last 4 Weeks

A user who does not have access to the premium application may wish to use the free Multex screener to generate alerts.

First, check the latest results for the Relative Value screen. If the stock is absent, the user might move on to a simpler shadow screen like this:

1. TTM P/E <= 25
2. Forward-Looking P/E < 20
3. Forward-Looking P/E/Projected Growth Rate <= 1.75
4. PYQ % EPS Growth Rate >= 5
5. PYQ % Sales Growth >= 5
6. TTM EPS Growth >= 10

If the stock also fails to make this relaxed value screen, treat that omission as an alert and move on to Sell Phase B (Update).

The preceding example involved a basic shadow screen, a less stringent approach to the same primary theme as used in the original screen.

There is an alternative. The following example is a general-purpose shadow screen that mimics the behavioral tests we'd use if we had a more sophisticated application. But, of course, its tests here are less stringent.

1. Stock Price % Change Last 4 Weeks >= 0
2. Mean Analyst Rating <= 2.5
3. Short Interest Ratio Now <= (Short Interest Ratio 1 Month Ago) * 1.1
4. Institutional Net Shares Purchased >= 0

We'll assume an alert is generated only if the stock fails to appear in the basic Relative Value screen and also fails to make this general-purpose behavioral shadow screen.

APPENDIX B TO CHAPTER 11

Spreadsheet Ticker-Matching Template

Figure 11B.1 illustrates a spreadsheet you can use to quickly determine which, if any, among the stocks you own are included among those con-

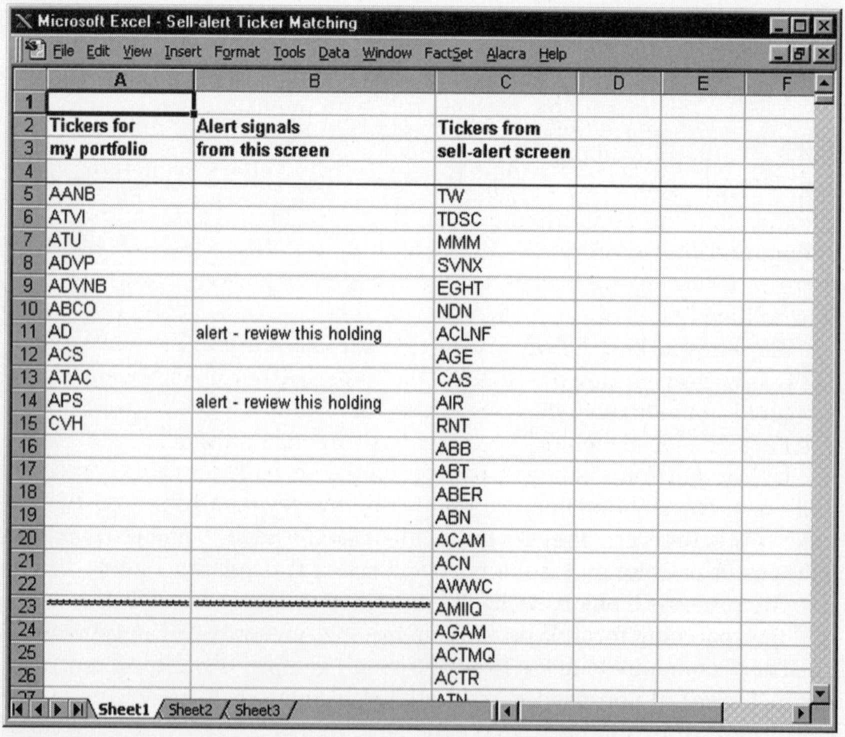

	A	B	C	D	E	F
1						
2	Tickers for	Alert signals	Tickers from			
3	my portfolio	from this screen	sell-alert screen			
4						
5	AANB		TW			
6	ATVI		TDSC			
7	ATU		MMM			
8	ADVP		SVNX			
9	ADVNB		EGHT			
10	ABCO		NDN			
11	AD	alert - review this holding	ACLNF			
12	ACS		AGE			
13	ATAC		CAS			
14	APS	alert - review this holding	AIR			
15	CVH		RNT			
16			ABB			
17			ABT			
18			ABER			
19			ABN			
20			ACAM			
21			ACN			
22			AWWC			
23	******************	******************************	AMIIQ			
24			AGAM			
25			ACTMQ			
26			ACTR			

FIGURE 11B.1 Spreadsheet Ticker-Matching Template

tained in a much larger list (presumably, a list of stocks appearing in a screen designed to produce sell alerts).

You could eyeball the large list to see which stocks you recognize. But results of sell alert screens can number in the hundreds, or even thousands, so a spreadsheet such as this can be a great time-saver.

Columns A and C contain ticker lists. In Column A, type (or paste) the tickers of the stocks you own. In Column C, paste the tickers appearing in the sell alert screen you are using. (Presumably, you will have generated the screen in an application that allows you to download the results in spreadsheet format. All you need do is copy the ticker column into your Windows clipboard and paste it into Column C of the template.)

Cell B5 contains the following formula:

=IF(ISNA(MATCH(A5,C$5:C$10004,0)),' ','alert - review this holding')

The key is the Excel MATCH function. In the formula above, Excel uses the ticker in Cell A5 as a starting point. It examines each ticker in Column C, rows 5 through 10,004 to see if there is a match with A5. If so, we'd normally see in B5 the row number (using the first cell in the row 5 to 10,004 range as 1) of the matching ticker. If no match is found, B5 would show Excel's #NA error message.

We do not care about the row number of the match; we just want to know whether any match exists. So we insert the matching activity into an IF-THEN function. Specifically, we want a yes-or-no answer to whether the cell contains the #NA error message. If #NA appears, we understand that there is no match and we can leave the cell blank. If there is a match, we flag it with a message that says "Alert—review this holding."

The lines in Row 23 of Columns A and B are there for convenience. They show how far down Column B the formula from B5 has been copied. We could immediately allow for larger portfolios, but the more formulas you have, the more memory your spreadsheet will consume.

If your portfolio is larger, use the spreadsheet functionality to insert additional rows above line 23. Then, copy the formula from Cell B5 into your new rows. The "$" sign indicators in the formula will make sure that each ticker in Column A is matched against each ticker in Column C, even if there are some blank rows in Column C.

The matching formula as specified should give you all the rows you'll need to accommodate any size screen result set (the biggest I've seen was in the 4,000s). If you need more than 10,000 rows, you can easily modify the formula, for example to make the match range C$5:C$12004 instead of C$5:C$10004.

APPENDIX C TO CHAPTER 11

Spreadsheet Template for Combining and Scoring Results of Several Screens

Figure 11C.1 illustrates a spreadsheet you can use to quickly determine if any among the stocks you own are included in either of two sell alert screens, and if so, set priorities by giving one screen more importance than the other.

There are some important similarities to the spreadsheet template presented in Appendix 11B. Column A contains the list of tickers for the stocks you own. As to tickers from sell alert screens, we now have two lists, one of which is pasted in Column F and the other in Column G. The portfolio size marker is again placed for convenience on line 23.

As with the Appendix 11B spreadsheet, the core is built around use of Excel's built-in MATCH and ISNA functions. Now, however, if we have a

	A	B	C	D	E	F	G
1				Individual-screen alert scores			
2				10	5		
3							
4		Total		short	price	Tickers from	Tickers from
5	Tickers for	Alert		interest	deterioration	short interest	price deterioration
6	my portfolio	Score		alert score	alert score	screen	screen
7							
8	AANB					TW	ATTY
9	ATVI	5			5	TDSC	FLWS
10	ATU					MMM	ISOL
11	ADVP	5			5	SVNX	FSBC
12	ADVNB	5			5	EGHT	TW
13	ABCO					NDN	TFSM
14	AD	10		10		ACLNF	TFHD
15	ACS					AGE	TCCC
16	ATAC					CAS	COMS
17	APS	15		10	5	AIR	THDO
18	CVH	5			5	RNT	MMM
19						ABB	TSIH
20						ABT	KDE
21						ABER	FDNX
22						ABN	SE
23						ACAM	IFLYQ
24						ACN	ACCO
25						AWWC	EGHT
26						AMIIQ	NDN
27						ACAM	TACV

FIGURE 11C.1 Spreadsheet Ticker-Scoring Template

match, we don't simply want a verbal message informing us so. We want a numeric score.

We input the scores in row 2. Cell D2 contains a score indicating our preferred level of importance for one screen (in this example, one of the screens using short interest data described on page 284), and Cell E2 contains our score for the other screen (in this example, one of the share price deterioration screens described on page 281). The scores assigned in Figure 11C.1 indicate that we place twice as much importance on the short-interest alert screen.

In Cell D8, we use the following formula.

$$=IF(ISNA(MATCH(\$A8,F\$8:F\$10007,0)),'\ ',D\$2)$$

Once again, if there is no match between the ticker in A8 and any ticker in Column F, rows 8 through 10,007 (i.e., if the spreadsheet calculates a #NA error message), Cell D8 will stay blank. If there is a match, Cell D8 will pick up the score we assigned to this screen, the number in Cell D2.

In Cell E8, we use the following formula.

$$=IF(ISNA(MATCH(\$A8,G\$8:G\$10007,0)),'\ ',E\$2)$$

This works the same as the preceding formula. The only difference is that it matches the ticker in A8 against screen tickers appearing in Column G, rather than Column F, and if a match is found, it picks up the score from Cell E2, rather than D2.

As with the spreadsheet presented in Appendix B, the use of "$" indicators in the formula is such as to preserve the integrity of the calculations even if you copy the formulas down to additional rows, as you would have to do if you insert new rows to accommodate a larger portfolio.

Cell B8 contains the following formula, which can be copied down to additional rows should you need to add more stocks to your portfolio.

$$=IF(SUM(D8:E8)>0,SUM(D8:E8),'\ ')$$

Essentially, it adds the scores, if any, in D8 and E8. The IF-THEN structure you see is designed for error handling. It leaves B8 blank if the ticker in A8 does not match any of those in Columns F or G. Absent the IF-THEN logic, you'd see error messages for any row that did not have matches between Column A and both Columns F and G. There is more than one way we could have handled such potential "errors." This approach was selected for cosmetic reasons.

Figure 11C.2 shows how this spreadsheet would look if you decide to add a third sell alert screen.

We paste the tickers for the newest screen (in this case, one of the estimate revision screens presented on page 283) in Column I. Then, we revise the analytic portions of the spreadsheet according to the following steps.

1. Insert a new column after E. This will push the original screens from Columns F and G to Columns G and H.

2. Paste tickers for the new screen in Column I.

3. Input the importance score for the new screen into Cell F2.

4. Copy the formulas in Column E (for however many rows you are using) to Column F. The "$" marker in front of Column A references will assure that the formula, as reproduced in Column F, will properly assume your portfolio is in Column A. As to the screen, you will note, after copying, that Excel assumes your portfolio is being compared to

X Microsoft Excel - Sell-alert Ticker Scoring - revised

File Edit View Insert Format Tools Data Window FactSet Alacra Help

	A	B	C	D	E	F	G	H	I
1				Individual-screen alert scores					
2				10	5	3			
3							Tickers	Tickers	Tickers
4		Total		short	price	estimate	short	price	estimate
5	Tickers for	Alert		interest	deterioration	cuts	interest	deterioration	cuts
6	my portfolio	Score		alert score	alert score	alert score	screen	screen	screen
7									
8	AANB						TW	ATTY	TW
9	ATVI	8			5	3	TDSC	FLWS	AIR
10	ATU						MMM	ISOL	ABB
11	ADVP	5			5		SVNX	FSBC	ABT
12	ADVNB	5			5		EGHT	TW	ANF
13	ABCO						NDN	TFSM	ABY
14	AD	10		10			ACLNF	TFHD	ACE
15	ACS						AGE	TCCC	ATVI
16	ATAC						CAS	COMS	ACTU
17	APS	15		10	5		AIR	THDO	AYI
18	CVH	5			5		RNT	MMM	ADBE
19							ABB	TSIH	ADIC
20							ABT	KDE	AEIS
21							ABER	FDNX	AMD
22							ABN	SE	AES
23							ACAM	IFLYQ	APD
24							ACN	ACCO	ARG
25							AWWC	EGHT	ALB
26							AMIIQ	NDN	AA
27							ACAM	TACY	ALKS

Sheet1 / Sheet2 / Sheet3 /

FIGURE 11C.2   Revised Spreadsheet Ticker-Scoring Template

the list of tickers in Column I and read the score from F2. The formula in F8 will look like this.

=IF(ISNA(MATCH($A8,I$8:I$10007,0)),' ',F$2)

5. Alter the score summation formula in B8 so that it looks like this. (On row 8, we now look to the sum of Columns D through F, rather than D through E.)

=IF(SUM(D8:F8)>0,SUM(D8:F8),' ')

Notice what the scoring does. Because of the scores we assigned, we see that it is more urgent to review AD, which appears in one sell alert screen, than ATVI, which appears in two screens. We also see that APS, which, like AD, appears in two screens, warrants closer attention because it has a higher score (it appears in the two screens we designated as being more important).

We have considerable discretion in how many stocks we review. Many of our stocks will very frequently appear on at least one sell alert screen. We want to focus our attention on the most important situations. In this example, we might decide to review only stocks having scores above 5, which means we would not update ourselves on ADVP, ADVNB, and CVH. If you think the price deterioration signal is, by itself, sufficient to warrant review, give it a higher score. That way, the only stocks to escape review would be those that appear on no screens, or only on the estimate cuts screen, which we ranked 3.

## CHAPTER 12

Holding and Selling: Case Studies

In Chapter 10, we applied our find-analyze-buy procedure to nine stocks. In two cases (Oracle and Group 1 Automotive), the stocks wound up on Decision Paths in the avoid zone. But the other seven turned out to be at least somewhat buyable. For purposes of this chapter, we'll assume those stocks were actually purchased and are now being reviewed pursuant to Step 4 (Sell).

In all cases, we'll assume Sell Phase A (Alert) was triggered by the passing of time.

- The two stocks we bought on April 20, 2000 (AAON Incorporated and Bebe Stores) will be reviewed based on information available on April 20, 2001.
- The four stocks we bought on April 20, 2001 (Engineered Support System, Graco, Sonic Corporation, and Patterson Dental) will be reviewed based on information available as of April 23, 2002.
- As of this writing, not enough time has elapsed to permit a one-year follow-up for our lone April 23, 2002, purchase (University of Phoenix Online). Hence it will be reviewed based on a six-month review using information available as of October 25, 2002.

Do not assume the reviews presented here are the first we would have made since purchasing the stocks. Recall from Chapter 11 that based on the shelf life of financial data, we should not allow more than three months to pass before a review. (We can, of course, do it sooner if screen or event-based alerts are generated.) Assume that the stocks to be discussed here were all reviewed previously and that in all cases the stocks wound up on Reconsideration Paths in the hold zone.

In reviewing these case studies, the same general points made early in Chapter 10 regarding the examples we explored there (letting the numbers carry the story, mixing qualitative with quantitative, etc.) apply here as well. And in the context of Step 4 (Sell), two additional points bear mentioning.

- **We will consider how our investments performed up till now,** even though our profit/loss status is not generally relevant to a sell-or-hold decision (see pages 277–278). We may thoroughly understand and accept the fact that a stock's future fortunes will be what they'll be without reference to whether we, individually, are ahead or behind. But we are human and accordingly cannot be expected to turn a completely blind eye toward this issue. Besides, prior share price performance can provide useful feedback about our earlier approach to the stock. Notice, though, that such considerations will not determine our ultimate hold-or-sell decision.
- **We'll pay closer attention to the fact that the Reconsideration Paths are used to set priorities,** rather than serve as a strict hold-versus-sell model. (The same can be said of the buy-oriented Decision Paths.) It is linguistically comfortable to describe stocks as buys, holds, or sells. But depending on what other stocks we're looking at, we may readily decide to sell stocks that fall on paths within what Chapter 11 referred to as the hold zone. For example, if we were choosing between holding Stock ABC, which falls on Reconsideration Path D, or buying Stock XYZ, which falls on Decision Path B, we'd wind up selling ABC and buying XYZ (assuming we don't have the funds to own both issues). On the other hand, if ABC were on subpath D1 and XYZ on subpath D3, we'd bypass XYZ and continue to hold ABC.

In Chapter 10, a decision whether to check the price before checking the merchandise or vice versa was based on whether the idea came to light through a good-stock or good-company screen. We could certainly establish our update sequence the same way. However, in this chapter we'll proceed in all cases by looking first at the price, based on the aforementioned emotional attachment to this factor we have when it comes to the stocks we already own. As before, we'll consistently assume a 5 percent risk-free rate of return and a 4 to 5 percent general equity risk premium.

Also, aside from information necessary to estimate growth capacity (in connection with the expectation analysis), updated checking-the-merchandise data tables will be presented only where there has been a noteworthy change. This is done solely for the sake of convenience; company-oriented data does not usually change as rapidly and dramatically as does data relating to stock valuation. But in real life, we would look at updated data with every bit as much thoroughness as we did during Step 2 (Analyze).

In all cases, the following abbreviations are used.

TTM	Trailing 12 months
MRQ	Most recent quarter
NA	Data is not available
NM	Data is not meaningful

AAON INCORPORATED (AAON)

AAON has not sparkled since I deemed it a buy following its April 20, 2000, appearance in my Growth at a Reasonable Price screen. Table 12.1 shows that the stock modestly outperformed the S&P 500, but considering this issue's micro-cap status, the Russell 2000 is a more relevant benchmark, and AAON trailed that index.

Updating the Price

In Chapter 10, I described the stock as being "dirt cheap" based on the April 2000 valuation metrics (Table 10.1). Now, a year later, Table 12.2 shows that it's even cheaper. Interestingly, I can't recompute the PEG ratio on an apples-to-apples basis because the lone analyst covering the stock did not publish estimates for the next fiscal year's earnings or long-term growth. So I created my own PEG ratio based on historic data. Under this approach, AAON's PEG ratio is still modest. More interesting, though, is the diminished interest on the part of the analyst.

TABLE 12.1 AAON Incorporated, Calculations as of April 20, 2001

	Date	Stock Price	S&P 500	Russell 2000
Buy	4/20/00	20.68	1,434.54	481.84
Review	4/20/01	19.00	1,242.98	466.71
% Change		−8.1	−13.4	−3.1

TABLE 12.2   AAON Incorporated, Updated Valuation Metrics Data as of
April 20, 2001

	Company	Industry	S&P 500
P/E based on estimate of next year's EPS	NA	—	23.99
Projected long-term EPS growth rate	18.14*	14.28*	17.71*
PEG ratio	0.506*	1.532*	1.603*
P/E (TTM)	9.17	21.88	28.38
P/E—5-year high	26.79	31.64	50.41
P/E—5-year low	8.85	12.40	17.31
Yield	—	—	—
5-year dividend growth	—	—	—
Yield + growth	—	—	—
Payout ratio (TTM)	—	—	—
Price/book value (TTM)	2.96	3.10	6.17
MRQ price/net working capital	14.534	7.228	NM
MRQ price/net cash (cash minus total debt)	NM	6.743	7.924
Return on enterprise value (%)	16.9	7.1	5.0

*Growth rate based on historic five-year sales growth; P/E is for TTM period.

Updating the Merchandise

This section of the update confirms that AAON is really falling off the
radar. Not only do we not have a complete set of estimates, but general
sentiment is lackluster even by standards of the so-so miscellaneous capital goods group. Interestingly, though, company fundamentals have
strengthened. The rhetoric surrounding AAON is still the same: Results
will suffer as commercial construction experiences a cyclical slowdown.
But through early 2001, that has not happened. Over the past year, AAON
handily beat estimates.

In Step 2 (Analyze), I cited Table 10.6 and noted AAON's industry-
lagging sales growth as a concern. But that comparison had reversed itself. Now, in the context of Sell Phase B (Update), we learn that AAON
achieved a 17.46 percent TTM sales growth rate, versus 9.72 percent for
the industry. AAON's margin and return characteristics remain strong, as
was the case in early 2000.

Still Getting Our Money's Worth?

Table 12.3 shows the updated expectation index for AAON. The predicted
relative P/E is based on an average of all the relative (company-to-S&P
500) P/E data appearing in the spreadsheet template (the numbers can be
seen in Table 12.2). Table 12.4 is the starting point for estimated growth ca-

TABLE 12.3 AAON Incorporated, Updated Analysis as of April 20, 2001

Expectation Analysis	
Time horizon (years)	6
Assumed risk-free return (annual %)	5.0
Assumed equity risk premium (annual %)	4.5
Beta	0.96
Current share price	8.44
Base-level EPS	2.38
Predicted future relative stock P/E	0.42
Predicted future market P/E	20.00
Predicted future stock P/E	9.10
Predicted future share price	32.43
Predicted future EPS	3.56
Expected annual EPS growth rate (%)	8.41
Estimated growth capacity (%)	18.80
Expectation index	1.85

TABLE 12.4 AAON Incorporated, Data as of April 20, 2001

% Returns on . . .		% Growth Rates	
Assets (TTM)	18.83	Sales (MRQ)	18.56
Assets (5-yr. avg.)	12.34	Sales (TTM)	17.46
Investment (TTM)	29.93	Sales (5-yr. avg.)	18.14
Investment (5-yr. avg.)	17.91	EPS (MRQ)	17.23
Equity (TTM)	37.55	EPS (TTM)	37.88
Equity (5-yr. avg.)	25.11	EPS (5-yr. avg.)	44.58

pacity. Before averaging the numbers, I eliminated the ones that appear most divergent from normal trends (the returns on equity, and the TTM and five-year EPS growth figures).

The Update Keys

1. **Is your original reason for buying the stock still valid?** Actually, the good-stock metrics are better than they were when the stock was purchased. The answer to this key is "yes."

2. **Are there any other factors you regard as positive?** The good-company data is likewise better than it was at the time of purchase. I'll answer "yes" to this key.

3. **Is the situation free of other factors you regard as negative?**
The expectation index now is stronger than it was a year earlier. Indeed, the expected growth rate has fallen so far as to leave us with a very healthy margin for error. But cyclical risk, an issue a year ago that generated a "no" answer to this key, causes a similar response now.

The Reconsideration Path

The yes-yes-no answer pattern we get for the AAON Update Keys corresponds to Reconsideration Path D, which is in the hold zone.

As we observed in Chapter 10, many stocks wind up on this path due to negative answers to the third key. However, within Path D, AAON remains on the top-priority subpath (Path D1) since the negative response does not stem from the expectation index or a value connection theme. All in all, AAON illustrates a situation where a sell losers strategy may not be constructive.

Postscript   From April 20, 2001, through April 23, 2002, AAON shares appreciated 136.8 percent versus declines of 13.4 percent and 23.1 percent for the S&P 500 and Russell 2000, respectively.

BEBE STORES (BEBE)

BEBE was a great company that hit a major pothole after its top-ranked merchandising executive departed. On April 20, 2000, I found the stock in my Contrarian Opportunities screen. Table 12.5 shows that it was a big-time winner.

Updating the Price

In Step 2 (Analyze), the valuation metrics were evaluated on the basis of downscale metrics. But the stock is no longer in the basement. I'll do the update based on middle-market criteria, which can be seen in Table 12.6.

TABLE 12.5 Bebe Stores, Calculations as of April 20, 2001

	Date	Stock Price	S&P 500	Russell 2000
Buy	4/20/00	9.69	1,434.54	481.84
Review	4/20/01	19.53	1,242.98	466.71
% Change		+101.5	−13.4	−3.1

TABLE 12.6 Bebe Stores, Updated Valuation Metrics Data as of April 20, 2001

	Company	Industry	S&P 500
P/E based on estimate of next year's EPS	15.30	15.13	23.99
Projected long-term EPS growth rate	19.50	17.06	15.67
PEG ratio	0.785	0.90	1.606
P/E (TTM)	20.20	20.11	28.38
P/E—5-year high	NA	48.65	50.41
P/E—5-year low	NA	11.50	17.31
Yield	—	—	—
5-year dividend growth	—	—	—
Yield + growth	—	—	—
Payout ratio (TTM)	—	—	—
Price/book value (TTM)	3.69	6.58	6.17
MRQ price/net working capital	5.33	NM	NM
MRQ price/net cash (cash minus total debt)	5.158	NM	7.924
Return on enterprise value (%)	10.6	9.3	5.0

The PEG ratio and the asset-oriented metrics still look good, albeit not as overwhelmingly so as a year earlier (see Table 10.30). The P/E ratios are marginally above average, but an above-par growth projection brings the PEG below the industry norm.

Updating the Merchandise

This is almost the reverse of AAON. Here, the stock rose sharply while BEBE's fundamentals seem to have headed south. The first quarterly earnings news after my April 2000 buy decision was fine. EPS came in at $0.22, a penny above the consensus estimate. But the next quarter was poor. EPS was $0.16 a share, well below the $0.30 result in the year-earlier period and the $0.32-a-share estimate in effect in April. The problem, which persisted through the time of our update, stemmed from merchandising miscues—exactly what the bears had been worried about. But as of April 2001, the rhetoric surrounding BEBE had improved. Many believed the company was getting back on track in terms of fashion decisions. But such improvement was not yet reflected in objective results.

Interestingly, although overall share price performance was excellent, the path has not been perfect. Table 12.7 shows that in recent weeks the stock has run out of steam, and Table 12.8 shows a noteworthy rise in short interest.

TABLE 12.7 Bebe Stores, Price Data as of April 20, 2001

	Price Performance			
Period	Actual (%)	Vs. S&P 500 (%)	Company Rank in Industry*	Industry Rank*
4 weeks	−11.0	−18.4	19	18
13 weeks	−23.0	−16.9	15	53
26 weeks	44.7	62.6	78	51
52 weeks	101.6	132.7	88	35
YTD	−8.6	−2.9	30	66

*Ranks are percentiles: 0 is worst, 99 is best.

TABLE 12.8 Bebe Stores, Short Interest Data as of April 20, 2001

	Short Interest			
	Shares (Millions)	% Outstanding	% Float	Days
Latest month	1.723	6.974	46.568	6.920
1 month ago	1.369	5.541	37.000	4.265
2 months ago	0.545	2.206	14.730	1.637
3 months ago	0.443	1.793	11.973	1.737

Still Getting Our Money's Worth?

Table 12.9 shows the updated expectation index for BEBE. The predicted relative P/E is based on an average of the relative TTM P/E and PEG ratios. Table 12.10 is the starting point for estimated growth capacity. Before averaging the numbers, I eliminated EPS figures, which seem more reflective of recent problems rather than long-term growth capacity. That resulted in a capacity estimate of 24.50 percent. This struck me as being too high, so I decided to stick with the 19.50 percent estimate I used in Step 2 (Analyze), based on the analyst consensus growth target. The expectation index falls below the 1.00 point of neutrality.

The Update Keys

1. **Is your original reason for buying the stock still valid?** The core fundamentals are still pretty good, so I'll stick with the "yes" answer I gave in Step 3 (Buy).

2. **Are there any other factors you regard as positive?** While I would not describe the stock as overpriced, it's hardly the irresistible bargain it once was. I'll answer "no" to this key.

TABLE 12.9 Bebe Stores, Updated Analysis as of April 20, 2001

Expectation Analysis	
Time horizon (years)	5
Assumed risk-free return (annual %)	5.0
Assumed equity risk premium (annual %)	4.5
Beta	2.147
Current share price	19.53
Base-level EPS	1.37
Predicted future relative stock P/E	0.60
Predicted future market P/E	20
Predicted future stock P/E	12
Predicted future share price	34.04
Predicted future EPS	2.84
Expected annual EPS growth rate (%)	19.95
Estimated growth capacity (%)	19.50
Expectation index	0.98

TABLE 12.10 Bebe Stores, Data as of April 20, 2001

% Returns on . . .		% Growth Rates	
Assets (TTM)	18.90	Sales (MRQ)	19.01
Assets (5-yr. avg.)	23.12	Sales (TTM)	11.45
Investment (TTM)	23.08	Sales (5-yr. avg.)	29.89
Investment (5-yr. avg.)	31.83	EPS (MRQ)	−5.67
Equity (TTM)	23.81	EPS (TTM)	−17.87
Equity (5-yr. avg.)	35.36	EPS (5-yr. avg.)	36.96

3. **Is the situation free of other factors you regard as negative?**
   This key merits a definitive "no." BEBE does not pass the expectation analysis. I'll admit it comes close. But I don't have strong convictions regarding the kind of assumptions I'd have to make to put it over the top. Also, risk surrounding merchandising remains present.

The Reconsideration Path

The yes-no-no answer pattern we get for the BEBE Update Keys corresponds to Reconsideration Path F, which is solidly ensconced within the sell zone.

Postscript   Our sell decision was not perfect. From April 20, 2001, through April 23, 2002, BEBE shares appreciated another 15.2 percent, versus declines of 13.4 percent and 23.1 percent for the S&P 500 and Russell 2000, respectively. But this paled by comparison with what the stock did in the year we "owned" it. So we did capture a hefty portion of the two-year gain. And as we'll see, the case studies from screens run on April 20, 2001, uncovered stocks that handily outperformed BEBE in the 2001–2002 time frame. So even though a decision to sell did not turn out to be strictly correct, we were able to live with an error like this because our value connection method provided more rewarding alternatives into which we could have reinvested proceeds from the sale of BEBE.

PATTERSON DENTAL COMPANY (PDCO)

I found PDCO on the April 20, 2001, list produced by the Fastest Turnover screen. Table 12.11 shows that over the succeeding year, it turned out to be a very successful investment.

Updating the Price

Table 12.12 shows the stock's valuation metrics as of our assumed April 23, 2002, one-year review date. In Step 2 (Analyze), I considered the valuation story solid if not spectacular. That's no longer the case. The stock cannot be described as overpriced, but now even "solid" would be too strong a word. Let's just say it's adequate.

Updating the Merchandise

In the year since PDCO flew through Step 3 (Buy) on Decision Path A (the highest one), the company performed as well as expected. Analysts were expecting the company to earn $1.33 a share in the fiscal year that would

TABLE 12.11   Patterson Dental Company, Calculations as of April 23, 2002

	Date	Stock Price	S&P 500	Russell 2000
Buy	4/20/01	30.00	1,242.98	466.71
Review	4/23/02	44.67	1,076.32	501.50
% Change		+48.9	−13.4	+7.5

TABLE 12.12 Patterson Dental Company, Updated Valuation Metrics Data as of April 23, 2002

	Company	Industry	S&P 500
P/E based on estimate of next year's EPS	27.94	25.33	22.40
Projected long-term EPS growth rate	18.14	16.74	13.54
PEG ratio	1.540	1.549	1.654
P/E (TTM)	34.28	44.49	29.33
P/E—5-year high	33.56	77.05	50.02
P/E—5-year low	21.27	23.21	17.60
Yield	—	—	—
5-year dividend growth	—	—	—
Yield + growth	—	—	—
Payout ratio (TTM)	—	—	—
Price/book value (TTM)	6.30	6.89	5.13
MRQ price/net working capital	10.023	NM	NM
MRQ price/net cash (cash minus total debt)	23.217	NM	NM
Return on enterprise value (%)	4.7	3.2	4.2

end April 30, 2002. At the time of the update, a few days before the end of that period, the estimate stood at $1.37 a share. PDCO looks good in cross-sectional TTM growth comparisons. For sales, PDCO grew 17.04 percent versus an industry average of 12.63 percent, and its EPS rose 20.09 percent versus a decline of 7.17 for the industry. All the data relating to footprints of success (margin, turnover, return) still look great.

The rhetoric was generally favorable at the time of the update. The company was continuing to grow nicely as more dentists were attracted to its ability to serve a broad range of dental needs (i.e., equipment-related). It had just announced the acquisition of a top-10 dental distributor, and was branching out into veterinary supplies.

Still Getting Our Money's Worth?

Table 12.13 shows the updated expectation index for PDCO. As I did in Step 3 (Buy), I computed predicted relative P/E based on all relevant P/E data and growth capacity based on an average of all the data in Table 12.14. That resulted in a bullish expectation index value of 1.20. In Step 2 (Analyze), I felt uncomfortable using PDCO's actual beta, which was 0.19; I manually changed the number to 0.60. This time around, the beta works out to 0.12 (showing my initial worries about assuming such low volatility were ill founded). If I stick with the 0.60 beta I used for the buy assessment, the index winds up at 1.01. I notice that the five-year high relative P/E is way out of line (on the low side) with the others. If I drop that from

TABLE 12.13   Patterson Dental Company, Updated Analysis as of April 23, 2002

Expectation Analysis	
Time horizon (years)	5
Assumed risk-free return (annual %)	5.0
Assumed equity risk premium (annual %)	4.5
Beta	0.60
Current share price	44.67
Base-level EPS	1.63
Predicted future relative stock P/E	0.995
Predicted future market P/E	20.0
Predicted future stock P/E	19.9
Predicted future share price	64.73
Predicted future EPS	3.25
Expected annual EPS growth rate (%)	18.85
Estimated growth capacity (%)	19.11
Expectation index	1.01

TABLE 12.14   Patterson Dental Company, Data as of April 23, 2002

% Returns on . . .		% Growth Rates	
Assets (TTM)	15.25	Sales (MRQ)	22.99
Assets (5-yr. avg.)	14.78	Sales (TTM)	17.04
Investment (TTM)	20.11	Sales (5-yr. avg.)	13.76
Investment (5-yr. avg.)	20.44	EPS (MRQ)	21.33
Equity (TTM)	20.46	EPS (TTM)	20.09
Equity (5-yr. avg.)	21.88	EPS (5-yr. avg.)	21.18

my calculation of the average, the predicted relative P/E rises to 1.103 and the index jumps back to 1.21.

The Update Keys

1. **Is your original reason for buying the stock still valid?** The good-company story is every bit as strong as it was a year earlier. I'll answer "yes" to this key.

2. **Are there any other factors you regard as positive?** The good-stock story hasn't been reversed by PDCO's strong market performance. But enough zest has been squeezed out of the picture to induce me to answer "no" to this Update Key.

3. **Is the situation free of other factors you regard as negative?**
The growth expectation and capacity estimates are both above where they were a year ago, but they are well aligned with one another. The expectation index is little changed versus a year ago. It's barely above 1.00, or higher depending on how we adjust assumptions. So I'll say PDCO passes this test. Meanwhile, I see no other noteworthy baggage, so I'll say "yes" to this key.

The Reconsideration Path

The yes-no-yes answer pattern we get for the PDCO Update Keys corresponds to Reconsideration Path B. That's not top-drawer, as was the case a year earlier. But it is still quite high within the hold zone.

Postscript   From April 23, 2002 through October 25, 2002, PDCO shares appreciated 21.3 percent versus declines of 16.6 percent and 20.0 percent for the S&P 500 and Russell 2000, respectively.

GRACO INCORPORATED (GGG)

On April 20, 2001, GGG appeared on my Relative Value screen. Table 12.15 shows this was a very sound investment.

Updating the Price

Table 12.16 shows GGG's updated (as of April 23, 2002) stock valuation metrics. Thanks to strong stock price performance, the valuation metrics we now see aren't as drastically low as they were a year earlier. But had we never seen Table 10.43 (featuring the previous spectacular metrics), we'd feel very positive about what we see in Table 12.16. And since we are trying to see these updates as if we were looking for the first time, we will

TABLE 12.15 Graco Incorporated, Calculations as of April 23, 2002

	Date	Stock Price	S&P 500	Russell 2000
Buy	4/20/01	27.60	1,242.98	466.71
Review	4/23/02	43.70	1,076.32	501.50
% Change		+58.3	−13.4	+7.5

TABLE 12.16 Graco Incorporated, Updated Valuation Metrics Data as of
April 23, 2002

	Company	Industry	S&P 500
P/E based on estimate of next year's EPS	16.95	18.53	22.40
Projected long-term EPS growth rate	15.00	13.69	13.54
PEG ratio	1.130	1.684	1.654
P/E (TTM)	20.45	27.06	29.33
P/E—5-year high	20.17	34.89	50.02
P/E—5-year low	10.21	12.20	17.60
Yield	1.01	1.42	1.82
5-year dividend growth	13.26	−5.27	8.25
Yield + growth	14.27	NM	10.07
Payout ratio (TTM)	19.28	21.22	30.47
Price/book value (TTM)	6.95	3.19	5.13
MRQ price/net working capital	17.424	NM	NM
MRQ price/net cash (cash minus total debt)	42.063	7.518	NM
Return on enterprise value (%)	7.7	5.2	4.2

pretend we didn't see Table 10.43, and describe GGG as being a solid good-
stock story.

Updating the Merchandise

Looking at the company leaves us feeling a bit colder. The risk of cyclical
slowdown that concerned us the first time around has become reality. The
company was not able to meet the earnings estimate that had already been
lowered ahead of time (see Table 10.45). In calendar 2001, the company
earned $2.07 (on April 20, 2001, analysts were looking for EPS to come in
at $2.27). The 2002 estimate has been cut from $2.59 to $2.27.

However, the weakened growth comparisons generally still are solid
compared to the industry averages. Table 12.17 shows that GGG comes up
short in terms of sales growth, but strong operational control produces
better EPS comparisons. (By this point in time, the company had ceased
buying back shares.)

Meanwhile, GGG's margin, turnover, return, and financial strength
comparisons remain as powerful as they were when we looked at them in
Step 2 (Analyze).

Still Getting Our Money's Worth?

Table 12.18 shows the updated expectation index for GGG. To compute
predicted relative P/E, I used all the historic P/E data in Table 12.16.

TABLE 12.17 Graco Incorporated, Growth Data as of April 23, 2002

Growth Comparisons (%)		
	Company	Industry
Sales MRQ vs. quarter 1 year ago	−1.78	1.34
Sales TTM vs. TTM 1 year ago	−2.30	3.17
Sales—5-year growth rate	3.83	10.70
EPS MRQ vs. quarter 1 year ago	15.40	2.96
EPS TTM vs. TTM 1 year ago	−3.26	−15.02
EPS—5-year growth rate	17.72	2.19
Capital spending—5-year growth	0.11	6.01

TABLE 12.18 Graco Incorporated, Updated Analysis as of April 23, 2002

Expectation Analysis	
Time horizon (years)	5
Assumed risk-free return (annual %)	5.0
Assumed equity risk premium (annual %)	4.5
Beta	0.38
Current share price	43.70
Base-level EPS	2.59
Predicted future relative stock P/E	0.468
Predicted future market P/E	20.00
Predicted future stock P/E	9.36
Predicted future share price	60.47
Predicted future EPS	6.46
Expected annual EPS growth rate (%)	25.67
Estimated growth capacity (%)	17.72
Expectation index	0.69

Growth capacity presented more of a challenge. Some return numbers in Table 12.19 are clearly too high. And most growth numbers are impacted by here-and-now cyclical conditions that are unlikely to be permanent. I decided to use the historic five-year EPS growth rate, which seems most representative of GGG's long-term capabilities. The end result is an index value of 0.69, far below the 1.23 computed in early 2001, and well below the 1.00 point of neutrality.

TABLE 12.19 Graco Incorporated, Data as of April 23, 2002

% Returns on . . .		% Growth Rates	
Assets (TTM)	25.11	Sales (MRQ)	−1.78
Assets (5-yr. avg.)	23.32	Sales (TTM)	−2.30
Investment (TTM)	34.89	Sales (5-yr. avg.)	3.83
Investment (5-yr. avg.)	34.26	EPS (MRQ)	15.40
Equity (TTM)	42.44	EPS (TTM)	−3.26
Equity (5-yr. avg.)	75.80	EPS (5-yr. avg.)	17.72

The Update Keys

1. **Is your original reason for buying the stock still valid?** The good-stock story remains valid, albeit less spectacular than it once was. I'll still answer "yes" to this key.

2. **Are there any other factors you regard as positive?** In Step 3 (Buy), I answered "yes" notwithstanding the presence of cyclical concerns because of the company's powerful returns, driven by an efficient operation and a tendency on the part of management to remove capital (through dividends and share buybacks) that could not be profitably deployed in GGG's business. The fact that the company was no longer buying back shares dims the story a bit, enough so that I'm willing to now answer "no" to this Update Key.

3. **Is the situation free of other factors you regard as negative?** The first time around, I answered "yes" to this key reasoning that this was the sort of company for which one could be willing to ride out a down cycle. I still feel that way. But now, GGG fails the expectation analysis to a wide degree. That merits an automatic "no" to this key.

The Reconsideration Path

The yes-no-no answer pattern we get for the GGG Update Keys corresponds to Reconsideration Path F, which is in the sell zone.

Postscript   From April 23, 2002, through October 25, 2002, GGG shares fell 7.2 percent versus declines of 16.6 percent and 20.0 percent for the S&P 500 and Russell 2000, respectively.

ENGINEERED SUPPORT SYSTEM (EASI)

EASI is another one of the stocks that was on the Relative Value screen on April 20, 2001. As can be seen in Table 12.20, this was an outstanding selection.

Updating the Price

Table 12.21 shows the April 23, 2002, updated stock valuation metrics for EASI. As with GGG, EASI's valuation metrics aren't as spectacular as they were the first time we looked at them. But they are still generally good.

TABLE 12.20 Engineered Support System, Calculations as of April 23, 2002

	Date	Stock Price	S&P 500	Russell 2000
Buy	4/20/01	23.51	1,242.98	466.71
Review	4/23/02	49.63	1,076.32	501.50
% Change		+111.2	−13.4	+7.5

TABLE 12.21 Engineered Support System, Updated Valuation Metrics Data as of April 23, 2002

	Company	Industry	S&P 500
P/E based on estimate of next year's EPS	17.45	18.53	22.40
Projected long-term EPS growth rate	17.67	13.69	13.54
PEG ratio	0.988	1.684	1.654
P/E (TTM)	25.52	27.06	29.33
P/E—5-year high	28.53	34.89	50.02
P/E—5-year low	8.41	12.20	17.60
Yield	0.07	1.42	1.82
5-year dividend growth	27.70	−5.27	8.25
Yield + growth	NM	NM	10.07
Payout ratio (TTM)	2.57	21.22	30.47
Price/book value (TTM)	4.36	3.19	5.13
MRQ price/net working capital	NM	NM	NM
MRQ price/net cash (cash minus total debt)	NM	7.518	NM
Return on enterprise value (%)	6.8	5.2	4.2

Updating the Merchandise

EASI did well in the April 2001 through April 2002 period. Earnings in the fiscal year that ended October 2001 came in at $1.83 a share, versus $1.44 a share in fiscal 2000 and the $1.68 analysts were expecting for 2001 back when we initially considered the stock. The fiscal 2002 estimate has been increased from $2.01 a share to $2.29. And as of the time of our review, the backlog remained healthy.

The fundamental growth, margin, turnover, and return comparisons remained generally favorable as they were in early 2001. The one notable difference was in financial strength. At first glance, Table 12.22 shows EASI's present balance sheet to be adequate but nothing to get excited about. However, this represents a stark improvement from a year earlier, when the company was financing acquisitions (see Table 10.64).

Still Getting Our Money's Worth?

Table 12.23 shows the updated expectation index for EASI. I calculate predicted relative P/E and growth capacity the same way I did back in Step 2 (Analyze). I averaged all the P/E data from the expectation spreadsheet template, and for capacity, I used only the return on assets and investment data (see Table 12.24), which strikes me as better representing a sustainable level of growth.

The result is a very low expectation index of 0.58. All of this is attributable to the higher growth expectation built into the stock price following the more than 100 percent rise. The capacity estimate is actually a bit higher than it was using the April 2001 data. Moreover, I do not see any plausible assumption changes I can make that would bring the index up to 1.00.

TABLE 12.22 Engineered Support System, Financial
Strength Data as of April 23, 2002

Financial Strength		
	Company	Industry
Quick ratio MRQ	0.64	1.34
Current ratio MRQ	1.72	2.39
Long-term debt/equity MRQ	0.31	0.56
Total debt/equity MRQ	0.49	0.65
Interest coverage TTM	7.72	12.93

TABLE 12.23 Engineered Support System, Updated Analysis as of April 23, 2002

Expectation Analysis	
Time horizon (years)	5
Assumed risk-free return (annual %)	5.0
Assumed equity risk premium (annual %)	4.5
Beta	0.43
Current share price	49.63
Base-level EPS	2.75
Predicted future relative stock P/E	0.633
Predicted future market P/E	20.00
Predicted future stock P/E	12.66
Predicted future share price	66.10
Predicted future EPS	5.22
Expected annual EPS growth rate (%)	17.39
Estimated growth capacity (%)	10.09
Expectation index	0.58

TABLE 12.24 Engineered Support System, Data as of April 23, 2002

% Returns on . . .		% Growth Rates	
Assets (TTM)	8.68	Sales (MRQ)	8.68
Assets (5-year avg.)	7.92	Sales (TTM)	7.92
Investment (TTM)	12.63	Sales (5-yr. avg.)	12.63
Investment (5-yr. avg.)	11.13	EPS (MRQ)	11.13
Equity (TTM)	20.44	EPS (TTM)	20.44
Equity (5-yr. avg.)	19.37	EPS (5-yr. avg.)	19.37

The Update Keys

1. **Is your original reason for buying the stock still valid?** The strong share price appreciation took some luster away from the good-stock story, but not enough to negate it altogether. I'll still answer "yes" to this key for the time being.

2. **Are there any other factors you regard as positive?** The good-company story has been strengthened by the improved balance sheet and the fact past acquisitions are now kicking in. I answered this key in the negative based on the early 2001 data. But now, in Sell Phase B (Update), I'll switch my answer to "yes."

3. **Is the situation free of other factors you regard as negative?** The poor showing in the expectation index generates an automatic

"no" to this key. And in an example of how the art and science of investing mix, I find the expectation analysis so weak as to leave me uncomfortable with my prior willingness to accept the good-stock story. Accordingly, I'll now revise my answer to Update Key 1 to "no."

The Reconsideration Path

The no-yes-no answer pattern we wind up with for the EASI Update Keys corresponds to Reconsideration Path G, which is far down in the sell zone.

Postscript   From April 23, 2002, through October 25, 2002, EASI stock was about flat, rising just 0.9 percent. But this was materially better than the declines of 16.6 percent and 20.0 percent we saw for the S&P 500 and Russell 2000, respectively. However, the stock was still sufficiently lackluster that we don't necessarily regret our decision.

SONIC CORPORATION (SONC)

SONC appeared on my Industry Leaders screen on April 20, 2001. It turned out to be a successful choice, as demonstrated by Table 12.25.

Updating the Price

Table 12.26 shows the April 23, 2002, updated stock valuation metrics for SONC. This stock is not exactly overpriced. But it can hardly be considered undervalued. The most favorable ratio, the PEG, will rise to the industry average if we change the consensus 18.88 percent SONC long-term growth rate to 15.11 percent, or raise the average industry growth projection from 14.43 percent to 16.64 percent. Long-term projections being what they are, I would not want to bet the farm on one assumption as opposed to another, especially when, as we'll see, my growth capacity projection for SONC works out to 14.91 percent.

TABLE 12.25   Sonic Corporation, Calculations as of April 23, 2002

	Date	Stock Price	S&P 500	Russell 2000
Buy	4/20/01	18.47	1,242.98	466.71
Review	4/23/02	29.20	1,076.32	501.50
% Change		+58.1	−13.4	+7.5

TABLE 12.26 Sonic Corporation, Updated Valuation Metrics Data as of April 23, 2002

	Company	Industry	S&P 500
P/E based on estimate of next year's EPS	22.60	19.83	22.40
Projected long-term EPS growth rate	18.88	14.43	13.54
PEG ratio	1.197	1.495	1.654
P/E (TTM)	29.47	27.14	29.33
P/E—5-year high	29.01	36.78	50.02
P/E—5-year low	14.49	18.04	17.60
Yield	—	—	—
5-year dividend growth	—	—	—
Yield + growth	—	—	—
Payout ratio (TTM)	—	—	—
Price/book value (TTM)	5.50	4.25	5.13
MRQ price/net working capital	NM	NM	NM
MRQ price/net cash (cash minus total debt)	NM	0.709	NM
Return on enterprise value (%)	5.6	6.0	4.2

Updating the Merchandise

The news flow coming out of SONC was positive. Earnings were strong, consistent with analysts' year-earlier projections (almost to the penny), and all the strategies discussed in connection with Step 2 (Analyze) appeared to be working a year later. The company's fundamental growth, margin, return, turnover, and financial strength comparisons looked pretty much like they did a year earlier, when the stock appeared on the screen.

Still Getting Our Money's Worth?

Table 12.27 shows the updated expectation index for SONC. The predicted relative P/E is based on an average of all P/E-related data in the expectation analysis spreadsheet template. The growth capacity estimate is based on an average of all return data appearing in Table 12.28.

The Update Keys

1. **Is your original reason for buying the stock still valid?** The good-company story remains very much in place. I'll answer "yes" to this key.

2. **Are there any other factors you regard as positive?** In early 2001, the good-stock story was not sufficient to prevent a negative answer to

TABLE 12.27 Sonic Corporation, Updated Analysis as of April 23, 2002

Expectation Analysis	
Time horizon (years)	5
Assumed risk-free return (annual %)	5.0
Assumed equity risk premium (annual %)	4.5
Beta	0.84
Current share price	29.20
Base-level EPS	1.31
Predicted future relative stock P/E	0.739
Predicted future market P/E	20.0
Predicted future stock P/E	14.78
Predicted future share price	44.48
Predicted future EPS	3.01
Expected annual EPS growth rate (%)	23.11
Estimated growth capacity (%)	14.91
Expectation index	0.65

TABLE 12.28 Sonic Corporation, Data as of April 23, 2002

% Returns on . . .		% Growth Rates	
Assets (TTM)	12.04	Sales (MRQ)	29.10
Assets (5-yr. avg.)	11.38	Sales (TTM)	25.98
Investment (TTM)	13.03	Sales (5-yr. avg.)	16.95
Investment (5-yr. avg.)	12.44	EPS (MRQ)	27.07
Equity (TTM)	21.40	EPS (TTM)	20.41
Equity (5-yr. avg.)	19.17	EPS (5-yr. avg.)	30.37

this key. Now, with the valuation metrics having diminished a bit, this key garners another "no" answer.

3. **Is the situation free of other factors you regard as negative?** The expectation index is way below the 1.00 neutral boundary. Even if I use the consensus SONC long-term EPS growth rate assumption (18.88 percent) in lieu of my more conservative approach, the index would only rise to a still-bearish 0.82. This poor showing garners an automatic "no" answer to this key.

The Reconsideration Path

The yes-no-no answer pattern we get for the SONC Update Keys corresponds to Reconsideration Path F, which is in the sell zone.

Postscript This sell decision turned out to be sound. From April 23, 2002 through October 25, 2002, SONC shares dropped 16.7 percent, in line with the 16.6 percent drop seen for the S&P 500 and a little better than the 20.0 percent drop in the Russell 2000. Strictly speaking, we could have lived with a hold, since SONC's decline was in line with the market. But had we really owned it, we would not have regretted a sell decision.

UNIVERSITY OF PHOENIX ONLINE (UOPX)

On April 23, 2002, UOPX appeared on my upscale High P/E Ratios screen. As of this writing, insufficient time has elapsed to allow for a one-year review. So we'll implement Step 4 (Sell) based on a half-year holding period, using data as of October 25, 2002. Table 12.29 shows how the stock performed. A 2.2 percent gain is not exciting, but considering that the buy occurred as the market was getting ready to fall off a cliff, we won't complain about UOPX's performance.

Updating the Price

Table 12.30 shows the stock's October 25, 2002 valuation metrics based on the same upscale criteria we used when we first looked at UOPX using

TABLE 12.29 University of Phoenix Online, Calculations as of October 25, 2002

	Date	Stock Price	S&P 500	Russell 2000
Buy	4/23/02	30.74	1,076.32	501.50
Review	10/25/02	31.42	897.65	372.64
% Change		+2.2	−16.6	−25.7

TABLE 12.30 University of Phoenix Online, Updated Valuation Metrics Data as of October 25, 2002

	Company	Industry	S&P 500
P/E based on estimate of next year's EPS	29.35	26.84	19.18
Projected long-term EPS growth rate	39.63	24.95	12.76
PEG ratio	0.741	1.108	1.243
P/E (TTM)	58.40	43.45	24.79
P/E—5-year high	NA	70.72	49.26
P/E—5-year low	NA	22.40	16.83
Price/sales (TTM)	10.87	5.85	2.98
Price/free cash flow (TTM)	47.90	37.46	26.12
Price/cash flow (TTM)	63.09	35.92	18.48

April 23, 2002 data. The shares still look richly valued based on the TTM metrics. The PEG ratio looks good, but bear in mind the number depends on an aggressive and hard-to-assess 39.63 percent long-term EPS growth projection.

Updating the Merchandise

Not much time has passed since we applied Step 2 (Analyze) for UOPX. It was widely understood that the company's blistering growth rates could not be sustained for a prolonged period, but through the first six months of our investment, UOPX has not yet downshifted. EPS estimates for the fiscal years ending August 2003 and 2004 rose from $0.57 and $0.82, respectively, to $0.75 and $1.04.

Still Getting Our Money's Worth?

Table 12.31 shows the updated expectation index for UOPX. The predicted relative P/E is an average of the relative PEG and TTM P/E ratios. Growth capacity is normally estimated from the data reproduced in Table 12.32. As you can see, it's hard to deem any of those numbers are being reasonably representative of what the company could achieve on a sustainable long-term basis. This same problem plagued us in Step 2 (Analyze), and we'll now do the same thing we did then. We'll ignore all the historic capacity data and simply plug in our own 25 percent assumption.

Interestingly, the index went up substantially, from 1.02 based on April

TABLE 12.31 University of Phoenix Online, Updated Analysis as of October 25, 2002

Expectation Analysis	
Time horizon (years)	5
Assumed risk-free return (annual %)	5.0
Assumed equity risk premium (annual %)	4.5
Beta	1.52
Current share price	31.42
Base-level EPS	1.04
Predicted future relative stock P/E	1.476
Predicted future market P/E	20.00
Predicted future stock P/E	29.52
Predicted future share price	54.98
Predicted future EPS	1.86
Expected annual EPS growth rate (%)	15.68
Estimated growth capacity (%)	25.00
Expectation index	1.59

TABLE 12.32 University of Phoenix Online, Data as of October 25, 2002

% Returns on . . .		% Growth Rates	
Assets (TTM)	35.47	Sales (MRQ)	77.69
Assets (5-yr. avg.)	63.32	Sales (TTM)	81.40
Investment (TTM)	49.45	Sales (5-yr. avg.)	58.58
Investment (5-yr. avg.)	201.79	EPS (MRQ)	140.00
Equity (TTM)	50.77	EPS (TTM)	124.17
Equity (5-yr. avg.)	NA	EPS (5-yr. avg.)	96.80

data to a solidly bullish 1.59 at the time we applied Sell Phase B (Update). The main difference is the base-level EPS, which benefits from the substantial upward analyst estimate revision.

The Update Keys

1. **Is your original reason for buying the stock still valid?** A good-stock story, anathema to the upscale screen that brought UOPX to light, produced a "no" answer to this key the first time around and it does likewise now.

2. **Are there any other factors you regard as positive?** The good-company story is at least as strong as it was before. This key merits a "yes" answer.

3. **Is the situation free of other factors you regard as negative?** The solidly bullish expectation index gets us off to a good start. My 25 percent growth capacity estimate is hardly carved in stone. But now we get the full benefit of the "solve for G" approach to this analysis. I don't really have to defend this assumption. Instead, I can defend a less bold assertion that UOPX shares would be reasonably valued if long-term EPS growth can at least equal 15.68 percent. It seems plausible that the company can do at least this well. Given the absence of any other noteworthy red flags, I'll answer this key "yes."

The Reconsideration Path

The no-yes-yes answer pattern we get for the UOPX Update Keys corresponds to Reconsideration Path C, which is solidly in the hold zone.

Postscript As of this writing, it's too early to evaluate our hold decision. But it has been looking good through mid-March. Over this short span, UOPX shares appreciated 25 percent, while the S&P 500 dropped 7 percent and the Russell 2000 fell 3.9 percent.

Conclusion

## CHAPTER 13

Benefits of the Value Connection

In the investment community, the topic of value is often controversial. Many are committed to the approach, believing that no other method is prudent. Others regard value as stodgy, past its prime, and so forth. I believe the value style is like most others. It can work well or poorly, depending on the way it is executed. For the following reasons, I believe the value connection is a method that implements this style in a constructive way that will enhance the probability of success.

THE METHOD IS WIDE-RANGING

As with any screen-based investment method, the value connection gives you an opportunity to discover any stock at any time. The only constraint is that the situation satisfy some tests relating to stock valuation metrics or company quality. But these are tests you choose when you create your own screen or select a preset screen created for use with today's screening applications. This is important because it reduces the role of coincidence or luck. You don't need to read the right newspapers or magazines, watch the right television broadcasts, talk to the right brokers, and so on. All you need do is look at the right data, something you can always do if you so choose.

Also, the wide-ranging nature of the method gives you the fortitude to do something everybody should do but many don't: walk away from a situation you don't understand. Many who held Enron shares undoubtedly wish they had done this. If ideas come to you in dribs and drabs, it's tempting to believe you must develop an understanding of the situation and come to a decision. In contrast, when stock screens produce hundreds of viable ideas at a time, it's easy to walk away from those that rub you the wrong way. There is always something else to look at.

THE METHOD IS SYSTEMATIC

I'm not a trader. But I've always marveled at the discipline they bring to the process. If you ask a trader why he or she bought or sold a particular stock at a particular price, you will always get a rational answer. You may not always agree with the method. You may not even respect the method. But you have to respect the fact that there *is* a method and that the trader will never respond to your inquiry with a confused look, a shrug of the shoulders, a grunt, or an answer made up on the spot.

I wish I could say the same for others. Sadly, many who wouldn't dream of short-term trading and insist on the virtues of long-term investing give the style a bad name. As indicated in Chapter 11, I hate the phrase "buy-and-hold." Traders are correct when they attack such practices as exemplifying a lack of diligence. The correct approach to long-term investing should more appropriately be labeled buy-and-review.

But it's not merely a question of semantics. Many investors do not use any sort of disciplined approach to determining whether a stock should be bought or whether it should be sold. Many are unable to articulate what they expect to achieve as a result of buying.

The value connection remedies those shortcomings and offers value investors a structured system that helps them to always explain why they bought the stock. Step 2 (Analyze) enables us to explain why we like the company, why we think the stock is reasonably valued, what expectations are built into the price we paid, and why we believe those expectations are credible. Step 3 (Buy) allows us to explain how we balance the pros and cons to reach a purchase decision. And Step 4 (Sell) allows us to explain why we continue to hold, or why we sold when we did.

This is not to say we will never allow emotion to enter the picture. We're human. We (even traders) cannot avoid that. The difference is that we'll know exactly when we're bowing to emotion. We'll never fool ourselves into believing we're acting based on facts when in actuality we aren't. We'll recognize when we're taking a plunge more for entertainment than serious investing. Accordingly, we'll keep our exposure to such situations manageably small, and we'll easily be able to avoid allowing grief over this part of our portfolio to influence how we handle the investments that we make on the basis of the value connection.

THE METHOD IS ACCESSIBLE

It's possible that you may at some point find yourself in the position of a customer, competitor, employee, or supplier of a company that has a lot more going for it than is believed in the investment community. If you ever have this good fortune, by all means apply your insight, so long as the information you possess does not run afoul of laws regarding inside information and disclosure. Even so, how far can such an approach take you? There are just so many companies about which most of us can gain this level of deep and legally proper knowledge. Unless you are in a position to earn enough from one or a few successful situation(s) to satisfy yourself for the duration of your investing life (i.e., you are able to act as a "raider" and make buyout offers), sooner or later you'll need a way to cope with a wider variety of situations.

Most investors, even professionals, cannot invest this way on a consistent basis. This screening method is unique in that we analyze companies and stocks based on questions we can answer. We won't all react to the answers the same way. We may ignore facts that in retrospect we realize we should have stressed, and vice versa. So this method contains no guarantees of success. What it does offer is full and fair opportunity for success, based on access to all the facts you need to make good decisions.

THE METHOD IS FREE OF RIGID VALUE STEREOTYPES

We saw earlier that value investing is plagued by many fictional stereotypes. One of the most frequently recurring is that as long as a stock looks cheap, value investors will buy anything. There's also folklore to the extent that low P/E ratios are always better than high P/E ratios, that P/E ratios should always be less than 20 or 25 or some other fixed threshold, or that PEG (P/E-to-growth) ratios should never be more than 1.00.

During the course of this book, we've eliminated all of these stereotypes, as well as many others. We have been scrupulous in our attention to company quality, even going so far as to offer screening strategies based primarily on this topic. We are not mindlessly contrarian. Instead, we are willing to use alternative screening themes based on sentiment among analysts and other constituencies within the investment community. And even if we don't screen based on such notions, we make them an integral part of Step 2 (Analyze).

Thanks to the notions of behavioral testing, we've even gone so far as to create a screen that seeks stocks with very high P/E ratios. We understand that great quality comes at high prices, and we are completely open to such upscale stock shopping experiences. What separates us from the momentum crowd is our insistence that high prices be justified by convincing showings of high quality.

THE METHOD IS COMPATIBLE WITH BASIC FINANCIAL THEORY

We recognize the valuation models that are based on classic financial theory. We understand that they are beneficial in that they inspire a disciplined focus on getting something for our money (we pay for a stock and in return we get a stake in corporate earnings and assets). But we also understand their shortcomings. The models often compel us to make assumptions that are unrealistic in the real world. A conspicuous example is the Dividend Discount Model, which requires us to assume a growth rate that can remain stable through the infinite future. We recognize practical alternatives (such as multistep variations to the Dividend Discount Model), but are also aware of our inability to make the assumptions they require.

Many investors react to such practical limitations simply by ignoring the theory. We did not do that. We adapted it in such a way as to mitigate the impact of troublesome assumptions as best we can. We understand why we are willing to value stocks based on EPS, as opposed to dividends. That knowledge helps us make reasonable choices regarding whether to use P/E ratios or other metrics based on sales, cash flow, and so on. And in the expectation analysis, we went so far as to recast the math in such a way as to minimize the problems we face being unable to forecast future growth rates. We simplify the task by computing a minimum growth target the company must achieve in order to justify investment at the current stock price. And we examine company fundamentals in order to help us make rational assumptions regarding the probability that the growth targets are achievable.

The bottom line is that however much we apply modern screening techniques and utilize reports generated by modern databases, we never stray too far from the basics. We do not use classic financial theory as a tether that limits us to companies whose stocks are priced low relative to EPS, book value, cash, working capital, and so on. Instead, we use theory as a bridge that helps us connect good stocks and good companies, or, in other words, acquire stakes in companies whose underlying merits are reasonable in light of the prices we pay for the shares. Ultimately, that is the goal of all value investors.

Index